D1571523

The Patent Crisis and How the Courts Can Solve It

The Patent Crisis and How the Courts Can Solve It

DAN L. BURK AND MARK A. LEMLEY

The University of Chicago Press
Chicago and London

Dan L. Burk is Chancellor's Professor at the University of California, Irvine, where he is a founding member of the law faculty. Professor Burk is internationally recognized for his scholarship on intellectual property, cyberlaw, and biotechnology law.

Mark A. Lemley is the William H. Neukom Professor at Stanford Law School and the director of Stanford's Program in Law, Science, and Technology. He is of counsel to the law firm of Keker & Van Nest and the author of six books and more than ninety articles on intellectual property and antitrust law.

The University of Chicago Press, Chicago 60637
The University of Chicago Press, Ltd., London
© 2009 by The University of Chicago
All rights reserved. Published 2009
Printed in the United States of America

18 17 16 15 14 13 12 11 10 09   1 2 3 4 5

ISBN-13: 978-0-226-08061-1 (cloth)
ISBN-10: 0-226-08061-7 (cloth)

Library of Congress Cataloging-in-Publication Data

Burk, Dan L.
    The patent crisis and how the courts can solve it / Dan L. Burk and Mark A. Lemley.
        p. cm.
    Includes bibliographical references and index.
    ISBN-13: 978-0-226-08061-1 (cloth : alk. paper)
    ISBN-10: 0-226-08061-7 (cloth : alk. paper)
    1. Patent laws and legislation—United States. 2. Patents—United States.
I. Lemley, Mark A., 1966– II. Title.
    KF3114.B97 2009
    346.7304'86—dc22

                                          2008040523

∞ The paper used in this publication meets the minimum requirements of the American National Standard for Information Sciences—Permanence of Paper for Printed Library Materials, ANSI Z39.48-1992.

Contents

Preface

This project has been more than a decade in the making. It began with a discussion we had in the Cayman Islands about the different ways courts were treating DNA and software cases. That discussion led to two articles—"Is Patent Law Technology-Specific?" in the *Berkeley Technology Law Journal* and "Biotechnology's Uncertainty Principle" in the *Case Western Law Review*—that discussed the differences in judicial treatment of patents in different industries. It also led to a broader discussion about industry-specific differences in the patent system, including differences in the economics of innovation and differences in how theorists conceive of the patent system. That broader conversation led to a third article, "Policy Levers in Patent Law," that appeared in the *Virginia Law Review*. This book has grown out of that third article and represents our effort to present the basic idea to an audience beyond law professors and tie it to the current fight over patent reform. We also hope to flesh out the economic analysis, discuss the rapid changes that have occurred since 2003, and respond to skeptics.

We thank the University of Toronto Faculty of Law Distinguished Visitor Program and the Centre for Innovation Law and Policy for their generous support of prior versions of this work. Kristen Dahling, Laura Quilter, Colleen Chien, and Bhanu Sadasivan provided research assistance. We are grateful to the following people, all of whom provided comments and advice on an earlier draft of this book or a related paper: John Allison, Bob Armitage, Michael Carroll, Rochelle Dreyfuss, Rebecca Eisenberg, Richard Epstein, Dan Farber, Brett Frischmann, Nancy Gallini, Wendy Gordon, Tom Grey, Rose Hagan, Bruce Hayden, David Hyman, Mark Janis, Brian Kahin, Dennis Karjala, Orin Kerr, Dan Lang, Clarisa Long, David McGowan, Rob Merges, Craig Nard, Judge Randy Rader, Arti Rai, Pam Samuelson, Herb

Schwartz, Polk Wagner, and participants at the Telecommunications Policy Research Conference, the Washington University Conference on the Human Genome, the Case Western Reserve Law and the Arts symposium, the University of Toronto Conference on Competition and Innovation, and faculty workshops at Stanford Law School, Boalt Hall School of Law at the University of California at Berkeley, and the University of Minnesota Law School. Our very special thanks go to our editor, David Pervin, who adopted our project and saw it through to completion. And, as always, we are eternally grateful to Laurie and Rose for their patience and support.

A Note on Usage. We refer to intellectual property rights collectively as "IP" rights throughout the book. There is considerable debate over whether IP rights are in fact "property" in any meaningful sense. We don't intend to engage in that debate here, but neither do we want to perpetuate the controversial assumption that they are by using the term.

PART ONE

The Problem

1

The Gathering Storm

The patent system is in crisis. The consensus in favor of strong patent protection that has existed since the 1982 creation of the Federal Circuit, the appeals court that hears virtually all patent disputes in the United States, has broken down. Patent owners—and the Federal Circuit itself—are beset on all sides by those complaining about the proliferation of bad patents and the abuse of those patents in court. Congress, the Federal Trade Commission, the National Academy of Sciences, industry leaders, the press, academics, and even the Patent and Trademark Office (PTO) itself have all gotten into the act. They point to example after example: silly patents granted by the PTO; lawsuits filed by people who invented something decades ago against companies who do something very different today; patent claims so confusing that no one can be sure what the patent covers, even after a district court holds hearings on the subject; and the ability of those who own a patent on a small component to get control over most or all of a much larger product.

Whether you think this crisis is real, or is instead a crisis of perception, probably depends on where you sit. There is a reason we are hearing this firestorm of criticism; the problems and examples are real. But the patent system described above—the one in crisis—is not the only one. There is another patent system in the United States today, one in which claims are clear, patents are subject to significant scrutiny, and strong protection is necessary to allow companies to recover hundreds of millions of dollars in investment. The prototypical industry that operates in this second patent system is the pharmaceutical industry, but other industries, including medical devices and chemistry, look more like this as well.

Talk to lawyers or businesspeople at technology companies about the patent system, and you will quickly get a sense of our two different patent systems. In the pharmaceutical industry, there seems to be a strong consensus (at least among innovative rather than generic pharmaceutical companies) that patents are critical to innovation. Their only complaint is that patents aren't strong enough. They don't last long enough to compensate for FDA delays, and the uncertain or probabilistic nature of patent scope and validity leaves them with uncertain protection for their enormous investment. Those in the biotechnology industry also see patent protection as critical to their survival, though they may also worry a bit about how the many different upstream patents owned by others might affect their ability to produce products at the end of the day.

Lawyers and executives in the information technology industries, by contrast, almost invariably see the patent system as a cost rather than a benefit to innovation. Even companies with tens of thousands of patents generally use those patents only "defensively," to minimize the amount they must pay other patent owners to permit them to sell their products. Ask most of these companies and in their candid moments they will tell you that they would be better off without any patent system, or at least with one that was radically changed and that left them alone to innovate.

Any doubts that the patent system is perceived by different industries in fundamentally different ways were dispelled during the course of congressional debates over patent reform in the four years beginning in 2005. The reform process ground to a halt because different industries couldn't agree on a single principle of reform. The reforms the pharmaceutical and bio-tech industries wanted—harmonization on first to file, the elimination of the best mode requirement, and the weakening of rules against inequitable conduct—were opposed by the IT industries. At the same time, the things the IT industry wanted—reforms to limit damages and injunctive relief in patent holdup settings, and an effective administrative process to oppose patents—were anathema to the biomedical industries.

Something very important is going on here. When some of the most innovative companies in the world think that they would be better off without a law whose entire purpose is to promote innovation, policymakers should sit up and take notice. At the same time, the fact that other innovators clearly rely on patent protection to fund research and development means that we can't simply get rid of the system. Clearly, patents are doing good in some circumstances, but they are also doing harm in others. Why is it that different industries focus on different effects? What should we do about it? Our effort to think through these problems is at the heart of this book.

We think that the problem is deeper than a question of which companies are on which side of particular cases at any given time. The economic evidence is overwhelming that innovation works differently in different industries, and that the way patents affect that innovation also differs enormously by industry. The question for patent policy is how to respond to those differences. In this book we suggest that the courts, not Congress, are best situated to deal with these differences, and indeed that they already have the tools to do so, provided they have the self-confidence to use them.

We hope, in short, to convince the reader of three things: (1) that a purely unitary patent system no longer fits the extraordinarily diverse needs of innovators in today's technology industries; (2) that the solution is not to split the patent system into industry-specific protection statutes, but to tailor the unitary patent rules on a case-by-case basis to the needs of different industries; and (3) that it is the courts, not Congress or the PTO, that are best positioned to do this tailoring.

Saying that the courts should have the power to tailor patent law to the needs of different industries will raise the hackles of many. To some, it smacks of judicial activism and raises questions about the institutional competence of the courts. To others, even those happy with the courts in charge, industry-specific rules will seem unworkable or a recipe for business uncertainty. We will consider these objections in detail later in the book, in chapter 8. But first, it is important to establish the need for such a system. We therefore begin in chapter 3 by examining the overwhelming evidence that innovation generally, and the relationship of patents to innovation in particular, differ by industry. A truly "unitary" patent law would therefore treat unlike things alike, which is neither fair nor likely to best encourage innovation across the range of industries. We then discuss the wide variance in theories of the patent system, pointing out how neatly they map to the different needs and understandings of different industries. Significantly, we explore the myriad ways in which the courts *already* treat innovation in different industries differently. The question, therefore, is not whether we should retain a unitary patent system—we don't have one now. The only question is whether we should acknowledge and embrace these differences, try to weed them out by fundamentally changing the law, or let the industry-specific characteristics of patent law develop accidentally. Given these alternatives, we think the right choice is clear.

We turn next to the most common objection to this flexible, industry-focused patent system: the idea that courts can't, or shouldn't, make these determinations. It is true that courts face some significant limits in their ability to tailor patent law to the needs of particular industries. But all advantages are comparative, and we suggest that neither the option of rigid uniformity nor the alternative of letting Congress or the PTO divide up the patent system is particularly attractive. A patent system that lacks the flexibility to deal with the radical differences between industries will break rather than bend. And a patent system whose only flexibility depends on particular industries lobbying Congress for specialized rules is unlikely to produce desirable rules. Certainly the lessons of recent efforts at patent reform are not encouraging for those who would rely on Congress.

The balance of the book begins the process of fleshing out our vision of a modular patent system. We begin in chapter 9 with some of the many industry-specific "policy levers" that courts now use to tailor the nominally unitary patent system to the needs of different industries. We talk about the ways courts in the last few years have begun to create new policy levers that treat different industries differently, and how those recent changes will alleviate some of the pressure that threatens to fracture the patent system. We then discuss in chapter 10 some other levers that courts have the power to use but currently do not, and some things Congress could do in the course of patent reform to facilitate the use of policy levers by the courts.

Some of the consequences of policy levers are fairly clear, especially for the two industries that today exist at opposite poles of the patent system—pharmaceuticals and information technology. But policy levers will also apply to other industries with more complex characteristics. As a result, in chapter 11 we offer preliminary assessments of the economics of one such industry—biotechnology—and discuss how policy levers can and do apply in biotechnology. Chapter 12 does the same for the information technology (IT) industries.

Our goal in these chapters—and in the book as a whole—is not to offer the last word in how the patent system works in different industries. Rather, it is to begin a conversation about how the patent system can best adapt to the diversity of the modern world. If we don't have that conversation in policy circles—and have it soon—the future of the patent system, and of the technological innovation that historically has flowed from the patent system, will be bleak indeed.

Foundations of the Patent System

The legal bundle of exclusive rights that we call a patent functions within a complex system of interlocking judicial, administrative, and legislative institutions. Much of the discussion of patents and innovation in this book takes for granted the background of the practices associated with these institutions. Readers who are familiar with the institutions and practices of the patent system may want to skip over this chapter, or skim it briefly to refresh their recollection. But for those who may be less familiar with the patent system, in this chapter we provide a brief overview of the legal and textual characteristics of the documents we call patents, as well as the institutions involved in granting and enforcing them. We focus primarily on the United States patent system, although with some local variation most of the features we discuss will be common to other patent systems around the world.

To decide whether this chapter is for you, take this simple test. Read the following four terms, and ask yourself honestly whether you know what they mean to a patent lawyer: anticipation, enablement, prior art, interference. If you know what these terms mean, skip this chapter: you'll be bored. If you don't know what they mean—if "anticipation" means only that you look forward to something, and "interference" only that someone is preventing you from enjoying it—by all means read on.

Why We Protect Inventions

The idea behind the patent system is simple: invention is a "public good" because it is expensive to invent but cheap to copy those inventions. If we don't do something to encourage invention by rewarding inventors, everyone will want to be an imitator, not an inventor.

At the same time, patents represent a significant departure from the norm of market competition. A patent gives its owner a legal right not only to prevent others from copying her idea but even the right to stop independent inventors from continuing to use ideas they developed themselves. So patents can not only encourage innovation, they can also interfere with it. And even if they don't, encouraging innovation by giving exclusive rights raises the cost of products to buyers. Drugs, for example, cost five to ten times as much when they are patented as they do when the patent expires and the drug manufacturer faces generic competition.

We cannot, then, think of patents as some sort of moral entitlement to one's invention. Rather, patents are deliberate government interventions in the market—a sort of mercantilist economic policy for artificially stimulating innovation. We think that this economic policy is on balance a good one. We need innovation, and in the long run we need it much more than we need price competition for existing goods. (If you don't believe us, ask yourself whether you'd rather have an iPod monopolized by a patent-owning Apple or very cheap eight-track tapes manufactured by a variety of companies in market competition). But the patent system is (and should be) designed to give sufficient incentive for invention, not perfect control. Perfect control does more harm than good. The result is that patents are limited in various ways—they expire after twenty years, for example—and that we must exercise care not to grant patents to people who don't deserve them or to grant rights broader than what the patentee actually invented.

The Nature of Patents

Intellectual property (IP) rights exist in many forms, but patents have distinct legal characteristics that distinguish them from other forms of IP, such as copyrights, trademarks, or trade secrets. Unlike copyright, which is primarily designed to protect aesthetic and artistic creations, or trademarks, which protect signifiers that allow consumers to identify the origins of goods and services, patents are specifically addressed to functional or utilitarian creations. In the United States, Congress has created a general class of patents, known as "utility" patents, and two specialized types of patents: plant patents, which cover asexually reproducing plant varieties (35 U.S.C. § 161.), and design patents, which cover nonfunctional product designs (35 U.S.C. § 171). These latter specialized patents are subject to some of the same rules as utility patents, but also have certain idiosyncratic quirks adapted to their specific subject matter. When most people speak of patents, they mean utility patents, and those more common patents are the focus of this book.

Utility patents may cover any new or improved machine, article of manufacture, composition of matter, or process (35 U.S.C. § 101), as long as the subject of the patent meets certain statutory criteria for novelty (35 U.S.C. § 102), nonobviousness (35 U.S.C. § 103), and utility (35 U.S. C. §§ 101, 112), and the inventor has adequately disclosed the invention. In the United States, the scope of potentially patentable subject matter has been extended quite far, to include living organisms, business methods, and anything else under the sun made by humans. The broad scope of patentability is controversial in many other countries, and has come under increasing fire here. Laws or products of nature that have not been created or altered by humans continue to be excluded from patent protection, even in the United States. But with that exception, "anything under the sun made by" human effort is patentable.[1] That broad conception of patentable things has brought patent disputes to many industries that were not traditionally affected by patents, including software and financial services. In doing so, it has contributed to the division in the patent system that is at the heart of our book.

Patents also differ substantially from other forms of IP in the way in which they are created. Many forms of IP protection arise spontaneously with the use or creation of the item protected. For example, in the United States copyright attaches to works of original expression at the moment the work is fixed in a tangible medium (17 U.S.C. § 102). Trade secrecy attaches to any valuable business information that is kept reasonably undisclosed from competitors. Trademark rights arise as the mark is used in commerce and becomes associated in the minds of consumers with a particular good or service. Patents, however, cannot come into being automatically. A patent right exists only if granted by the federal government after a review of the claimed invention to determine whether it meets relatively rigorous statutory criteria (35 U.S.C. § 131).

To facilitate this examination process, a federal agency, the Patent and Trademark Office (PTO), has been organized to review applications for patents (35 U.S.C. § 1) Inventors who wish to obtain a patent must submit an application to the PTO that sets out the nature and details of the invention to be covered by the patent (35 U.S.C. § 111). This applications and review process is termed the "prosecution" of the patent. Prosecution is not especially rigorous—the PTO is inundated with applications, and spends no more than sixteen to eighteen hours on average examining each application—but it can take three or more years to get a decision from the PTO.

Patents cannot be obtained for inventions that have already been published or disclosed to the public or are in public use (35 U.S.C. § 102[a]).
In much of the world, patents follow a standard of absolute novelty—any
disclosure of the invention to the public precludes obtaining a patent. However, the United States gives the first inventor a one-year grace period to file
a patent after the invention has been disclosed publicly (35 U.S.C. § 102[b]).
Since the clock on the one-year period may be started by someone other
than the inventor, possibly even without the inventor's knowledge, this creates a significant incentive for inventors to file an application for a patent as
soon as possible, even if they believe they may have a year or more to do so.

Even if the patent applicant is the first to have invented a particular technology, they cannot have a patent on that invention if it is "obvious"—that
is, if a scientist of ordinary skill in the field would have been able to come
up with the invention without undue experimentation. Finally, the inventor of a new and nonobvious patent must teach people in the field how to
make and use the invention, both to prove to us that the inventor herself
understood and was in possession of the invention and to make sure that
the public can use the knowledge in the patent once it expires.

Anatomy of a Patent

The application for a patent is a highly specialized and stylized document
conforming to the rules set out by the Patent Office. These rules allow, and
in some cases require, specific elements to be present in the application,
most of which also appear in a final published patent. The cover page of the
application sets out a variety of classifying and indexing data. The name
of the inventor or inventors appears here, as well as the name of any entity
to which the patent may be assigned. Information about the date of application, and, eventually, the date and number of patent issue appears here.
Numerical designations corresponding to international technological clas-
sification categories are set forth. A list of prior art references also appears
on this page, as well as an abstract summarizing the features of the invention being claimed.

Patents also generally contain one or more drawings illustrating aspects of the invention and keyed to a textual description of the invention
(35 U.S.C. § 113). Typically, a "background" section will describe the state of
the prior art, that is, of the technology up to the development of the invention claimed in the patent. The background section will also typically explain
or highlight the limitations of the prior art. A description of the invention

follows, explaining how the claimed invention overcomes the limitations, defects, or shortcomings of the prior art. Following this section there is often a more detailed description of the invention, which may include working examples explaining how to make or to use the invention, data about its efficacy, or technical specifications about its characteristics.

The patent application, which is the basis for the patent that is eventually published as a public record, must set forth a description of the invention that is sufficiently detailed to teach someone of ordinary skill in the art how to make the invention (35 U.S.C. § 112). But an inventor need not have actually "reduced to practice" the invention—that is, need not have built or physically tested the claimed invention in order to file a patent application. A "paper patent"—one without an actual reduction to practice—is sufficient if it contains enough detail to allow the invention to be actually made and used. We will see these "paper patentees" again under the guise of "patent trolls" who enforce patents, because they play a significant role in some industries. But there is a risk to filing "paper patents"—if the disclosure lacks sufficient information, or the information proves to be wrong, then the patent will be invalid.

The heart of the patent application is actually found at the end of the document: the claims. The claims take the form of numbered paragraphs, each containing a single sentence that is intended to delineate the outer bounds of the technology claimed. Claim language has over time evolved to include highly specialized terms of art that are intended to be recognized by courts and by other inventors as having those particular meanings. The structure of claim sentences is fairly standardized, beginning with a preamble that indicates the type of invention, a transitional verb that indicates the inclusiveness of the claim elements, and a series of elements recited in a particular relationship to one another. For example, a fanciful patent claim might read:

> I claim:
> 1) A widget comprising a main frammistat fastened lengthwise to a runcible renoberator.

Here the preamble indicates that the invention is a "widget," and the elements of the widget are a "frammistat" and a "renoberator," placed in a particular relationship to one another. The transitional term "comprising" signals that this claim is in "open" format, that is, that the claim covers widgets having *at least* these elements. An open claim is not limited to exclusively these elements; for example, it might cover widgets built of a frammistat, a renoberator, and a frawlpin. Even though such a widget would contain an additional element, so long as it had the elements recited by the claim, it would be covered by the claim.

Patent applicants get multiple shots at defining their invention in patent claims. To calibrate the scope of a patent, claims may be drafted as stand-alone, independent paragraphs that can be understood on their own, or as dependent claims that rely upon the stand-alone claims. Typically the patent will have a series of claims, some dependent and some independent. The format of the fanciful claim discussed above would be termed "independent," as its terms can be read and understood standing by itself. A dependent claim relying on such an independent claim might read:

2) The widget of claim 1, wherein the renoberator burbles uffishly.

Claim 2 "depends" from the first, independent claim, that is, its terms incorporate by reference the first claim. The dependent claim can only be understood by referring to the independent claim on which it relies. The dependent claim is also narrower or more specific than the general, independent claim; the dependent claim focuses the "renoberator" element of the independent claim to a particular type of "renoberator" that has more specific characteristics. The dependent claim can be more specific, adding additional limitations, without repeating every word of the independent claim.

These particular examples use made-up or invented terms (borrowed with apologies to Lewis Carroll, Berkeley Breathed, Roger Zelazny, and Edward Lear) to describe the invention. Inventors are in fact free to coin their own terminology so long as the terms are somehow clear to the reader, for example, by defining the terms elsewhere in the patent specification. As the patent law saying goes, the inventor can be "his own lexicographer," using any terms he pleases, as long as he defines those terms. More commonly inventors will use terms that are common in the vernacular of the relevant technical field, terms that would be understood by those of skill in that art.

The critical thing to understand—and what drives a lot of the problems in some industries—is that what the patentee owns is what they claim, *not what they actually built or described.* Thus, the critical issue in a patent case is what the patent claim terms mean. A court attempting to understand unclear or difficult patent claims would look first to the disclosure of the patent itself, to see if definitions of the terms are offered there and to understand the context of the invention. The court might also look to see how the terminology is used by practitioners of the relevant technology, including the use in standard texts or journal literature. A court will also look to the correspondence between the inventor and the Patent Office, to see if a particular term was discussed or considered in the course of granting the patent. The documents generated by the examiner and by the inventor in response to the examiner are preserved and referred to as the "prosecution history" or the "file wrapper history." If the inventor responded to an examiner's objection regarding the terms of a particular claim, either by amending the claims or by commenting on the term, this may offer important clues as to the meaning that the inventor intended.

Many patent claims are ambiguous, notwithstanding these interpretive sources. Parties disagree not only over the meaning of specialized technical terms but also over the meaning of such seemingly straightforward words as "a," "or," "when," and "through." As a result, while courts sometimes analogize the claims of a patent to the boundaries of a deed establishing who owns a particular piece of land, in fact the patent claim gives the public much less information than a real property deed about what the patentee does and does not own.

Patent Prosecution

Once received by the Patent Office, the application is routed to the proper office division or "art unit" for examination. Examiners will review the application to determine whether the invention meets the statutory criteria for obtaining a patent. First, the invention must fall within the subject matter of patentability: any useful invention made by a human is eligible, but products of nature or attempts to claim natural laws are excluded. This in turn requires that the invention must be useful—it must have some practical benefit. Third, as mentioned above, the invention must be novel; if it has been previously known or used by the public in the United States, or described in a patent or printed publication anywhere in the world, it is disqualified from patenting. The examiner will also determine whether the patent has been filed within the one-year grace period after a public disclosure.

Unlike other nations around the world, the United States at the time of this writing is a "first to invent" jurisdiction, that is, U.S. law seeks to confer the patent for a given invention on the person who invented it earliest (35 U.S.C. § 102[g]). Elsewhere, when more than one person claims a patent for an invention, the dispute is settled on the basis of who first applied for the patent. But unlike "first to file" jurisdictions, the United States resolves the dispute through an administrative proceeding in the Patent Office, called an "interference" (35 U.S.C. § 135). In the interference, each claimant presents evidence as to the dates she though of, or "conceived" the invention, and the dates she perfected or "reduced to practice" the invention. Much as in a trial, such evidence may take the form of documents, witness testimony, or affidavits. Interferences may arise between two co-pending applications in the Patent Office, or between an application and an issued patent, or even between two issued patents. If applications are pending at the time of the interference, examination is suspended until a decision as to priority is made.

The largest statutory barrier to obtaining a patent is the requirement of nonobviousness, which outside the United States is referred to as the "inventive step" requirement. The invention must not only be new, it must be a significant advance over what was previously known. Patents are not intended to be conferred upon inventions that could easily be developed by just anyone. If a person having ordinary skill in the technological field of the invention would have regarded the invention, taken as a whole, as obvious at the time it was invented, then it is ineligible for a patent.

To assess the application against the statutory criteria, the examiner will conduct a search of the relevant "prior art": previous patents and publications that may be identical or similar to the invention defined in the claims. She will read those references, as well as any references the applicant may have submitted, and compare them to the patented invention. The examiner will write an Office Action, which may allow or reject the application (35 U.S.C. § 132). Applicants start out with a significant advantage—they don't need to prove their entitlement to a patent. An examiner must grant the patent unless they can find some reason to reject it. If the Office Action issued by the examiner rejects or raises objections to the application, the applicant may respond in several ways. The applicant may choose to give up or abandon the application, either by not responding or by explicitly filing a document with the Patent Office stating the intent to abandon the application. The applicant might choose to abandon the application for a variety of reasons, including a change in business strategy, lack of further interest, or lack of funds to pursue a patent further.

Alternatively, the applicant may respond with arguments intended to answer the examiner's objections and persuade her that a patent should issue. The inventor may make technical arguments, pointing out features in the application that the examiner may have misconstrued or misunderstood in relation to the prior art. The applicant may also make legal arguments, pointing out or disputing the examiner's application of the statutory legal standards to the application. Since examiners are engaged for their technical expertise rather than for their legal expertise, and typically have only minimal legal training, explanation or clarification of the application's technical features may prove more fruitful. Finally, the applicant may amend his claims in response to the rejection, adding a limitation designed to distinguish the invention from the prior art or to limit the scope of the claims to correspond to what the application actually teaches. The examiner will in turn respond with another Office Action, which will either allow the patent or reject it once again.

Eventually the action of the examiner will be made "final." But the term *final* is a misnomer. There are administrative procedures for keeping an application alive after a final action, such as by filing a "continuation" of the application based on the disclosure of the originally filed document. These procedures are commonly used; nearly one third of patent applications filed in 2001 were continuations of a prior application. Applicants dissatisfied with the outcome can file an unlimited number of continuations, meaning that there is no way for the PTO ever to truly finally reject a patent application. But because the term of the patent is calculated from the date the application is filed, applicants often want to reach a resolution of the application as quickly as possible in order to maximize the time they own the patent.

Examiners face a heavy workload; at this writing there were over a million patent applications waiting to be processed, and four hundred thousand new applications are filed every year. Each examiner has on average only eighteen hours to devote to the entire process of patent prosecution, including reading the application, searching for and reading the prior art, writing several office actions, reading the applicant's responses, and perhaps engaging in an interview with the applicant. Given this limited time and the ability of patent applicants to come back an unlimited number of times, it is not surprising that a large majority of patent applications—roughly 75 percent—ultimately issue as patents, and many of the ones that don't are abandoned for business reasons.[2]

Nonetheless, some patent applications are rejected. The ultimate denial of the application may be contested by an internal appeal within the Patent Office to the Board of Patent Appeals and Interferences (35 U.S.C. § 134). If the patentee remains unsatisfied by the board's decision, she may appeal the decision out of the Patent Office to the United States Court of Appeals for the Federal Circuit (35 U.S.C. § 141). If the patentee remains unsatisfied with the decision of the Federal Circuit, she can request review by the United States Supreme Court, which has the authority to review the Federal Circuit ruling, but very few patent cases are accepted by the Supreme Court.

Patent Enforcement

Once a patent has been granted, the patent owner has the exclusive right to make, use, sell, offer for sale, or import the claimed invention into the United States (35 U.S.C. § 271[a]). The term of these rights lasts for twenty years from the date the patent application is filed, with special term extensions available if the prosecution of the patent was unreasonably delayed or if regulatory approval of a drug consumed a portion of the patent term (35 U.S.C. §§ 154(a)(2), (b); 155–56). Patents confer only the right to exclude others from engaging in these activities, or to collect royalties by allowing these activities. The patent confers no affirmative right upon the patent holder to practice the invention. Manufacturing or distributing the invention might require government approval, as with drugs, or might violate other laws, such as environmental or safety regulations. Practicing the invention might even be prohibited by another, overlapping patent, as in the case of "blocking" patents—overlapping patents that exclude one another.

Actions to enforce a patent must begin in a United States District Court having appropriate geographic jurisdiction over the case—typically, in a district court where the patent owner resides or where the allegedly infringing acts were committed (28 U.S.C. § 1338). Because even one sale of an infringing product can give rise to jurisdiction, patentees can generally sue anywhere in the country. The parties to the action may demand a jury trial, or they may agree on a "bench" trial where the case is decided by a judge. In either case, the United States Supreme Court has held that the construction and interpretation of the patent claims is a matter to be determined by the judge.[3] If the trial is a jury trial, the jury will decide the facts of the case that may be in dispute. Patentees have discovered that juries are more likely to rule for them, and so they are increasingly requesting jury trials, which have increased from 4 percent of patent cases in the 1940s to over 70 percent today.

When we spoke of the patent as a right to exclude, we were speaking approximately. In fact, a patent is a right to *try* to exclude a competitor. To exclude a competitor, a patent owner must persuade a court that what the defendant is doing infringes the patent, and the court will also consider whether the patent should have been issued in the first place. A court deciding an infringement case is required to find every element of the invention described in the patent claims in the defendant's product. In some cases, the accused device may escape literal infringement because some element of the claimed invention is lacking, but still constitute substantially the same invention, by making a trivial variation or replacing some element with a known substitute. Such accused devices may still be found infringing under the "doctrine of equivalents," which is intended to prevent infringers from making an "end run" around the patent claims via trivial substitutions.[4] Patent holders may also enforce their patents against those who do not themselves infringe but who assist others in infringing or supply to others materials that have no substantial use other than to infringe the patent.

Defendants who are accused of infringement may raise defenses or counterclaims, chiefly that the patent was improperly granted, and so is invalid (35 U.S.C. § 282). The defendant may attempt to show that the patented invention is obvious or anticipated or otherwise statutorily defective despite the Patent Office's approval. Issued patents are entitled to a presumption of validity, so defendants seeking to invalidate a patent carry a heavy burden of proof (35 U.S.C. § 282). Potential infringers can also proactively seek to prove noninfringement or invalidity of a patent by filing a "declaratory judgment action" in federal court. Although the declaratory judgment plaintiff must carry the same heavy burden of proof, this option alleviates the uncertainty of waiting for a patent holder to sue first.

If infringement is found, the patent owner may be entitled to an injunction to prevent further infringement and to damages compensating for past infringement (35 U.S.C. § 283–84). The damages awarded will typically be either the profits the plaintiff can prove it lost due to infringement or a reasonable royalty, as if the infringer had taken a license from the patent holder by negotiation rather than infringing the patent claims. But although the damages provision seeks to make the *patent owner* as well off as if a license had been negotiated, it may not be desirable to make the *infringer* as well off as if a license had been negotiated—that would simply invite infringement with no special penalty for being caught. Consequently, courts may triple damage awards for deliberate or willful infringement (35 U.S.C. § 284).

If the parties are dissatisfied with the decision of the trial court, they may choose to appeal the decision. In the U.S. system of federal courts, appeals from the district courts are typically taken to one of the dozen or so geographically situated circuit courts in which the particular district court is located. But in the case of patents, nearly all patent appeals go to a single circuit court located in Washington, D.C., no matter where the case originated geographically—the same Court of Appeals for the Federal Circuit that reviews administrative decisions of the Patent Office (28 U.S.C. § 1295). About half the docket of the Federal Circuit consists of patent cases. Consequently, between appeals from the Patent Office and appeals of patent enforcement cases from around the United States, the judges of the Federal Circuit develop considerable facility with the law of patents.

A Federal Circuit decision regarding patent infringement, like an interference or patent denial, may be reviewed by the Supreme Court. In the early years of the twenty-first century, the Supreme Court appeared to be accepting a somewhat larger number of patent cases, perhaps in recognition of the growing importance of this area of law. Additionally, having given the newly formed Federal Circuit approximately two decades without significant interference to develop a coherent body of patent law, the Supreme Court may have decided to pay more attention to the Federal Circuit's jurisprudence. Several recent Supreme Court cases appear to limit or curtail the Federal Circuit's power, such as a case requiring the Federal Circuit to give greater deference to the factual findings of the Patent Office[5] and another case holding that some decisions involving patent counterclaims may be appealed to appellate courts other than the Federal Circuit.[6]

Postgrant Proceedings

Given the expense of a lawsuit—legal fees now average $5 million per side for high-stakes cases—and the possibility of an injunction that would shut the defendant down, the threat and uncertainty of patent litigation could deter many entrepreneurs from adopting technologies that might be covered by a patent or that are covered by a patent of doubtful validity. One way to reduce the cost and uncertainty of patent litigation is to give a potential defendant an opportunity to challenge the patent before the PTO. Many nations conduct administrative proceedings in their patent agencies after the grant of a patent, in order to adjudicate disputes over the granting of the patent. Such postgrant opposition proceedings allow outside parties to challenge the patent, producing evidence and arguments as to why the patent should not be granted or why it should be narrowed.

The United States does not presently have such a procedure. For the most part, challenges to an issued patent must be brought before a court. But the United States does have some postgrant administrative procedures. Issued patents may be subjected to a review process, called reissue, which the patent holder may initiate when he believes that a substantive error was made that resulted in a patent that was either broader or narrower than deserved (35 U.S.C. §§ 251–52). The reissue process is essentially identical to the process of examination. However, due to the potential for surprise or abuse, reissue of broadened claims is limited to two years from the original patent issuance, and it has only limited infringement applicability to those who might have relied upon the claims of the original patent in conducting their business.

A second type of postissuance review of the patent, called reexamination, can be triggered by any interested party able to show a new and substantial issue not originally considered by the Patent Office (35 U.S.C. §§ 301–07). Reexamination may result in claims that are narrower than those of the original patent or in cancellation of the entire patent—the entire patent is put at risk. But unlike reissue, reexamination cannot result in broadened claims. As of this writing, reexamination exists in two forms. The classic form of reexamination may be initiated by an outside party, but once the reexamination is under way, it proceeds ex parte, just like the original examination—essentially as a dialog between the examiner and the inventor, without participation by any third party.

A newer form of reexamination has also been instituted, paralleling in some respects the opposition practice that exists in many countries (35 U.S.C. §§ 311–18). In many countries, third parties may contest the issuance of a patent and participate actively in the administrative proceeding, called an "opposition." Many observers believe that these administrative proceedings are less expensive and more efficient than challenging bad patents in litigation. Consequently, the United States Congress altered reexamination to look somewhat more like an opposition, allowing a form of reexamination in which a third party can actively participate, producing evidence regarding the patentability of the inventor's claims. However, Congress forced third parties who wished to participate in the reexamination proceeding to make a choice: in order to participate in reexamination, they would have to renounce their ability to later challenge the patent in court. As a consequence, this form of reexamination is seldom used, as few challengers wish to surrender their right to sue in court.

The International Context

We have primarily described the system in the United States, with some comparison to other countries. This is because patents are at present a national affair. No worldwide or international patent system exists. Patent protection exits country by country; the protection given under the laws of a particular nation typically end at that nation's borders. Although the European Union has for a number of years conducted negotiations on creating a regional patent that would cover all the EU member states, such negotiations have to this point proved unsuccessful. Even the European Patent Office—an entity entirely separate from the European Union—is authorized by treaty to issue a "bundle" of patents from the signatory nations, and each national patent in the bundle is enforceable only in that particular country. Typically patent applicants must make strategic choices about the countries in which they will seek patents. Filing patent applications in every country of the world is impractical due to the expense of multiple examinations. This expense can be ameliorated somewhat under the Patent Cooperation Treaty, or PCT, administered by the World Intellectual Property Organization, or WIPO, a subsidiary agency of the United Nations.[7] This treaty facilitates certain savings in time and effort for patent applicants; it acts as a coordinating mechanism for international patent applications but still requires filing in the individual nations where the applicant desires to obtain patent protection.

Although no worldwide patent is available, international harmonization efforts have made the character of national patents increasingly similar. In particular, the international treaty on Trade Related Aspects of Intellectual Property (TRIPS) has gone far toward standardizing national patents.[8] TRIPS is integral to membership in the World Trade Organization; nations that wish to join the WTO are required to sign and abide by the terms of the TRIPS agreement. Many, although not all, major jurisdictions around the world have joined or are seeking to join the WTO—for example, as of this writing, Russia was not a signatory. The treaty specifies certain minimum standards for patent protection by signatory nations. For example, they must recognize similar categories of patentable subject matter, must apply legal standards similar to the U.S. standards for nonobviousness, utility, and novelty, and must offer to the citizens of other signatories the same opportunity to obtain a patent as they offer their own citizens. Some national variation is permitted; for example, the treaty allows countries to decline to recognize as patentable subject matter inventions that are contrary to good public order or morals; the United States generally does not make such exceptions, but other countries may make exceptions based on their perception of public order. The treaty also allows certain exceptions and delayed implementation of patent standards for least developed nations.

3

Cracks in the Foundation

Our patent system has stood for over two hundred years. A patent act was one of the first laws passed by the first Congress that the United States ever had, and the patent statute has in one form or another been in force ever since. There have been changes in the legal requirements to obtain patents and in the structure and organization of the governmental agencies responsible for administering patents, but for most of its history, the patent system has served innovators—and those of us who depend on innovations—rather well.

By most accounts, that is changing. Public policy circles are replete with arguments that the patent system is broken, perhaps irretrievably. Nor are these complaints the province solely of legal scholars or of a few disgruntled litigants. The Federal Trade Commission, the National Academy of Sciences, leading members of Congress from both parties, the head of the Patent and Trademark Office itself, the *Wall Street Journal,* top economists, and many of the most innovative companies in the world—and those who obtain the most patents—have joined in a chorus of calls to reform the patent system. That chorus is not unanimous, of course. Plenty of industry players—to say nothing of organized groups of patent lawyers—have weighed in with the view that things are just fine, and that patent reform will destabilize American innovation. But when that many people with that many different perspectives have decided something is wrong, it is time to sit up and take notice. In this chapter we tell the story (or perhaps more accurately, *a* story) of how the patent system found itself in crisis.

The Patent Flood

We begin with perhaps the most dramatic difference between the Patent Act of 1790 and the patent system we have today: Modern patent law is a mass-production business. The original patent system contemplated that three cabinet officials would personally review each application for a patent and collectively decide whether to grant it. Even by 1793, it became clear that that system was unworkable. Today it is unthinkable. The PTO received 456,154 patent applications in 2007,[1] more than four times the number it received as recently as 1984.[2] It granted 157,283 patents in 2007, and since patents last for up to twenty years there are approximately 2.4 *million* patents potentially in force today.[3]

This flood of new patents has a number of important consequences. Among other things, it means that the popular image of the PTO as a group of scientists in white lab coats meticulously testing each invention to see if it works is, indeed *must be,* a myth. It also means that if you want to find out whether there is a patent out there that affects your business, you have a hard and perhaps even impossible task ahead of you to sort the wheat from the chaff. Finally, although there is no way to prove it, the existence of these millions of patents also leads us to suspect that the PTO has been more lenient in granting patents in recent decades than it was in the past. Perhaps that's wrong— perhaps there really are 2.4 million new and nonobvious inventions developed in the last twenty years—but we're skeptical. Even if the world is more innovative than it used to be, we doubt it is four times more innovative than it was in the 1980s, or that it is nearly twelve times as innovative as the 1870s, a decade that saw the development of the telephone, the lightbulb, and enormous railroad innovation, among other innovations.[4] The more logical explanation is that it is simply easier to get a patent today than it used to be, and that we are granting patents on more obvious inventions than in the past.

THE OVERBURDENED PTO

Regardless of why we have so many more applications than we used to, one consequence of the patent flood is that the PTO is overburdened. When Alexander Graham Bell filed his patent application on the telephone in 1876, he got a patent in less than four weeks. Today, by contrast, patent applications spend an average of three years or more pending in the PTO,[5] and nearly 10 percent of all the applications filed in January 2001 were still pending more than five years later, in May 2006.[6]

The fact that the PTO spends three to five years deciding whether to issue a patent does not mean that the patent examiner is actively working on the application during that period. Instead, it is generally more than a year, and sometimes more than two years, before the examiner even picks the application up off the pile.[7] Once the examiner does begin to look at an application, he or she spends surprisingly little time actually assessing whether a patent should issue. The patent prosecution process is ex parte—the only participants are the applicant seeking a patent and the examiner, who is both judge and devil's advocate.[8] Although patent applicants must submit to the PTO relevant prior art of which they are aware,[9] they are under no obligation to *search* for prior art, and a large number do not. The examiner, then, has the burden of reading the application, searching for and identifying the relevant prior art, reading the relevant prior art, deciding whether the application should be allowed by comparing the claims to the prior art, and writing an Office Action explaining the reasons why any claims are rejected. After the applicant writes a response to that office action, perhaps amending the claims, the examiner must return to the application (usually many months later), review it again, and write another office action. This back-and-forth with the applicant may happen yet again. The examiner may also conduct an interview with the applicant in which they discuss allowability in person or over the phone. Finally, there are technical matters that the examiner must identify and attend to before the patent application is in condition for allowance. The *total* time the examiner spends on all these tasks in fits and starts over the years of patent prosecution is eighteen hours on average.[10] It is not surprising, therefore, that the PTO issues many patents that, had they had perfect knowledge, would have been rejected. This is particularly true since much of the most relevant prior art isn't easy to find—it consists of sales or uses by third parties that don't show up in any searchable database and will not be found by examiners in a hurry.

There are also reasons to worry that when examiners make mistakes, those mistakes are disproportionately ones that favor granting rather than denying patents. Patent examiners have notoriously heavy caseloads and they are rewarded by the civil service system only for an initial response to a patent application and for finally disposing of an application.[11] As a result, an examiner has no incentive to spend more time on harder cases. Quite the contrary—their incentive is to dispose of cases as quickly as possible. And for reasons we explain below, the easiest way for an examiner to dispose of a patent application is to grant rather than to deny a patent. There is reason to worry, therefore, that when reviewing patents with multiple claims and a lot of prior art, the PTO will pay less (not more) attention to each claim or piece of prior art, and will tend in doubtful cases to grant rather than reject the application. Small wonder, then, that the PTO grants patents to approximately 75 percent of those who apply.[12]

DO-OVERS AT THE PTO

The structural tendencies for the PTO to grant patents, and the limited time examiners have to find prior art they can use to reject patents, are exacerbated by one of the oddest things about the U.S. patent system: the fact that it is impossible for the PTO to ever finally reject a patent application. While patent examiners can refuse to allow an applicant's claims to ownership of a particular invention, and can even issue what are misleadingly called Final Rejections, the patent applicant always gets another chance to persuade the patent examiner to change her mind. Even stranger, perhaps, is that the PTO doesn't even possess the power to finally *grant* a patent. Even when the examiner concludes that an invention is patentable and issues a "notice of allowance," the patent applicant always retains the right to abandon the application that was deemed patentable and start the process over again. Alternatively, an applicant can take the patent awarded by the PTO and, at the same time, seek additional or broader claims arising out of the same patent application.

In all three cases, the culprit lies in what is known as the "continuation" application.[13] Applicants dissatisfied with the course of patent prosecution can abandon an application and file a continuation. Alternatively, a patentee can prosecute one or more patents to issue and also keep a continuation application on file, hoping to win a better patent from the PTO in the future.

Continuation practice has a number of pernicious consequences. First, at a minimum, continuation practice introduces substantial delay and uncertainty into the lives of a patentee's competitors, who cannot always know whether a patent application is even pending and can never know for sure whether the patent will issue with claims that cover their technology. Second, allowing the applicant an unlimited number of do-overs means that the error costs of the patent system are systematically skewed in an applicant's favor: an erroneous grant leads to a patent, while an erroneous denial merely leads an applicant to try again. The result is that applicants can sometimes obtain a broad patent not because they deserve one, but because the examiner made an error in their favor or simply because the examiner lacks the incentive to continue to argue the matter. Third, continuation practice can be—and has been—used strategically to gain advantages over competitors by waiting to see what product the competitor will make, and then drafting patent claims specifically designed to cover that product. Finally, some patentees have used continuation practice to delay the issuance of their patent precisely in order to surprise a mature industry, a process known as "submarine patenting."

The result of all this is a patent prosecution process that lets bad patents issue, and one that may well let a lot of bad patents issue. Every patent lawyer has their own stable of favorite silly patents that the PTO actually issued, whether it is a method of exercising a cat with a laser pointer[14] or a method of twisting a swing[15] or a hyper-light-speed antenna that facilitates time travel.[16] More problematic are bad patents that issue on important technologies to people who did not in fact invent those technologies. Patentees regularly lay claim to be the inventor of multimedia, or video on demand, or Voice over Internet Protocol, or electronic commerce, or dozens of other significant new innovations. The problem isn't that those inventions shouldn't be patentable; it is that the PTO is granting patents that allegedly cover those things to people who do not appear to have invented any such thing.

We don't mean to suggest that the PTO is responsible for the flood of bad patents. As we have seen, patent examiners work under enormous time constraints and are subject to rules that bias the system in favor of granting rather than denying patents. Given the constraints of that system, it is surprising that the PTO does as good a job as it does, managing to reject a small but nontrivial percentage of the applications it receives and to narrow the scope of the claims in many of the patents it does issue.[17] And in recent years the PTO has worked hard to try to improve the prosecution process, creating (so far unsuccessful) rules to restrict continuation practice, soliciting prior art from third parties through the Peer-to-Patent system, and setting up a pilot program to encourage applicants with important inventions to opt into accelerated examination. The problem isn't that the PTO is badly managed or incompetent; it isn't. Rather, the problem is systemic. As long as the PTO is beset with a flood of applications and little time to review them, and as long as the incentives are to grant rather than deny patents, the PTO will continue to issue bad patents.

The problems with the patent system don't stop with some bad patents on the books. Those patents are increasingly being taken to court. And it is in the court system, where patents are enforced, that the current patent crisis becomes most apparent.

LITIGATION FLOODS AND UNCERTAINTY

The flood of patents has been accompanied by a flood of patent lawsuits. It itself, this shouldn't be surprising; a patent is a legal right that must be enforced in court, so as the number of patents issued has skyrocketed in the last twenty-five years, it makes sense that the number of patent lawsuits has kept pace. In fact, however, the number of lawsuits is accelerating *faster* than the already dramatic increase in the number of issued patents. Most academic studies of the issue measure the rate of litigation per thousand patents, a measure that accounts for the increase in patenting over time. Using that measure, Jean Lanjouw and Mark Schankerman found that between 1978 and 1984 the rate of patent litigation was nineteen suits per thousand patents. By 1991–95 it had risen to twenty-two suits per thousand patents,[18] and Deepak Somaya and John Allison et al. report that it rose again in the late 1990s to thirty-two suits per thousand patents.[19] Because the number of patents issued also increased significantly during this time, Bronwyn Hall and Dietmar Harhoff correctly point out that the absolute numbers of patent lawsuits increased more significantly during this period.[20]

More significant than the absolute number of lawsuits is the rise of what Carl Shapiro has termed the "patent thicket"—a nest of overlapping rights that any company that wants to produce a technology must find its way through. This patent thicket results not only from more patents and more patent lawsuits but from changes in the nature of the technology those patents cover. The patent system was designed for an era in which a patent covered a machine, and a machine was a fairly basic thing. As Rob Merges puts it, one hundred years ago "if you put technology in a bag and shook it, it would make some noise."[21] The kinds of things subject to patent protection had a fairly uniform character.

That uniform character is gone. We now have a patent system that, while unitary in nature, has to accommodate pharmaceuticals and biotechnology, DNA, mechanical devices, medical devices, computer software, computer hardware, and the Internet. Notably, more than half of all the patent applications being filed in this century are in the information technology sector, broadly defined to include the Internet, semiconductors, telecommunications, computer hardware, and computer software. And the most notable fact about IT is the multiplicity of patents that developers must deal with. This is not a problem pharmaceutical companies generally encounter. Although sometimes a drug requires multiple patented inputs—and there have been efforts to try to obtain multiple patents on the same drug —generally, one patent covers one drug. By contrast, in the IT industries, there are usually multiple patents—sometimes hundreds or even thousands—on each new product.

There are, as we have seen, roughly 1.5 million patents in force right now in the United States, and that doesn't count the substantial percentage that are dropped for failure to pay maintenance fees at some time in their lives. These 1.5 million are just the ones that people are willing to continue paying money to hold onto because they think they might turn out to be useful. A significant percentage of these patents are in the IT sector. Hundreds of thousands of patents cover semiconductor, software, telecommunications, or Internet inventions.

There are so many IT patents because of the nature of these technologies and the ways in which they interact; it is almost always the case that a product in the IT field combines a number of different components and therefore a number of different patents. Therein lies the basic problem. In the pharmaceutical industry, the medical device field, or the traditional mechanical field, an individual may only have one or two patents covering his invention. In IT, however, one product regularly involves the combination of fifty, one hundred, even one thousand, or—as Intel lawyers themselves say with respect to their own core microprocessor—five thousand different patent rights. All of those patent rights must be cleared, designed around, or somehow avoided in order to get the product to market.

But it is far from simple to decide *which* five hundred or five thousand patents might cover your new technology. Patent claims are meant to define the scope of an invention. But, while they do this reasonably well in some fields, such as chemistry or DNA, they are notoriously poor at telling the world exactly what a patent in the IT field actually covers.[22] Deciding what the patent covers becomes a linguistic exercise, in which we break a patent claim into its elements and parse the words used to define each element. But there are no hard and fast standards in the law by which to make the "right" decision as to either the size of the textual element that will be evaluated for meaning or the level of abstraction at which it will be evaluated. Indeed, the indeterminacy is so acute that courts generally don't even acknowledge that they are engaging in either inquiry. They define an element almost arbitrarily, and even when judges disagree as to the proper definition they offer no principled basis for doing so. The problem may be worse than a simple failure to acknowledge subconscious decisions that affect the scope of a patent, however. This indeterminacy may well be inherent in the process of mapping words to things, as modern literary theorists suggest. While courts purport to rely on the "ordinary" or "plain" meaning of the words of a patent claim, there may simply be no such thing.[23] The only way to find out whether a patent covers what you are doing is to go to court—and ultimately to the appeals court, because the data suggest that when judges do construe patent claims they are reversed approximately 40 percent of the time.[24]

Nor does the fact that the company developing the product did all its own work help it. Unlike copyright or trade secret law, which hold a defendant liable only if they copied from the plaintiff, patent law forbids even independent invention. And indeed preliminary evidence suggests that the overwhelming majority of patent lawsuits—more than 95 percent outside of the pharmaceutical industry—are filed not against defendants alleged to have copied ideas or technology from the plaintiff, but against defendants who developed that idea on their own.[25]

In practice, this means that a company that wants to sell a new product in the IT space cannot know who will assert a patent against it, whether that patent is one that really should have issued, or whether the patent actually covers what they are doing. And this uncertainty is a major contributor to the rise in patent litigation. It is well understood in legal circles that litigation, for patents or other disputed rights, is usually an outcome due to mutual mistake. If both parties know the real value of their disputed claims, it is in their interests to settle the dispute privately and avoid the costs of litigation.[26] And most legal disputes in most areas do in fact settle without a trial. Only when there is a substantial difference in their estimates of value will the disputants turn to a third party, such as a court, to adjudicate their differences. Greater uncertainty as to the nature and scope of patents will inevitably lead to more such adjudications.

PATENT HOLDUP AND LITIGATION ABUSE

The uncertainty we just described is a problem for patent plaintiffs as well as defendants, although the uncertainty for plaintiffs takes a slightly different form. If a patentee cannot know what her patent covers or whether it is valid, she cannot know who to license or sue. Standing alone, therefore, the indeterminacy of patent validity and scope may lead to more good-faith litigation, but doesn't necessarily lead to abuse of the patent litigation process.

Unfortunately, the patent remedy rules as currently designed give patent owners more than they should be entitled to as a matter of good patent policy. The combination of injunctive relief, patent damages that do not take sufficient account of the contributions made by others, and the prospect of treble damages for willful infringement even if the defendant developed its product on its own, all lead to a litigation system that is skewed in favor of patent plaintiffs, and that therefore encourages patent owners to roll the dice of litigation in hopes of reaping a large reward.

The first problem is injunctive relief. The prospect that a patent holder will obtain an injunction that will force the downstream producer to pull its product from the market can greatly affect licensing negotiations, especially in cases where the injunction is based on a patent covering one small component of a complex, profitable, and popular product. Injunction threats often involve a strong element of *holdup* in the common circumstance in which the defendant has already invested heavily to design, manufacture, market, and sell the product with the allegedly infringing feature. Companies that sell a complex, multicomponent product risk losing the ability to sell that product at all, at least for a time, if they are enjoined from selling even one small component in that product. As Mark Lemley and Carl Shapiro show, the threat of an injunction that cripples a larger product can enable a patent holder to negotiate royalties far in excess of the patent holder's true economic contribution.[27] The threat that the patent holder will obtain an injunction causes the negotiated royalty rate to exceed the true economic contribution of the patent holder, especially if the value of the patented technology is small relative to the value created by the product as a whole. (They also show that designing around the patent in advance of litigation won't help much, since those design-around investments will be wasted whenever the patent turns out to be invalid or not infringed). These royalty overcharges act as a tax on new products incorporating the patented technology, thereby impeding rather than promoting innovation.

The second problem is royalty stacking. Royalty stacking refers to situations in which a single product (again, usually a complex, multicomponent product of the type common in the IT industries) potentially infringes on many patents, and thus may bear multiple royalty burdens. The term "royalty stacking" reflects the fact that, from the perspective of the firm making the product, all of the different claims for royalties must be added or "stacked" together to determine the total royalty burden borne by the product if the firm is to sell that product free of patent litigation. As a matter of simple arithmetic, royalty stacking magnifies the problems associated with injunction threats and holdup, and greatly so if many patents cover the same product. In this key sense, the problems of injunction threats and royalty stacking are intertwined. But the problem also resides in legal rules for royalty calculation that do not sufficiently account for the presence of other inventions included in the infringing product.[28] Unfortunately, the rules commonly used by the courts to assess reasonable royalties perform especially poorly in the combined presence of injunction threats and royalty stacking.[29] The "reasonable royalty" that courts calculate should logically take into account all the other things that contribute to the success of the defendant's product, including other inventions included in that product and the contributions the defendant makes to the success of the product. But as a practical matter, juries never get to hear that evidence, and a jury that has focused attention for several weeks on the plaintiff's invention is likely to come away with an inflated sense of the relative value of that invention. As a result, royalty rates in court cases are surprisingly high—13 percent on average[30]—and give patentees a disproportionate share of the value of the defendant's product. These royalty rules have led to multibillion dollar verdicts,[31] to settlements in the hundreds of millions of dollars, and to a generation of patent plaintiffs with dollar signs in their eyes.

In 2006, the Supreme Court helped put the brakes on patent holdups when it decided *eBay v. MercExchange,* holding that a victorious patent plaintiff isn't always entitled to an injunction. In the wake of that decision, district courts have been limiting the right to injunctive relief to circumstances in which the plaintiff competes with the defendant, an approach that seems logical. But it remains to be seen how the Federal Circuit will implement the rule, and one recent decision may undo the benefits of *eBay* altogether by allowing patentees to obtain up to *fifty times* their actual damages in the form of a royalty fee in lieu of an injunction.[32] If the Federal Circuit decides to punish defendants for continuing to sell products when it has refused to order them to stop selling those products, it may as well have ordered an injunction. And in any event the problem of patent holdup will remain as long as courts refuse to apportion damages so that they bear some relation to the value of the patented invention.

The Bottom Line: Costs and Benefits

The combined effect of these problems, according to a number of economists who have studied the patent system, is that the system is broken. At least three major economic studies in the last five years have suggested that the patent system may actually do more harm than good to innovation, because the assertion and litigation of too many bad patents against companies that make innovative products ends up raising their costs and reducing their innovation more than the existence of those patents spurs new innovation. For James Bessen and Michael Meurer, the problem is a classic example of the prisoner's dilemma, in which individuals all make rational choices that collectively lead to disaster. In the modern patent system, they argue, the individual decision to obtain a patent is a rational one for most innovators, because the private benefits *of that patent* exceed the costs of obtaining it. But the collective costs those millions of patents impose on other innovators mean that, in every industry except chemicals and pharmaceuticals, the private costs to innovation *of the patent system as a whole* far exceed the private benefits those patents confer.[33] In other words, their data suggest the rather remarkable conclusion that in most industries innovators as a whole would be better off without a patent system. Bessen and Meurer don't jump to that conclusion, preferring instead some rather modest improvements designed to fix one of the problems identified above—the uncertainty associated with patent rights. But other economists have gone further. Jaffe and Lerner propose more significant efforts at patent reform, including steps to make it harder to get patents and easier to challenge them in hopes of stemming the patent flood at the source. And Michele Boldrin and David Levine have argued that we should be rid of the patent system altogether.[34] We think that goes too far. The patent system is in crisis right now for the reasons we have described. But we should be wary of cures that may be worse than the disease. In particular, two things concern us about the Boldrin-Levine proposal: it doesn't take account of how the real world might "design around" the inefficiencies in the current system, and it doesn't deal with Bessen and Meurer's most striking finding—the dramatic differences in the value of patents by industry.

Backlash: Ignoring Patents

Given these problems, it's a wonder companies make products in patent-intensive industries at all. And yet they do. Companies do not seem much deterred from making products by the threat of all this patent litigation.[35] Intel continues to make microprocessors, Cisco routers, and Microsoft operating system software, even though they collectively face nearly one hundred patent-infringement lawsuits at a time and receive hundreds more threats of suit each year. Companies continue to do research on gene therapy, and even make "gene chips" that incorporate thousands of patented genes, despite the fact that a significant fraction of those genes are patented.[36] Universities and academic researchers continue to engage in experimentation with patented inventions despite the now clear rule that they are not immune from liability for doing so.[37] John Walsh's study suggests that threats of patent infringement are not in fact responsible for deterring much, if any, research.[38]

What's going on here? The answer is straightforward, if surprising: both researchers and companies in component industries simply ignore patents.

Virtually everyone does it. They do it at all stages of endeavor. Companies and lawyers tell engineers not to read patents in starting their research, lest their knowledge of the patent disadvantage the company by making it a willful infringer. Walsh et al. similarly find that much of the reason university researchers are not deterred by patents is that they never learn of the patent in the first place.[39] When their research leads to an invention, their patent lawyers commonly don't conduct a search for prior patents before seeking their own protection in the Patent and Trademark Office.[40] Nor do they conduct a search before launching their own product. Rather, they wait and see whether any patent owner claims that the new product infringes their patent. Even then, it is common in many industries characterized by a significant number of "patent trolls" to ignore the first cease-and-desist letter one receives from a patent owner, secure in the knowledge that patent litigation is expensive and uncertain and that some letter writers will never follow up with a serious threat of a suit. Finally, and most significantly, companies in component industries that in fact get sued for patent infringement essentially never pull their product off the market pending the outcome of the suit. Rather, they decide to take their chances in court and hope that they can avoid infringement or invalidate the patent. Even if they embark upon a product redesign to avoid infringing the asserted patent, the redesign rarely replaces the original product unless and until the patent is held valid and infringed.[41]

There is, to be fair, one industry in which the patent system doesn't look much like anything we've described so far in this chapter: the pharmaceutical industry. Patent owners in that industry identify all the patents they have covering a drug by listing them in the *Orange Book*.[42] Entry by generic pharmaceutical companies is strictly regulated by the FDA. Once the FDA grants approval, the generic must tell the patent owner it plans to enter and give the patent owner an opportunity to sue. If they do sue—and they essentially always do—patent owners are entitled to automatic preliminary injunctions pending the outcome of patent litigation.[43] Even once that automatic preliminary injunction expires, generic entrants are often afraid to enter "at risk" without a final determination that the patent is invalid or not infringed, just as people are afraid to build houses on land they don't own. Those patent lawsuits rarely involve real disputes over infringement or claim construction, because the definition of a chemical claim is relatively straightforward and because the generic was required to copy the patentee's active ingredients (though there are sometimes disputes about the dissolution profile of a drug—the rate at which it dissolves—or about the inclusion of inactive ingredients). If a title-search system works in the pharmaceutical industry, why won't it work just as well in other industries?

The answer will lead us into the next part, and to the diagnosis of the problems with the patent system. The characteristics of the pharmaceutical industry are quite different than the component industries in which it is common to ignore patents. The need for strong patent rights is greater in that industry because of the cost and delay associated with FDA approval.[44] Virtually all patent owners in the industry are market competitors who rely on the exclusivity of the patent system coupled with the exclusivity that FDA approval provides.[45] The scope of the patents is generally quite clear, as they are defined in terms of chemical structure, and disputes over what the patent means are less common than in information technology. Pharmaceutical innovation is rarely cumulative, so the need for further research on a particular drug after FDA approval, while not zero,[46] is not particularly high. Further, the patent owner identifies up front the patents that cover a particular product. It can do that because market entry is delayed for years and even decades by the FDA approval process, with the result that all parties involved will generally know what patent rights exist before the generic seeks to enter.

All of these characteristics, particularly those that flow from the FDA regulatory structure, make the need for strong patent protection greater, the resulting patent rights clearer, and the costs of that protection less than they are in other industries, and particularly than they are in the IT industries. It is those interindustry differences that hold the key to effective reform of the patent system.

PART TWO

The Diagnosis

4

The Diversity of Innovation

There is virtually unanimous agreement that the purpose of the patent system is to promote innovation by granting exclusive rights to encourage invention. The standard account of the patent system recounts how such exclusive rights address the public goods nature of inventions—the fact that they are expensive to produce but easy to appropriate. The consensus position has been that patents are justifiable if they offer a net benefit to society, trading the disutility of restricted output and higher prices for the greater social utility of inventions that might otherwise not be produced. There is no unanimity, however, about whether the patent system actually succeeds. Among legal and economic theorists, the patent system has staunch defenders,[1] vocal critics,[2] and those who cannot decide whether the system is good or bad.[3] The most memorable statement of the uncertainty of the merits of patent law came from Fritz Machlup in 1958. Asked by Congress to conduct a detailed review of the patent system and the prospects for its reform, Machlup concluded that if we did not have a patent system, it would be irresponsible to create one, but since we have one, it would be irresponsible to eliminate it — hardly a ringing economic endorsement of the patent system.[4]

As late as 1986, George Priest complained that economists could tell lawyers virtually nothing about IP, and that the ratio of empirical evidence to speculation in the field was close to zero.[5] Although empirical studies of the patent system have blossomed in the years since Priest's observation, the positions of proponents and opponents of patenting, seen in recent legislative skirmishes over patent reform, seem to be no different than those at the time Priest wrote. In other words, both defenders and critics of the system seem to have adopted their positions about the patent system's merits or demerits as articles of faith rather than as conclusions drawn from hard evidence.

But we no longer lack for empirical evidence on innovation. In the last twenty years, legal and economic scholarship has provided valuable evidence about the complex process of innovation and how the patent system affects innovation. Rather than resolve the debate over how well the patent system works, however, this evidence has painted a more complex picture.[6] Different industries vary greatly in how they approach innovation, the cost of innovation, and the importance of innovation to continued growth. For innovation, one size definitely does not fit all.[7] This observation is graphically illustrated by examples from several industries, whose characteristics we sketch here and will develop further in the last part of the book.

It is important to understand that these differences are growing and changing over time. The history of innovation in this country begins with a fairly homogenous set of mechanical devices and, to a lesser extent, processes. As Rob Merges colorfully put it, in the first hundred years of the republic, "if you put technology in a bag and shook it, it would make some noise."[8] Industry-specific characteristics of innovation began to develop during the Industrial Revolution, when first railroads and then aircraft presented unique challenges to the patent system.[9] Even as late as 1978, the majority of all inventions fit comfortably into the category of mechanical devices. But innovation today is remarkably diverse, taking place in industries as different as telecommunications and proteomics. The process of innovation simply doesn't work the same way in those very different industries. And as we will see, neither do patents.

What do we mean when we say innovation works differently in different industries? The industry-specific components of innovation fall into several categories.

Differences in the Costs
of Research and Development

First, the cost of R&D varies widely from industry to industry and from innovation to innovation. Some inventions are accidental or the result of a flash of insight and require essentially no research budget. Canonical examples include the Post-it note,[10] which was originally a failed attempt to make an adhesive, and penicillin, which was discovered by accident when bread mold contaminated a petri dish. Other inventions, by contrast, require years of work by large teams of scientists methodically trying different approaches to a problem. A first-order approach to incentives might take the position that we need patents in the second case but not the first, since there is no need to encourage investment in serendipity. We think that oversimplifies the problem. Even serendipitous invention requires that the researcher be in a position both to think of and to appreciate the invention. Frequently, such a scientist will be part of a larger R&D project. Nonetheless, it certainly seems intuitive that patent protection will be more important in industries that require a large investment in R&D than in industries that don't need such an investment, because the public goods problem the patent system is trying to solve is much greater for those large investments.

Although there are examples of both types of inventions in many industries, notably in inorganic chemistry, some industries spend significantly more on R&D than others. In the pharmaceutical industry, for example, the R&D, drug design, and testing of a new drug can take a decade or more and cost, on average, hundreds of millions of dollars. Some—probably most—of this cost is a result of the labyrinthine regulatory process and the detailed study that is required to determine that a drug is safe and effective for humans so the FDA will approve it. A major additional part of the cost stems from the uncertainty of the R&D efforts. Pharmaceutical companies may try hundreds of compounds before identifying a possible drug, and they may not know for years whether they have chosen the right one for testing. The precise statistics are disputed: PharmA, the industry trade group, says the average cost of developing a new drug is $802 million, while Ralph Nader's consumer group argues that the average cost is only $110 million per drug. Part of the dispute centers on what components of cost should be included. The pharmaceutical industry tends to include marketing costs, which can be substantial but which should not count as innovation-related expenditures. But for our purposes who's right doesn't really matter. Even $110 million per drug is still an awful lot of money, and drug companies need some way to get a return on that significant investment.

Another example of an industry where invention requires significant investment is semiconductors. As microprocessors have gotten smaller, their design as well as the facilities and processes needed to create them have grown exponentially more complex. Building a new microprocessor requires not only painstaking work on circuit design—work that can cost tens of millions of dollars—but also the design and construction of an entirely new fabrication process in a new facility. The need for both highly skilled labor and a dedicated physical plant makes microprocessor development highly resource intensive. Ultimately, the design of a new generation of microprocessor takes years of planning and construction and can cost more than four billion dollars.[11] Although some aspects of semiconductor invention have recently been disaggregated into specialty design firms,[12] a significant part of the invention in semiconductors lies in the field of process, which still requires substantial investment. And even semiconductor design inventions rely on significant investment by downstream firms.

By contrast, other industries require significantly less investment in R&D. In the software industry, for example, it has long been possible for two programmers working in a garage to develop a commercial software program. Steve Jobs and Steve Wozniak are famous for having started Apple Computer in a garage, and Bill Hewlett and David Packard for starting Hewlett-Packard in the same way. Michael Dell started Dell Computer from his college dorm room.[13] The cost of writing code has gone up in recent years, particularly for operating systems. Operating systems tend to be more complex than applications programs, because they must be written to run a variety of computer programs and to control various hardware devices. But it is still possible in many cases to hire a team of programmers to write a new applications program for less than a million dollars. Although debugging a new program is still a significant undertaking, writing such a program takes considerably less time than developing a new drug or producing a microprocessor.

Further, in software and in many other industries, particularly biotechnology and the manufacture of machines and consumer products, much of the innovation process has been automated in the last fifteen years. Although computer-assisted design and manufacturing tools (CAD/CAM) do not replace the need for innovative ideas, they make the process of prototyping and testing those ideas much easier and faster. Similarly, powerful bioinformatics databases and the development of mass-production techniques like polymerase chain reaction (PCR) have revolutionized the biotechnology industry, making the identification of gene sequences and the development of related therapies much cheaper and quicker than they were in preceding decades. The use of automated tools that actually generate sections of code to help design simple programs such as websites has made computer programming simpler.[14] The result of this automation is that industries in which traditional innovation was largely an iterative process of optimizing prototypes today require less R&D expenditure than those that require either live testing or a new manufacturing process.

Economic evidence has also shown industry-specific variation in the corporate nature of innovation. The prototypical innovation contemplated by the patent law is made by an individual inventor working in his garage after hours. Alexander Graham Bell is in many ways the icon of the patent system. Vestiges of the patent law's focus on individual inventors can be found in the rule that patents can issue only in the names of individuals, not companies (35 U.S.C. § 118) and in the different response to individual and corporate excuses for delays in reducing an invention to practice.[15] But innovation in most industries today is generally collaborative, and much of it requires large laboratories. The overwhelming majority of patents today are granted to large corporations,[16] and even those granted to individuals and small corporations are often incubated in large research universities.[17] The role of individual inventors is much greater in some industries, such as mechanics and software, than in others, such as biotechnology and semiconductors.[18] And not surprisingly, corporate innovation tends to cost more than innovation by individuals.

The systematic variation in R&D expenditures across industries naturally affects the need for patent protection. Industries that must spend more time and money in R&D generally have a greater need for patent protection in order to recoup that investment. That doesn't mean that the patent system has no place for cheaper inventions; they may still facilitate market transactions in new innovations. But it means that certain industries have a stronger claim than others to need the incentives patents provide.

Differences in Firm Size

A related issue is the relationship between firm size and innovation. There is some economic evidence supporting the idea that small firms and large firms innovate differently, with small firms disproportionately likely to engage in breakthrough innovations and large firms more focused on "routine" (though still significant) improvements.[19] The evidence is disputed, and patterns are not entirely clear, but it does seem that small firms are more efficient innovators and that they are disproportionately responsible for the most important innovations.[20] By contrast, large firms, while engaging in significant innovation, tend to focus their innovative efforts on incremental improvements.[21]

If true, this general relationship would itself point to different patterns of innovation in different industries, since the scale required to engage in efficient research and development is, as we have seen, very different in the pharmaceutical and semiconductor industries than in software and the Internet. And the importance of these disruptive inventions may provide a justification for patent protection of small inventors even if they don't make a substantial research investment. But the situation is even more complicated, because evidence suggesting that the relationship between firm size and significance of innovation is not universal, but is itself industry-specific.

Thus, Keith Pavitt et al. find an extremely negative correlation between firm size and significant innovation, but they also find significant variance by industry in the strength of that correlation.[22]

Differences in Appropriability

The importance of patent protection in an industry is not simply a linear function of R&D cost. It is also dependent on the ability of an inventor to appropriate the returns from her invention through means other than patent law. Appropriability is itself an amalgam of a complex set of variables, many of which are themselves industry-specific. As Jonathan Barnett explains, alternatives to patents can often be more important appropriability mechanisms than patents themselves, "especially in what the innovation literature calls 'complex' technology sectors, in which innovations tend to arise and operate interdependently, and less true in what the innovation literature calls 'discrete' technology sectors."[23]

One such variable is the cost and speed of imitation. Some products disclose their know-how on their face. A seller of such a product necessarily gives its competitors information on how to imitate the product.[24] The inventor of the paper clip can't protect it as a trade secret, for example.[25] Once the paper clip is sold on the open market, anyone can see how to make one. Pam Samuelson's *Manifesto* points to software as an example, arguing that certain types of software innovations are disclosed on the face of the product and are therefore easy to imitate, and that new legal regimes are needed to protect such innovation.[26] Other inventions may be more effectively concealed within a product. Even if the product clearly contains the invention—if the results are visible, for example—competitors may face an arduous and uncertain process of reverse engineering in order to discover how the invention works. The standard example of such an invention is the formula for Coca-Cola, which according to conventional wisdom has not been successfully reverse engineered by competitors despite repeated efforts. Some software inventions also have this character, particularly if the code is released only in object code format. Process as opposed to product inventions may be even easier to protect without patent protection, because competitors have no legal opportunity to observe the process even once it is in use, and trade secret law will prevent efforts to sneak a look at the process.[27] Indeed, survey evidence from R&D managers across a range of industries shows that some industries rely more heavily on trade secrets than on patents to protect their innovation, particularly the chemical industry, which emphasizes process innovation.[28]

Appropriability is also a function of the speed of change in an industry and the importance of first-mover advantages. Even if imitation is possible, the inventor may recoup significant returns during the period before that imitation occurs. Innovators who are first to market often enjoy substantial advantages over later imitators even when access is not physically, electronically, or legally restricted.[29] This first-mover advantage is not premised on any direct effort to restrict access to proprietary information; it results from practical limitations on access and delays associated with incomplete knowledge. In fast-moving industries, particularly those with relatively little absolute R&D cost, inventors may be able to capture sufficient returns during the initial period before imitators enter the market to justify the investment they made in inventing. Empirical data shows that such first-mover advantages function as innovation incentives. For example, one study of large corporations in various industries concluded that head-start advantages, including the establishment of production and distribution facilities, were more effective than the use of patents in enabling firms to reap returns from innovation.[30] Some computer software fits into this category.[31] By contrast, in other industries an invention requires a significant initial investment that can only be recouped over the medium to long run—think of steel or glass manufacturing, for instance.

A second overlay is the ability of companies to leverage an initial first-mover advantage into a long-term benefit even during the period of imitation. FedEx, for example, was the first in this country to come up with a guaranteed overnight package-delivery system. At the time, that business method invention was not patentable, though it might be today.[32] Nonetheless, FedEx retains a significant advantage from being the first mover, because it established a significant brand name that draws customers even in the presence of competitors who provide quite a similar service. Similarly, Gideon Parchomovsky and Peter Siegelman have shown that pharmaceutical manufacturers actually sacrifice profits at the end of their patent term in order to strengthen their brands, because doing so gives them constrained power over price even after generic companies can sell an identical product.[33] Whether companies can take advantage of their first-mover status is industry-specific because it depends on the speed of change in the industry and on the structure of the market.

R&D cost and imitation cost are obviously interrelated. A more refined measure of the need for innovation incentives might be the ratio of R&D cost to imitation cost.[34] If imitation is impossible even in the absence of patent protection, there is little need for the incentives patents provide. Even in such a case, patent law would sometimes provide more protection than trade secret law because a patent forbids even independent discovery by a competitor. But it does not follow that patents would be optimal for society in such a case. Preventing independent discovery is a side effect of the patent system, not its goal. If imitation cost is enormous, innovators will be able to recoup even very large R&D costs without the need for patent protection.

Even assuming imitation is possible, if it is sufficiently expensive or time consuming the inventor may be able to make enough money to justify the cost of R&D. Whether this will be true depends on the time and cost of imitation—factors that are likely to differ by invention and by industry—as well as on the importance of first-mover advantages in an industry. In some industries, being first to market is critically important, either because it allows the first entrant to establish strong brand recognition or because network effects reward those who are first to build a customer base.[35] In those industries, even a modest amount of lead time resulting from the cost of imitation may provide enough incentive to innovate.

The ratio is of course also dependent on the size of the numerator, R&D cost. As the cost of R&D goes up, innovation without patent protection requires higher and higher imitation costs. All other things being equal, the need for patent protection is greatest where the ratio between R&D cost and imitation cost is highest. Since both R&D cost and imitation cost vary from industry to industry, so too will the ratio.

Other Incentives to Innovate

Another significant factor affecting the importance of patent protection in an industry is the availability of alternative incentives to create. IP promises a market-based reward for creativity, but it is not the only possible ex post reward system. Inventors may be motivated by the prospect of prestige among peers, by prizes (such as the Nobel) based on inventive activity, or by the academic rewards of promotion and tenure. They may also be motivated by the desire to do good, particularly in fields such as medicine, or by the love of science.[36] Indeed, there is a significant literature on the economic value of prizes as an alternative to IP rights for prompting innovation.[37]

It seems clear that at least some innovation would continue in the absence of any patent protection. Nineteenth-century experiments by Switzerland and the Netherlands in eliminating patent protection confirm that innovation will occur even in the absence of patents, though the evidence is mixed on the success of these experiments—that is, how much innovation we would lose if we abolished the patent system, and what we would gain.[38] In large measure, innovation in the absence of patent protection can be attributed to a variety of alternative means of appropriating returns, a list that includes "contractual agreements, joint ventures, technological opacity, copy-prevention technologies, secrecy practices, . . . various branding, product bundling, learning-by-doing and other commercial strategies that exploit a first-mover innovator's lead-time advantage."[39] These nonmarket rewards are more common in some industries than in others—there is no Nobel Prize in business or in semiconductors. They are also more likely to motivate certain types of invention than others. Prizes tend to motivate individual rather than corporate achievement, and the desire to do good or save lives works better in medicine (or perhaps some forms of computer software) or in university departments than in automotive or optical innovation.

In addition to ex post rewards for successful innovation, there are a number of ex ante subsidies to support R&D. Government agencies such as the National Science Foundation and the National Institutes of Health spend billions of dollars funding R&D; the National Institutes of Health alone spent approximately $21.6 billion to support research in fiscal year 2002 (an estimate based on 93 percent of the total budget of $23.2 billion being spent for research).[40] Universities spend even more—about thirty billion dollars in direct research support, as well as other forms of indirect research support, such as faculty salaries.[41] Numerous private foundations such as the American Heart Association or the American Cancer Society also invest substantial funding into biomedical and related research. University research is further assimilated into the private sector through spin-off companies incubated in universities supported by the Bayh-Dole Act (35 U.S.C. § 200 et seq). These rewards and subsidies encourage R&D even in the absence of patent protection.

There is good reason to believe that the effects of these alternative incentives vary by industry. The government spends far more on health-related research than on semiconductor or software R&D, for example. Indeed, unlike governmental funding of biomedical research, governmental forays into research subsidies for technologies such as semiconductors have been notably unsuccessful. Consortia such as SEMATECH, founded in the 1980s to help the U.S. semiconductor industry stay competitive in the international environment, have not generated substantial new innovations, and in the meantime the U.S. semiconductor industry did quite well on its own.[42] As a result, the level of nonpatent incentives to innovate varies by industry. Rebecca Eisenberg and others have explored in detail the tension between the system of reputational rewards and that of IP rights in the scientific research community.[43] It is no accident that they focus on the biomedical field, where ex ante incentives play the largest role.

Finally, the existence of regulatory barriers to entry in certain markets, especially the regulations imposed by the Food and Drug Administration (FDA), can benefit the regulated party as well as costing it money. Pharmaceutical, biotech, and (to a lesser extent) medical device manufacturers must spend years and large sums of money establishing the safety and efficacy of their products before they can sell them. Those regulatory barriers raise the cost of developing a new product in those fields, and therefore increase the need for companies to recoup those investments. At the same time, however, the existence of those regulatory barriers means that imitation of those products is also more costly. No one can simply copy or design around an FDA-regulated product; they must seek regulatory approval as well. If the copier wants to make the same drug the patentee is making, they can take advantage of an abbreviated new drug application process, but they are then subject to a variety of limits on entry, including an automatic thirty-month stay of entry if the patentee files suit for infringement and a variety of FDA-determined exclusivity rules in addition to patent-based exclusivity. If the generic wants instead to design around the patented invention, the fact that it is making a different drug means that it must go through the same multi-year safety and efficacy review as the original drug. As Bill Ridgway points out, this regulatory process itself provides protection for the original patent owner, since it both delays and raises the costs of imitation (especially improvement or design-around), and therefore reduces the need for legal exclusivity to allow the original developer to capture rents during that period of delay.[44]

Spillover Effects

Another significant factor in determining innovation incentives is the question of positive externalities or "spillovers." In most industries, innovation by one firm will leak out to others at some point, naturally subsidizing the productivity of other firms without direct governmental intervention. It is well established that the social returns to innovation exceed the private returns.[45] In part, this is because the benefits of innovation "spill over" to other firms in ways that cannot be fully internalized. Although one might think that spillover effects discourage innovation, because they mean that the inventor doesn't capture the full social value of her invention, in fact it is not necessary to capture positive externalities in order to justify investment in R&D; all that is required is that inventors capture sufficient returns to justify the investment. Indeed, there is good reason to believe that the fact that firms can't capture the full social value of their innovations is a good thing: these spillovers are actually driving, not impeding, innovation. [46]

Important recent work by Dietmar Harhoff has demonstrated that the level of these spillovers also varies by industry.[47] Further, he shows that sector-specific productivity is directly and positively related to the level of spillover.[48] In other words, the inherent "leakiness" of IP law has a positive effect on innovation. And because leakiness varies by industry, that positive effect will occur in some, but not all, industries. Relatedly, Ashish Arora and others argue that the "patent premium"—the additional payoff to a private firm of patenting an invention—has a differential effect on R&D in different industries. They find that increasing patent protection gives a substantial boost to R&D in drugs and biotechnology but leads to much less additional innovation in other fields such as electronics and semiconductors.[49] Using different metrics, Jim Bessen and Mike Meurer find much the same thing.[50]

Cumulative Nature of Innovation

Industries differ in the importance of continued innovation. Innovation is, in general, socially valuable. In many industries, especially young ones, innovation is critical to welfare. But innovation works very differently in different industries. In some industries, notably pharmaceuticals, innovation tends to be a stand-alone process generating a single finished product. Once a drug is developed and tested, it tends not to be improved. At most, pharmaceutical companies will improve the delivery system or patent obvious chemical variants such as metabolites. By contrast, in computer software cumulative innovation is extraordinarily important. It is received wisdom among software consumers that you shouldn't buy version 1.0 of any program. The expectation is that the programs will be incrementally improved over time. These differences have great significance for patent policy, because they bear on the importance we should attach to pioneer innovation as opposed to improvements.

The Risks of Innovation

A related, somewhat counterintuitive fact is that innovation is not always a good thing. Although it has significant social benefits, innovation may also impose costs. It may inhibit standardization, and therefore slow product adoption in a network market.[51] Innovation in interrelated fields such as computer software may affect product stability, since each new component can interact in unpredictable ways with existing components. And innovation in the biomedical and nanotechnology fields, while critical to human health and the environment, also poses concerns for health and safety until the long-term effects of new drugs and molecules can be determined. Each of these concerns is industry-specific.

Further, even leaving aside the potential social harm of some kinds of innovation, more innovation is not always a good thing. There is an optimal level of innovation in any given industry. Granting IP rights and subsidizing research generally encourage more innovation, at least by pioneers. Whether that is a good or bad thing depends on whether we think we've reached the optimal level of innovation, so that encouraging further investment in research and development in an industry might actually divert investment away from more productive uses. One study suggests we may already have reached that point in agricultural biotechnology, for example.[52]

In short, innovation differs by industry in a variety of ways. Each distinct technology displays an idiosyncratic profile of technical and economic determinants for research, development, and return on investment. Given this, there is no a priori reason to believe that a single type of legal incentive will work best for every industry. Indeed, there is every reason to believe that achieving optimal innovation in different industries will require greater or lesser measures of legal incentive, and in some cases perhaps even no legal incentive at all.

The Industry-Specific Nature of the Patent System

In the last chapter, we established that innovation is not all of a piece. Innovation varies greatly in a number of ways, and many of those ways differ systematically from industry to industry. The relationship between patents and innovation is at least as complex as the profile of technological and economic factors that determine innovation. There is no simple or universal correlation between the availability of patents and the incentive to innovate. Indeed, as Bob Hahn puts it, "the most general lesson to be gleaned from the patent literature is that there are few general lessons."[1] This is due in part to the fact that the patent system interacts with industries at several different points in the innovation process. Recent evidence has demonstrated that this complex relationship is industry-specific at each stage of the patent process: deciding to seek protection, obtaining a patent, setting the scope of the patent that results, deciding to enforce a patent, and determining litigation outcomes. Not surprisingly, in view of this, different industries put very different values on patents and the patent system. In this chapter, we explore each of these industry-specific characteristics in turn.

Deciding to Seek Patent Protection

Companies in different industries vary widely in the importance they attribute to patents and in the cost and effort they expend to obtain them. The differences begin with efforts to seek patent protection. Numerous economic studies over the last forty-five years have shown that a firm's propensity to obtain patents differs by industry in systematic ways.[2] The pharmaceutical industry, for instance, is often cited as a major consumer of patents.[3] Major cross-sectoral studies by Richard Levin and Wesley Cohen have shown that some industries rely more than others on patents to appropriate the returns from innovation. Both studies surveyed technology managers at companies in different industries, seeking evidence about why they innovate. Both studies found that patents play a major role in supporting innovation in only a few industries, most notably in chemistry and pharmaceuticals.[4] This self-reported data is bolstered by evidence suggesting that start-ups in certain industries, most notably biotechnology, spend far more of their budgets on patents than companies in other industries.[5] Indeed, one venture capitalist with whom we spoke estimated that his biotechnology companies spent 5 to 10 percent of their total budget on patent protection.

Given these facts, it is notable that the significant growth in the number of patents being obtained worldwide seems to be driven by the semiconductor, computer, and electronics industries, and not the chemical or pharmaceutical industries.[6] Indeed, Mark Lemley and Bhaven Sampat studied patent applications filed in 2001 and found that half of all applications filed were in the information technology industries, broadly defined, while only 4 percent were in pharmaceuticals.[7] This is likely explained by the importance of building patent portfolios in the IT industries, a development we discuss below.

Industry-specific variation thus affects which companies choose to apply for patents, how many patents they apply for, and how much effort they put into those patents.

The Patent Prosecution Process

Once a firm decides to seek patent protection, the process it will have to go through to obtain a patent depends on the industry in which the invention is located. John Allison and Mark Lemley studied the patent prosecution process and found that it varied dramatically from industry to industry.[8] They concluded:

> The U.S. patent prosecution system is not unitary. Rather, different entities experience very different sorts of patent prosecution. For example, chemical, pharmaceutical, and biotechnological patents spend much longer in prosecution than other types of patents. Chemical, medical, and biotechnological patents cite much more prior art than other patents, and are abandoned and refiled much more frequently. . . . These differences suggest that it is unwise to think of prosecution as a whole when setting patent policy. Objections and proposals for reform that are tailored to the needs of one industry may not fit another well at all.[9]

Doug Lichtman has further documented the industry-specific differences in patent prosecution by showing that examiners require more amendments to patent claim language in some industries than others.[10] This in turn means that patents in some industries—he cites nanotechnology as an example—will be less likely to qualify for protection under patent law's doctrine of equivalents.

In further work, Allison and Lemley determined that this heterogeneity in the patent prosecution process is a recent development. They found that the patent prosecution system was largely unitary in the 1970s, and indeed that the technologies themselves were not as diverse then as they are today. By the 1990s, new and different industries such as software and biotechnology experienced the patent system in fundamentally different ways.[11] Getting a patent is quicker, cheaper, and easier in some industries than in others.

The reasons for these differences are not entirely clear. In some respects the differences in patent prosecution may be inherent in the nature of particular industries. For example, the PTO has access to some forms of prior art—notably prior patents and some online journals—but not to other kinds, such as product catalogs and computer source code. The kinds of prior art the PTO traditionally searches are far more prevalent in some industries than others. Mechanical and chemical inventions may tend to show up in these available sources. This in turn means that the PTO is likely to cite much more prior art in these fields.[12] By contrast, in fields such as software the most important sources of prior art are not published in sources accessible to the PTO. As Julie Cohen explains:

> [I]n the field of computers and computer programs, much that qualifies as prior art lies outside the areas in which the PTO has traditionally looked—previously issued patents and previous scholarly publications. Many new developments in computer programming are not documented in scholarly publications at all. Some are simply incorporated into products and placed on the market; others are discussed only in textbooks or user manuals that are not available to examiners on line. In an area that relies so heavily on published, "official" prior art, a rejection based on "common industry knowledge" that does not appear in the scholarly literature is unlikely. Particularly where the examiner lacks a computer science background, highly relevant prior art may simply be missed.[13]

To some extent, therefore, we should expect that patent prosecution in certain industries will be more difficult and time consuming than in other industries because the PTO will be better able to evaluate patent applications in those industries. Other differences may be more random. Doug Lichtman finds, for example, that examiners simply differ in their individual proclivity to require amendment.[14] And Mark Lemley and Bhaven Sampat find that new examiners conduct much more thorough searches and are more likely to reject patents than more experienced examiners.[15] Because they also find that there are many more new examiners in the IT industries than in other fields, the result is that even the seemingly random distribution of "tough" and "easy" examiners can in fact have industry-specific characteristics.

Still other differences stem from the different value that patent applicants in different industries place on the patents they will receive. John Allison et al. show that patent applicants have a fairly good sense ex ante as to which of their patents will likely be the most valuable. As one general counsel of a major software company put it to us, "We pretty much know which twenty of the six hundred patents we file are critical, and which 580 it would be nice to have." For critical patent applications, companies go to greater lengths to try to "bulletproof" the resulting patents in litigation or licensing. To do this, they are likely to draft more claims. Claims cost money, but they give patentees multiple chances to cover a defendant's product in subsequent litigation. They are also likely to cite more prior art to the PTO. Empirical research has shown that patents are less likely to be invalidated in court on the basis of prior art that has already been considered by the PTO.[16] This makes intuitive sense—it is harder to persuade a jury to second-guess the PTO's judgment than it is to convince them that the PTO would have rejected a patent application if they had been aware of a critical piece of prior art. The result is that the owners of critical applications often cite a great deal of art to the PTO in an effort to strengthen their patent in litigation—particularly in the pharmaceutical and biotechnology fields, where patents are considered particularly important.[17] Finally, the owners of critical patent applications are more likely to fight for broad claims. This may mean that the patents spend more time in prosecution and generate more continuation applications and Requests for Continued Examination (RCEs), since the patentee can use these procedures to come back to the examiner an unlimited number of times in an effort to either hone the language of its claims or to persuade the examiner to allow those claims. Although this variation between patents whose value is known ex ante and those for whom a patent is a lottery ticket would seem to be an independent explanation for differences in prosecution, Mark Schankerman has found that distribution of value itself varies systematically by industry, with the chemical and pharmaceutical industries holding patents with more consistent value and mechanical and electronic patents showing high variance in patent value that is more consistent with treating a patent like a lottery ticket that may or may not pay off.[18]

Whether the heterogeneity in the patent prosecution process is attributable to the PTO, the patentee, or both, it seems indisputable that different industries experience the patent prosecution process quite differently, both in terms of what they put into it and what they get out of it. Although the patent office has nominally uniform procedures for all types of subject matter, and applies nominally uniform standards from a statute that covers all types of subject matter, the outcome varies systematically according to the subject matter.

The Scope of Patents

The effective scope of patents that do issue also varies tremendously by industry. This variance results from the relationship between a patent and a product. Much conventional wisdom in the patent system is built on the unstated assumption of a one-to-one correspondence in which a single patent covers a single product. For example, we speak of patents covering products: in common parlance, Eli Whitney patented the cotton gin, Thomas Edison patented the lightbulb, Alexander Graham Bell patented the telephone, and the Wright brothers patented the airplane. Modern patent law also assumes such a one-for-one correspondence in its decision to measure damages by the profits lost in the sale of infringing products.

Such a correspondence is the exception rather than the rule in the modern economy, however.[19] Machines of even moderate complexity are composed of many different pieces, and each of these components can itself be the subject of one or more patents. No inventor could patent a modern car, for instance. Rather, they would be required to patent a particular invention—say, intermittent windshield wipers[20]—that is only one small piece of a much larger product. This correspondence may have been overstated even in the classic inventions mentioned in the last paragraph. The Wright brothers did not in fact patent an aircraft; their patent actually covered the use of a vertical rudder and a fixed wing (the "aeroplane"). Edison's patent was an improvement on an existing lightbulb that claimed a particular class of incandescent filaments. Still, the traditional mechanical nature of invention was more susceptible to the one patent–one product correspondence than the more complex modern environment.

The strength of this correspondence varies by industry. In some industries, such as chemistry and pharmaceuticals, a single patent normally covers a single product—a new chemical or a new use for that chemical. In industries such as semiconductors, by contrast, new products are so complex that they can incorporate hundreds and even thousands of different inventions—

inventions frequently patented by different companies. A patent covering one of those hundreds of components will not effectively protect a product; it is useful, if at all, only as a licensing tool. Further, this difference means that we cannot simply apply the remedy rules from one industry to patents in another; if damages are calculated correctly patents in the semiconductor industry will tend to generate much lower royalty rates than in the single-patent product industries. (Mark Lemley and Carl Shapiro offer evidence that courts do not fully take these differences into account, but they still find industry-specific variation in royalty rates).[21] Still other industries fall somewhere in between. Products in biotechnology or software may require the integration of several different patents, but not hundreds of them. The correspondence between patents and products obviously affects the significance of patents in protecting R&D. Individual patents are inherently more powerful when they correspond to products than when they correspond to small components of a product. At the same time, patents on small components of large products may be uniquely useful in patent "holdup" of companies that must integrate the inventions into a working product.

Correspondence can sometimes work in the opposite direction. If products change fast enough, a single patent right that lasts twenty years from the filing of a patent application may cover not just one product but several different generations of products. Thus, although in some industries many different patents must be aggregated to produce a single product, it can also be the case that a single patent can cover multiple products. For obvious reasons, the value of a patent in encouraging R&D will vary depending on how much protection that patent gives to products that are sold for revenue in the real world.[22]

Patent Portfolios

Complicating the story of industry-specific correspondence between patents and products is the development of patent portfolios—large blocks of patents surrounding a particular technology. Gideon Parchomovsky and Polk Wagner have studied the growth of patent portfolios.[23] They argue that portfolios have value greater than the sum of their individual patents, because they hedge against the risks of patent invalidity and narrowing of scope. Although there is a strong chance of invalidating any given patent, it is hard to knock out a hundred different patents. Jean Lanjouw and Mark Schankerman find that the result is that the owners of large portfolios don't need to file suit as often as individual patent owners or those who hold small portfolios.[24]

While Parchomovsky and Wagner do not study the question directly, it seems quite clear that the construction of patent portfolios is an industry-specific matter. The companies acquiring the most U.S. patents each year are almost all in the computer hardware and electronics industries—IBM, Hitachi, Motorola. Most portfolio behavior occurs in the semiconductor and computer industries.[25] Rosemarie Ziedonis finds that companies in fragmented technology markets respond by patenting aggressively, creating their own defensive patent portfolio to avoid running afoul of someone else's portfolio.[26] By contrast, portfolios are rare in industries with a one-to-one patent-to-product correspondence, even in industries such as pharmaceuticals that consider patents extremely important. Pharmaceutical companies may seek a few patents covering the same pharmaceutical product—patenting metabolites, extended-release formulations, enantiomers, or processes of use. But these patents are usually used to try to extend patent life under the peculiar rules of the Hatch-Waxman Act, not to create a "thicket" of patents surrounding a complex of products.

We can gain indirect evidence on industry-specific variation in portfolio ownership by looking at whether large or small companies own patents in a particular industry. Although small as well as large companies can own patent portfolios, it is far more common for large companies to do so. Allison and Lemley find that individual inventors and small companies are much more likely to own patents in certain industries—notably mechanics and medical devices—than in other, "higher technology" industries, such as biotechnology or semiconductors.[27] And Judge Kimberly Moore has shown that foreign patentees—who are much more likely to be large companies with significant patent budgets than small companies or individuals— are more likely to own chemical, electronics, and mechanical patents than pharmaceutical patents.[28] Whether this reflects variation in who is doing the inventing in those industries, or who is choosing to patent, there can be little question that the outcome is industry- and technology-specific.

Use and Enforcement of Patents

Heterogeneity is also endemic to the enforcement of patents. Although the basic theory of patent law posits that a patent's value lies in the patentee's enforcement of the right to exclude competitors, or at least to compel a license fee, recent work makes it abundantly clear that most patents are never enforced. Indeed, the data show that less than two percent of all patents are ever litigated, and less than 0.2 percent reach the courtroom.[29] Scholars recognizing this fact offer a variety of alternative ways in which patents might contribute value to their owners,[30] but none of them is entirely persuasive.[31]

The decision to enforce a patent—and hence to make the traditional use of patents—is far more likely to occur in some industries than in others. For example, a study by Allison et al. found that patentees in the medical device and software industries are far more likely to bring suit than patentees in other industries, such as chemistry or semiconductors. The variation they find is so great that patentees in other industries are three times as likely as semiconductor patentees to file suit. Lanjouw and Schankerman find that pharmaceutical patents are more likely to be litigated than other types of patents.[32] And Deepak Somaya finds that patents in the drug and medical industries are more likely to be litigated in proportion to the number of patents issued, while patents in the electronics, computers, and chemical industries are less likely to be litigated.[33] When computer patents are litigated, they tend to be litigated in portfolio groups, and are more likely to trigger counterclaims of patent infringement, a finding that Somaya suggests is consistent with the idea that any given patent is less valuable in the computer industry than in the medical field.[34] Patents in semiconductor and other industries that tend not to litigate their patents presumably have some value to their owners (at least potential value ex ante), but that value appears to lie in signaling facts about the patentee to third parties or in defensive use rather than in excluding competitors or demanding licenses.

There is further evidence of industry differentiation in litigation and licensing as well. As noted above, individuals and small inventors are much more likely to own patents in mechanics and medical devices than in industries such as biotechnology and semiconductors. And recent studies have demonstrated that individual inventors and small companies are much more likely to enforce their patents,[35] while foreign owners are much less likely to do so,[36] meaning that all other things being equal, litigation is more likely in those industries with many individual inventors and small companies and less likely in industries dominated by foreign patent owners. Michael Meurer has argued that opportunistic patent litigation by nonmanufacturing "trolls" seeking to extract royalties is more common in some industries than others;[37] this may be correlated in part with patent ownership by individuals and small licensing shops. And it is reinforced by the portfolio effect we described above; companies with large patent portfolios are unlikely to sue other companies with large patent portfolios, because both sides are likely to lose in such a war. Instead, these large patent owners tend to cross-license their patents, which means that in the industries in which portfolios are common (semiconductors, telecommunications, computers) patent lawsuits tend to be filed by the outsiders.

Likelihood of enforcement is in part a function of the speed of change in an industry, because speed of change will affect the effectiveness of patent enforcement. Patent protection tends to be rather slow. It takes a while after an invention for inventors to hire a patent lawyer and draft and file a patent application,[38] close to three years on average for the Patent and Trademark Office to process that application,[39] and then still more time to identify infringers and bring a case through the litigation process to court. Although Allison et al. find that patent owners tend to file suit relatively quickly after the patent issues,[40] litigation still takes several years, and appeals even longer. Allison and Lemley found that patents litigated to actual judgment in a reported decision took 12.3 years on average from the time the application was first filed until the case was finally resolved.[41]

This rather substantial delay has significant effects in some industries. Software is an obvious example. It is very difficult for a software inventor to use patent law to prevent competitors from using her invention. By the time she has filed for, obtained, and enforced a patent, the software industry has moved on. Indeed, it may well be that several product generations have passed before the case is resolved. As a result, patent litigation in the software industry tends to be brought by companies who are no longer at the top of the industry, and are either seeking past damages based on infringements that no longer occur or are trying to apply their patent to new product generations, either by imaginatively reinterpreting their patent or perhaps by using the doctrine of equivalents.[42] By contrast, patentees in the biotechnology and pharmaceutical industries are less likely to be troubled by the delays in the patent system, because these delays are dwarfed by the labyrinthine approval process of the Food and Drug Administration. Patents in those industries are most useful at the end of their term, and delay in obtaining patent protection is therefore not a problem because the patented drug is rarely on the market yet when the patent issues. Delay in litigation is also not a problem for patent owners, because patentees in those industries are entitled to an automatic thirty-month preliminary injunction against the production of generic drugs under the Hatch-Waxman Act. And it is also the case that drugs tend to have more market staying power than software or semiconductors, which rapidly become obsolete as improved versions are introduced into the market. Not surprisingly, Schankerman finds that the value of patents depreciates rather sharply over time in the electronics industry, and stands up well over time in the chemical and pharmaceutical fields.[43]

When a patent does make it to litigation, the importance of the issues in that litigation also turns out to differ by industry. We begin with claim construction (the process of figuring out what the patent claims mean), arguably the most important determination a court will make in a patent case. It turns out that patent claims in some industries are relatively straightforward to understand, while in other industries they are almost completely opaque. A patent claim that sets out a DNA sequence or a chemical structure has a defined meaning to one of ordinary skill in those industries. By contrast, in many other industries patent claims turn out not to be so clear, whether because of the inherent difficulty of mapping words to things or because of deliberate efforts by the patent owner to draft ambiguous claims. In those industries, including software, hardware, telecommunications, the Internet, and, to a lesser extent, mechanical devices, the central issue in a patent lawsuit is figuring out what the patent actually covers.

Even beyond claim construction, the most important issues in a patent case depend on the industry in which the case is filed. Empirical evidence suggests that while challenges based on the asserted obviousness of an invention are common to all industries, challenges to the sufficiency of the disclosure a patentee made in her application are much more common in the chemical and pharmaceutical industries than in others, and are much more likely to succeed in those industries.[44] Whether or not this is a result of differences in how courts apply the law in those industries, as we have argued elsewhere,[45] or reflects differences in claim drafting, does not matter for our purposes here. Either way, both the question of what a patent covers and the question of whether or not it is valid depend in significant part on the industry and technology at issue in the case.

To the extent lawyers and patent owners understand and internalize the different legal treatment of different industries, that understanding will affect their decisions to seek and enforce patents in those industries. Even if lawyers don't expressly know that their industry is being treated differently than others—a very real prospect, given that in-house counsel and patent prosecutors generally work only within a single industry—they will react to the perceived treatment of their industry by the PTO and the courts. Biotechnology patent lawyers behave differently as a result of the outcome of biotechnology patent cases, for example. Their reaction to the cases they care about is likely to be very different than the reaction of software patent lawyers to the cases of interest to them.

Bargaining in the Shadow of Patents

Industry-specific use extends beyond litigation. Empirical evidence suggests that in industries characterized by cumulative innovation, such as computers and semiconductors, virtually no patent licensing occurs ex ante. Rather, companies in these industries innovate first and sort out rights later. Put another way, companies in complex, multicomponent industries tend to ignore patents unless and until they are forced to pay attention to them.[46] By contrast, ex ante licensing is more common in the chemical and pharmaceutical industries, where it is virtually impossible to ignore patents.[47] Arora has found that markets for patent licensing are more likely to develop under some industry structures than others.[48] This makes sense for many of the same reasons that litigation differs by industry.

Further, some of the nontraditional uses of patents are likely to be industry-specific. Some scholars have suggested that patents serve as metrics to measure and manage innovation in large bureaucratic companies.[49] To the extent that patents do serve that purpose—something about which Parchomovsky and Wagner are skeptical[50]—they will do so only in industries where patent owners tend to be large companies with significant patent portfolios, not industries where patents are owned by individuals or small companies. Others consider patents important in deciding which companies to invest in.[51] Those uses are naturally limited to small companies in industries in which venture financing plays a substantial role.

Not only patent enforcement, then, but licensing practices and the importance of other uses of patents differ significantly by industry.

Industry-Specific Patent Law

In the few cases in which patents are litigated to judgment, the law increasingly treats patents from different industries differently.[52] The most striking examples arise in biotechnology and computer software. In DNA-related biotechnology cases, the Federal Circuit has gone to inordinate lengths to find biotechnological inventions nonobvious, even if the prior art demonstrates a clear plan for producing the invention. At the same time, the court has imposed stringent enablement and written description requirements on DNA patents that do not appear in its jurisprudence regarding other technologies. In computer software cases, the situation is reversed. The Federal Circuit has essentially excused software inventions from compliance with the enablement and best mode requirements, but in a manner that raises serious questions about how stringently it will read the nonobviousness requirements.[53]

Even a casual juxtaposition of the biotechnology and software cases shows dramatic differences in applying what are nominally the same legal rules. Commentators have observed that the Federal Circuit's biotechnology written-description cases apply a standard quite different from the written description precedent in other areas.[54] District courts have recognized the difference, applying the Federal Circuit rules in different ways depending on the technology at issue.[55] The easiest way to see this may be to imagine the court's language from one discipline applied to another. In *Fonar,* for instance, the court said:

> As a general rule, where software constitutes part of a best mode of carrying out an invention, description of such a best mode is satisfied by a disclosure of the functions of the software. This is because, normally, writing code for such software is within the skill of the art, not requiring undue experimentation, once its functions have been disclosed.[56]

Replace software with DNA, though, and the following would result:

> As a general rule, where [DNA] constitutes part of a best mode of carrying out an invention, description of such [DNA] is satisfied by a disclosure of the functions of the [DNA]. This is because, normally, [identifying such DNA] is within the skill of the art, not requiring undue experimentation, once its functions have been disclosed.

This is *exactly* antithetical to the actual rule in biotechnology cases, as stated by *Eli Lilly:*

> A definition by function . . . is only an indication of what a gene does, rather than what it is. It is only a definition of a useful result rather than a definition of what achieves that result. Many such genes may achieve that result. The description requirement of the patent statute requires a description of an invention, not an indication of a result that one might achieve if one made that invention. Accordingly, naming a type of material generally known to exist, in the absence of knowledge as to what that material consists of, is not a description of that material.[57]

Conversely, of course, application of the biotechnology rule to software would radically change the law. The legal rules are the same, but the application of those rules to different industries produces results that bear no resemblance to each other.[58] The Federal Circuit and its predecessor court have been forthright in describing the different treatment given to a related disclosure doctrine, enablement:

In cases involving predictable factors, such as mechanical or electrical elements, a single embodiment provides broad enablement . . . In cases involving unpredictable factors, such as most chemical reactions and physiological activity, the scope of enablement obviously varies inversely with the degree of unpredictability.[59]

Nor are obviousness, disclosure, and patent scope the only doctrines that show such an industry-specific variation. The requirement that an invention have general utility, which has been all but eliminated in most fields of technology,[60] is alive and well in the life sciences. The Supreme Court imposed a stringent requirement on pharmaceutical inventions in *Brenner v. Manson*.[61] The Federal Circuit has relaxed that requirement somewhat,[62] but the court still requires more proof of experimentation in order to satisfy the utility requirement in biotechnology and pharmaceuticals than it does elsewhere. For example, in *In re Fisher* the Federal Circuit held that "expressed sequence tags (ESTs)," gene fragments used solely to help map the human genome, were not "useful" within the meaning of the patent statute.[63] Just a few years earlier, the same court had held that a drink machine that made customers think they were getting a drink from a visible source when in fact they were getting it from elsewhere was useful and therefore patentable.[64] Those two decisions can coexist only because the utility doctrine is applied in an industry-specific manner.

These categorical differences in the legal treatment of patents do not simply affect the validity of particular patents in particular industries. Patent scope is necessarily interrelated with obviousness and enablement.[65] The Federal Circuit's treatment of software validity issues implies that while the court will find relatively few software patents nonobvious, those that it does approve will be entitled to broad protection. The Federal Circuit's decisions strongly suggest that a patent is nonobvious only if it is the first program to perform a given function.[66] Of course, most patents will not meet this test—that is, most issued software patents are likely invalid for obviousness. Those that do, however, will not be constrained by prior art to claim only their particular implementation of a function—they can claim the function itself. The fact that they give little or no description of how to achieve this function will not bar the broad claims because the Federal Circuit has proven remarkably unwilling to require software patentees to disclose details. As a result, we should expect the first programmer to implement a new idea in software to write patent claims that encompass the entire category of software, regardless of how second-comers actually implement the same concept.[67] And indeed the pattern of software litigation in this decade has shown exactly that. Time after time, inventors of one specific, now-obsolete technology assert their patent claims against technologies developed years later—including e-commerce, VoIP (Voice over Internet Protocol), video on demand, Internet search—that seem to bear only a passing resemblance to what the inventor originally built or described.

The conceptual linkage of obviousness and disclosure similarly dictates a predictable result for the availability and scope of biotechnology patents, at least those involving DNA. The result is the opposite of that in the software cases: DNA patents will be numerous but extremely narrow. Under the Federal Circuit's precedent, a researcher will be able to claim only sequences disclosed under the stringent written description rules—the actual sequence in hand, rather than a group or genus of DNA sequences. And as Judge Learned Hand observed long ago, a claim that covers only the thing invented is a weak claim indeed.[68] At the same time, the inventor is shielded from obviousness by the lack of such explicit and detailed disclosure in the prior art. This lack of effective prior art seems to dictate that anyone who has isolated and characterized a novel DNA molecule is certain to receive a patent on it. But the inventor is certain to receive a patent only on the particular molecule described, as the Federal Circuit appears to regard other related molecules as inadequately described until their sequence is disclosed.[69] And since the obviousness threshold is so low, many different companies can patent different sequences, cabining rather closely the freedom of movement of patent owners.

Aside: Does It Matter Whether the Courts Intend to Treat Industries Differently?

Polk Wagner has argued that the differences we identify in the text need not concern us greatly, because they are merely case-specific differences rather than systematic variations by industry.[70] We do not find that reading of the cases persuasive. The court's systematic conclusions in different cases, its reliance on industry-specific precedent from case to case, its focus on uncertainty in the biotechnological arts, and its emphasis in biotechnology cases on proof of structure—a discussion totally absent from the software cases— all point in the direction of industry-specific rather than fact-specific differences in legal rules. This was strikingly confirmed in *In re Wallach* when the Federal Circuit once again applied the strict "possession of the DNA sequence" rule in 2004, notwithstanding the intervening developments in the science since 1997.[71] Indeed, *Wallach* seems to go even further than *Lilly,* holding that possession of a partial amino acid sequence is not enough to claim even the full protein, much less the DNA sequence coding for that protein. It is true that non-DNA cases in biotechnology are more lenient in their application of the written description doctrine, and it is also true that the court has started to apply the doctrine in other fields. But the rules the Federal Circuit has created for DNA seem to apply to no other technology.

In reaching these industry-specific results, the court is applying a nominally neutral patent law. It is possible that Wagner is right in one sense—that the Federal Circuit is not acting consciously to treat biotechnology and software differently, but is simply driven by its understanding of the facts of the cases. Even if that is true, we think that understanding itself is based on factors that will lead to industry-specific results. In a prior article, we have explained how the application of the same general legal standards can lead to such different results in diverse industries.[72] Much of the variance in patent standards is attributable to the use of a legal construct, the "person having ordinary skill in the art" (PHOSITA), to determine obviousness and enablement. The more skill those in the art have, the less information an applicant has to disclose in order to meet the enablement requirement—but the harder it is to meet the nonobviousness requirement. One reading of the biotechnology and computer software cases is that the Federal Circuit believes computer programmers are extremely skilled, while biotechnology experts know very little about their art. This implication is closely tied to the Federal Circuit's designation of some technologies as belonging to the "unpredictable arts"; the court treats biotechnology as if the results obtained in that art are somehow outside the control of those of skill in the art, whereas computer science is treated as if those of skill in the art have their outcomes well in hand. We discuss the industry-specific use of the PHOSITA in more detail in chapter 9.

Even where the courts don't apply legal rules in an industry-specific fashion, the interaction between those rules and the technological characteristics of different industries can produce anomalous results. Thus, William Kingston argues that the obviousness doctrine was created with the chemical industry in mind, and that its application outside of that industry is fraught with danger:

> [Nonobviousness] has shown itself to be incapable of developing organically to deal with other industries, other kinds of information and new ways of inventing. It works poorly for engineering products and is disastrously wrong for biotechnology. It should never have been applied to computer software. In complex technologies, it allows vast numbers of patents to be granted to firms which have no need of patent protection to innovate.[73]

To Kingston, the risk is not so much that the law will be applied differently in different industries as it is that nominally uniform application will have very different effects because of the different nature of those industries.

The breadth of patent protection is in part a function of how different the invention is from the prior art. Lowering the obviousness threshold and granting many different patents may actually constrain the freedom of patentees to operate, because they will be subject to more patents owned by different entities. As Jay Thomas puts it, "[a] lenient view of nonobviousness is ordinarily seen as inventor-friendly and pro-patent. But this trend allows the patenting of marginal inventions, increasing the possibility that primary inventors will have to share the rewards of their pioneering inventions with follow-on inventors of improvements."[74] Further, patent claims are invalid if they are not fully described and enabled by the patent specification, so the permissible breadth of a patent will be determined by how much information the court determines must be disclosed to enable one of ordinary skill in the art to make and use the patented invention. The range of claim equivalents is also a function of obviousness and enablement, since a patentee is not permitted to capture claim scope under the doctrine of equivalents that she would not have been permitted to capture at the time of prosecution.[75] Because a patentee can capture later-developed technologies under the doctrine of equivalents but cannot capture inventions in the prior art, the functional scope of a patent is more closely tied to obviousness than to enablement. Several scholars have noted that there is an equilibrating tendency between obviousness and patent scope—strengthening obviousness will make patents harder to get, but more valuable and therefore more attractive to seek, while weakening obviousness will narrow patents and therefore will make them less desirable.[76] This equilibrating tendency creates tradeoffs in the use of policy levers, but it does not mean—as Wagner might be read to suggest—that the effects of any given change in patent law are inherently indeterminate.

The total effects of the differences we have reviewed are quite striking. Numerous studies find that the contribution of patents to appropriability depends significantly on the industry in question.[77] The overall "patent premium"—the value patent ownership contributes to a company's market value—is modest but positive. But virtually all of the contribution of patents to industry value—and virtually the entire role they play in stimulating innovation—comes from only a few industry sectors.[78] Bessen and Meurer use the premium to calculate an "equivalent subsidy rate"—the amount of money that a government would have to provide to a company to replace the value of the patents that company owns. The rate is about 12 percent of R&D expenditures overall, or about $12 billion per year.[79] They find, however, that the actual patent premium varies significantly by industry. The premium is greatest—that is, patents are most valuable—in the pharmaceutical industry. Computers, mechanical devices, and chemicals all derive significant value from patents as well. By contrast, the premium is near zero in the electrical and electronics industries. That is, patents in those industries don't contribute significantly to the market value of the companies that own them; the industry would do just as well if patents didn't exist. And in a few industries, Bessen and Meurer find that the patent premium is actually negative—that patent owners would be better off without patent protection.

There are similar differences in the *social* as opposed to private value of patents by industry. Bessen and Maskin find that even if owning particular software, semiconductor, and computer patents contributes to the owner's bottom line, the role of patents more generally is to retard rather than enhance innovation, or at least R&D spending in those industries.[80] By contrast, it seems clear that pharmaceutical and biotech R&D spending is heavily dependent on patent protection.

We have shown that innovation occurs differently among different industries and that those differences extend to the way in which industry players experience every stage of that system. The basic message of chapters 4 and 5 is that it makes little sense to speak generally about innovation or about patents. The evidence is overwhelming that, at virtually every stage of both the innovation and patent processes, different industries have different needs and experience the patent system differently. We do not have a unitary patent system today, if by unitary you mean one system that works the same way everywhere. We have one set of legal rules, but the industries affected by those rules operate in very different patent systems. In chapters 6 and 7, we argue that these differences are so great that they affect the way that even theorists think about the purpose and effects of the patent system. For scholars as well as lawyers and businesspeople, where you stand depends on where you sit, and that fact helps to explain the theoretical confusion that exists today in patent law.

Heterogeneity in Patent Theory
Why We Can't Agree Why We Patent

Over a decade ago, John Wiley famously wrote that "the doctrine of patent law coheres while the doctrine of copyright does not."[1] His basic premise was economic: patent law was coherent because it started from a widely shared utilitarian baseline. Copyright law, by contrast, has produced no similar agreement on goals, with the result that, as Jamie Boyle put it, "in copyright law—to a greater extent than in most other fields of legal doctrine—there is a routine *and acknowledged* breakdown of the simplifying assumptions of the discourse, so that mundane issues force lawyers, judges, and policymakers to return to first principles."[2]

Wiley's premise is correct as far as it goes. To a greater extent than any other area of IP, courts and commentators widely agree that the basic purpose of patent law is utilitarian: we grant patents in order to encourage invention.[3] Although there is a second utilitarian justification—encouraging the disclosure of inventions that might otherwise be kept secret—it is clearly subordinate to the primary incentive goals,[4] and has little explanatory power in a world where very few scientists get their technical information from patents and scientists at many companies are discouraged even from reading patents. The corollary to the premise that we grant patents in order to promote innovation is that we should grant patents only to the extent necessary to encourage such innovation,[5] and patent lawyers and scholars are in general agreement about the need to walk the narrow line between too much protection and not enough. By contrast, copyright scholars and courts regularly offer both utilitarian and entitlement-based justifications for copyright law, and those justifications point copyright policymakers in very different directions. It is not surprising, therefore, that recent Supreme

Court jurisprudence suggests that even though congressional power to create patents arises from the same constitutional clause as the power to create copyrights, copyright and patent can be treated differently under the Constitution.[6] (The court's ultimate resolution of the copyright question in that case, *Eldred v. Ashcroft,* was quite surprising, but that's another story).

It is true that there have been a few theories of patent law based in moral right, reward, or distributive justice,[7] but to be blunt they are hard to take seriously as explanations for the actual scope of patent law. Patent law routinely gives control over products never built or contemplated by the patent owners.[8] This occurs in four basic ways. First, the scope of a patent is defined by its claims, and a patentee can claim to own a class or genus without having actually built or tested all of the species in that genus. Second, the doctrine of equivalents provides a means for broadening the scope of a patent beyond the literal language of the claims, and hence beyond the invention originally made by the patent owner. Third, patent claims may reach new and unanticipated inventions made after the patent issues, but which fall within either the literal language of the claims or the doctrine of equivalents. Finally, the patent law permits inventors to obtain patents based entirely on a written description of the invention, without actually constructing or selling the products embodying the invention.[9]

This extensive control, taken together with the short term of patent protection[10] and the broad right to prevent even independent development of an idea,[11] are all difficult to square with the idea that a patentee "deserves" to own the rights granted by the law in some natural law sense of the word.[12] Surely an inventor has no moral right to prevent someone who independently comes up with an idea that is in many respects better than the inventor's from making or selling those independently conceived products, yet patent law countenances just such a result. At the other extreme, if one believes in a natural law theory of ownership of the fruits of one's labor, it is hard to see why a moral right to prevent the copying of one's invention should suddenly evaporate fifteen to twenty years after it was granted. It seems far more logical to think that patents are what they claim to be— temporary grants of exclusive control over a product given by the government as part of a social project to encourage innovation.

Consistent with this understanding of patent theory, courts have treated patent law as utilitarian, not as a moral entitlement. Agreement on basic utilitarian goals has not, however, translated into agreement on how to

implement them. Despite a surface commitment to basic normative principles, different theories of patent law offer widely disparate explanations for
the role of patents and very different predictions as to their optimal division
and scope. The major theories of patent law, which we review in this chapter,
reach conclusions that seem to be fundamentally at odds with one another.
Scholars and practitioners disagree significantly about the proper scope,
availability, and even the very need for patents to optimize innovation.

The growing body of economic literature on patent theory has developed
at least five distinct approaches to the proper scope and allocation of patent rights.[13] These approaches exist in considerable tension. The approaches
range from theories contemplating "sole and despotic" control over new inventions to theories at the other extreme that contemplate minimal or no
property rights in inventions. In between these extremes lie several theories
that consider patents as both facilitators of and potential impediments to
innovation. The theories make different and conflicting predictions about
the effect of patents on innovation and dictate different and conflicting prescriptions for the parameters of patent law.[14]

Theories of Patent Law

As noted above, the classic utilitarian theory of patent law is one in which
inventors are encouraged to invest in research and development by the
prospect that their invention will be patented and that they will therefore
own the right to exclude others from practicing the invention for a limited
period of time. This right to exclude can either be waived in exchange for
money or exercised by a patentee who makes and sells her own products at a
price in excess of marginal cost. In either event, patents give entrepreneur-
ial individuals and companies a financial incentive to invent a commer-
cially successful product. At the same time, because patent law grants such
an exclusive right, it raises the cost of new products to consumers, and can
make it more difficult to engage in follow-on innovation. Patent law therefore attempts to balance the costs and benefits of exclusive rights, granting
sufficient incentive to invent but not perfect control.

The theories we discuss in the balance of this chapter are not so much
alternatives to this classic incentive-to-invent story as they are efforts to understand how the incentive works in practice and to balance the costs and
benefits in the light of economic evidence about how innovation and patent
incentives work. (The first theory, prospects, is a partial exception to this
rule: it is a theory designed to replace or at least supplement the incentive-
to-invent story).

PROSPECT THEORY

In 1977, Edmund Kitch offered a new theory of the patent system that he believed would "reintegrate the patent institution with the general theory of property rights."[15] This prospect theory of IP is rooted in many of the same economic traditions as the classic incentive-to-invent story, but its focus is not on ex ante incentives to create. Rather, it is an ex post theory that emphasizes the ability of IP ownership to force the efficient management of inventions and creations through licensing once they are made.[16] The fundamental economic bases of this approach are the "tragedy of the commons" and the hypothetical Coasean world without transactions costs.

The tragedy of the commons is a classic economic story in which people with access to common property overuse it because each individual reaps all of the benefits of his personal use but shares only a small portion of the costs.[17] For example, lakes open to the public are likely to be overfished, with negative consequences for the public (to say nothing of the fish!) in future years. Likewise, common fields will be overgrazed with similar unfortunate consequences. Any other exhaustible public resource may be similarly overused. Although in theory it is possible for cattle owners to agree to limit their grazing in the public interest, any such effort at agreement is likely to run into insurmountable problems. Not only will organizing and policing such an agreement take effort that will not be rewarded, but individual grazers have an incentive to free ride, reaping the benefits of reduced grazing by others while refusing to reduce their own grazing.[18]

The conventional economic solution to the tragedy of the commons is to assign resources as private property. If everyone owns a small piece of land (or lake) and can exclude others (with real or legal "fences"), then the private and public incentives are aligned. People will not overgraze their own land because if they do, they will suffer the full consequences of their actions. Further, if deal making between neighbors is costless, as Ronald Coase postulated but did not believe,[19] transactions will allow neighbors with large cattle herds to purchase grazing rights from others with smaller herds. Such transactions should occur until each piece of land is put to its best possible use.[20]

In the context of IP, Edmund Kitch's argument remains one of the most significant efforts to integrate IP with property rights theory.[21] Kitch argues that the patent system operates not (as traditionally thought) as an incentive-by-reward system, giving exclusive rights to successful inventors in order to encourage future invention, but as a "prospect" system analogous to mineral claims. In this view, the primary point of the patent system is to encourage further commercialization and efficient use of as yet unrealized ideas by patenting them, just as privatizing land will encourage the owner to make efficient use of it. Perhaps the best—certainly the most extreme— example of the prospect approach is a patent granted in Edwardian England to the philosopher's stone—the mythical catalyst that would change lead into gold.[22] The idea behind the patent was not a reward for an invention already made, but the theory that the prospect of exclusivity would concentrate the patentee's incentive to search for it.

Fundamental to this conclusion are three assumptions. First, Kitch postulates that

> a patent "prospect" increases the efficiency with which investment in innovation can be managed. . . . [T]echnological information is a resource which will not be efficiently used absent exclusive ownership. . . .
>
> [T]he patent owner has an incentive to make investments to maximize the value of the patent without fear that the fruits of the investment will produce unpatentable information appropriable by competitors.[23]

This is analogous to the tragedy of the commons argument in that only with private ownership do private incentives match social incentives. In the tragedy of the commons, the private incentive to "invest" in a field—for example by letting it lie fallow, or limiting grazing, in order to permit it to grow—is less than the social value of such an investment. In the patent context, Kitch makes an analogous argument: that the private incentive to improve and market an invention will be less than the social value of such efforts unless the patent owner is given exclusive control over all such improvements and marketing efforts.

Second, Kitch assumes that

> [n]o one is likely to make significant investments searching for ways to increase the commercial value of a patent unless he has made previous arrangements with the owner of the patent. This puts the patent owner in a position to coordinate the search for technological and market enhancement of the patent's value so that duplicative investments are not made and so that information is exchanged among the searchers.[24]

The Coase theorem is doing Kitch's work here. Under that theory, giving one party the power to control and orchestrate all subsequent use and research relating to the patented technology should result in efficient licensing, both to end users and to potential improvers—assuming, that is, that information about the existence of patents is perfect, all parties are rational, and licensing is costless.[25]

Finally, to maximize social benefit, the property owner must make the invention (and subsequent improvements) available to the public at a reasonable price—ideally, one that approaches marginal cost. It is not possible to price IP *at* its marginal cost and still stay in the business of producing new works, since developing those new works requires a fixed investment of resources (time, research money, and so forth) that frequently dwarfs the marginal cost of making and distributing copies of the idea once it has been developed. A property owner will have no incentive to reduce his prices toward marginal cost, however, unless he faces competition from others. If the property owner is alone in the market, he may be expected to set a higher monopoly price for his goods, to the detriment of consumers and social welfare.

Kitch notes this problem, but does not resolve it. He merely points out that not all patents confer monopoly rights, and that in some cases the creators of IP rights will face competition from the makers of other fungible goods and therefore their individual firm demand curves will be horizontal rather than downward-sloping. If one assumes such competition, IP owners may be expected to price competitively, just as producers of wheat do. Kitch is surely correct that the vast majority of IP rights do not confer monopoly power in a relevant economic market.[26] It is equally true, however, that IP rights must confer some power to raise prices above the marginal cost of production if they are to serve their acknowledged primary purpose of encouraging creation. Indeed, the "incentive to manage" argument that Kitch adopts also depends on giving patent owners some measure of power over price; without that power, there could be no incentive. IP most commonly gives this power by permitting some product differentiation and therefore some increase in price. The price is constrained by competing goods, but those goods are imperfectly competitive and so they do not limit price to marginal cost.

Kitch's prospect theory strongly emphasizes the role of a single patentee in coordinating the development, implementation, and improvement of an invention. The analogy to mining is instructive: Kitch reasons that if we consolidate ownership in a single entity, that entity will have appropriate incentives to invest in commercializing and improving an invention. Indeed, based on Kitch's theory one might think it appropriate to assign rights to prospect for inventions to companies even before they have invented anything, just as we do for the owners of prospecting rights, because doing so will give them the monopoly incentive to coordinate the search. Of course, patent law does not preassign patent rights, in part because we are unsure whether and when the basic assumptions underlying the prospect theory truly apply to innovation. Critics have charged that early assignment of rights may substantially interfere with downstream innovation, especially if the Coasean model of costless transfer does not apply. Transaction barriers may quickly accrue around exclusive patent rights to create the monopoly problems that Kitch elides. More generally, it is unclear whether the rationale for coordination and management of exhaustible resources can be sensibly applied to intangible, inexhaustible concepts.[27]

Kitch's prospect theory draws on economic literature in the Schumpeterian tradition, which in its strong form holds that companies in a competitive marketplace have insufficient incentive to innovate. On this view, only strong rights to preclude competition will effectively encourage innovation.[28] Further, on this theory only central control will allow effective coordination and marketing of inventions. A prospect theory therefore suggests that patents should be granted early in the invention process and should have broad scope and few exceptions.

COMPETITIVE INNOVATION

The Schumpeterian monopoly model of innovation has not gone unchallenged. In an influential article, Kenneth Arrow has argued that competition, not monopoly, best spurs innovation because, to simplify greatly, companies in a competitive marketplace will innovate in order to avoid losing out to a competitor, while monopolists can afford to be lazy and will fear that new inventions will steal their own markets.[29] Furthermore, unlike tangible property, information is a public good for which consumption is nonrivalrous—that is, one person's use of the information does not deprive others of the ability to use it. As a result, there is not likely to be a tragedy of the commons problem with ideas.[30] An idea cannot be overgrazed, because using it will not deplete it. Prospect theory is wrong, on this view, because it rejects the fundamental teaching of economics that competition, not monopoly, will most efficiently allocate resources. The only reason we need IP rights in the competition model is to create ex ante incentives to innovate. Even there, the case for IP rights is far from airtight. If inventors would still develop their ideas without the lure of a monopoly over the resulting product, so much the better.

Empirical evidence offers some support for Arrow's thesis. As a descriptive matter, it is clear that the overwhelming number of patents do not confer strong rights in an economic market. Rather, they protect particular ways of competing in the market.[31] Innovation still occurs in those markets. Indeed, many have argued that in some industries the freedom from patents is much more important to innovation than the incentive provided by patents.[32] There are clearly industries in which competition, not monopoly, has spurred dramatic leaps—the software industry in the 1970s and the Internet in the 1990s are but two obvious examples. There is some empirical evidence suggesting that competition is a better spur to innovation than monopoly even in the telecommunications industry, one which requires significant long-term investment in facilities.[33] And William Baumol has argued that oligopoly, rather than either perfect competition or monopoly, is the best spur to innovation more generally.[34]

Arrow's argument suggests a much more limited role for IP rights. If patents are justified at all on Arrow's theory, they should be narrowly circumscribed to particular implementations of an invention and should generally not give the patentee the right to control competition in an economic market.[35]

CUMULATIVE INNOVATION

Both Schumpeter's monopoly incentive theory and Arrow's competition theory involve somewhat stylized models of innovation involving single inventions. A growing number of economists and legal scholars have focused on cumulative innovation, in which a final product results not only from an initial invention but from one or more improvements to that invention. Where innovation is cumulative, patent law must decide how to allocate rights between initial inventors and improvers.[36] One way to allocate those rights is to give them all to the initial inventor, as prospect theory would do. But as Mark Lemley has argued, consolidating the rights in such a way is unwise if there is reason to believe either that competition among improvers will work better than centralized control of innovation or that patent owners and potential improvers will not necessarily come to terms.[37]

Robert Merges and Richard Nelson have offered an alternative model that tries to allocate rights between initial inventors and subsequent improvers.[38] Their theory of "tailored incentives" stands in opposition to prospect theory. Merges and Nelson dispute the assumption of prospect theorists that rivalry in innovation is wasteful. They believe that competition, not monolithic ownership, promotes invention most efficiently. They suggest that "when it comes to invention and innovation, faster is better"[39] and that "we are much better off with considerable rivalry in invention than with too little."[40] At the same time, however, they do not deny the importance of IP rights and the incentives they offer both to initial inventors and to improvers. Merges and Nelson offer empirical evidence to support their position in a variety of industries.[41] Merges has further elaborated this structure in his discussion of blocking patents and the reverse doctrine of equivalents.[42]

Merges and Nelson's approach is consistent with the traditional utilitarian story of patents, in which IP is a creation of limited rights by the government for a specific purpose.[43] Even William Landes and Richard Posner, noted advocates of property rights in other contexts, treat IP as primarily concerned with the balancing of incentives rather than the initial allocation of property interests:

> Copyright protection—the right of the copyright's owner to prevent others from making copies—trades off the costs of limiting access to a work against the benefits of providing incentives to create the work in the first place. Striking the correct balance between access and incentives is the central problem in copyright law. For copyright law to promote economic efficiency, its principal legal doctrines must, at least approximately, maximize the benefits from creating additional works minus both the losses from limiting access and the costs of administering copyright protection.[44]

Whereas prospect theory assigns broad initial rights and then leaves the parties to bargain to an efficient outcome, the tailored incentives approach pays closer attention to the particular allocation of rights between initial inventors and improvers. Merges and Nelson's approach, if valid, undermines the fundamental tenets of a property rights approach to IP because, at least in the industries they study, invention and creation are unquestionably cumulative activities.[45] Rather than granting rights to one party and leaving others to bargain for rights, cumulative innovation theory suggests that because markets often fail, we must be concerned with the allocation of rights *among* inventors.

Cumulative innovation's rejection of prospect theory does not mean that it rejects patents or even their status as "property" in a different sense: the "property rule–liability rule" framework for remedies introduced by Guido Calabresi and Douglas Melamed in their famous article, "Property Rules, Liability Rules, and Inalienability: One View of the Cathedral."[46] Under this framework, "property rules" refer to legal regimes that confer a right to prevent an injury, rather than merely a right to collect damages for an injury. As should be evident from even a cursory review of IP cases, successful plaintiffs in IP cases benefit from a strong "property rule"—they are entitled to injunctive relief in the ordinary case, assuming that they actually sell products in the market.[47] Merges makes a strong argument for the use of property rules in IP cases: it is extremely difficult for courts to put a value on IP rights. Employing property rather than liability rules allows the parties rather than the courts to make such valuation decisions.[48]

Establishing that IP remedies are governed by a "property rule" in the Calabresi-Melamed sense does not, however, tell us the extent to which original creators are entitled to real-property-like control over improvements within the scope of their original work. The literature on cumulative innovation argues that patent rights are important, but that they should not confer unlimited power to exclude. There are at least three strands to this argument. First, for a variety of reasons, society cannot rely on pioneers to efficiently license to improvers the right to compete with them.[49] Second, positive "spillovers" from innovation that cannot be appropriated by the innovator actually contribute to further innovation.[50] Third, granting strong IP rights encourages rent-seeking, which may dissipate the social value of the property rights themselves. In the patent context, giving too strong a right to first inventors could encourage wasteful patent races or holdup-based lawsuits.[51]

Although initial inventors will sometimes be entitled to patent claims that cover later improvements, the later improver also needs incentives to innovate. The cumulative innovation literature argues that granting patents to both initial inventors *and* improvers—so-called blocking patents—will normally balance incentives correctly, but that in some cases improvers should be protected from liability under the reverse doctrine of equivalents.[52] How the balance should be struck depends on the relative importance of the initial invention and the improvement.[53] Scholars who discuss cumulative innovation also imply that unfinished products, early versions, and improvements to a subset of a product should all be patentable—indeed, were it otherwise, there would be few cases in which the initial inventor and the improver would both be entitled to patents. Thus, cumulative innovation theory contemplates patents on smaller inventions, but it would give less complete rights over those inventions than would prospect theory.

THE ANTICOMMONS

Although the economic literature on cumulative innovation has generally suggested the grant of divided entitlements as a means of encouraging innovation by both initial inventors and improvers, a more recent body of scholarship points out the limits of divided entitlements in circumstances in which transaction costs are positive. Far from solving the tragedy of the commons, allocation of property rights can in some contexts produce its own inefficiencies.[54] Consider how problematic walking through your neighborhood would be if every piece of sidewalk were privately owned by a different person and you were required to obtain permission to take each step.[55] Relying on Michael Heller's description of what he calls the "anticommons,"[56] a number of patent scholars have argued that granting too many different patent rights can impede the development and marketing of new products when making the new product requires the use of rights from many different inventions.[57] Underlying this argument are concerns about transactions costs and strategic behavior, which these scholars argue will sometimes prevent the aggregation of the necessary rights.

The anticommons is characterized by fragmented property rights that must be aggregated to make effective use of the property.[58] Although these fragmented rights might represent an instance of cumulative innovation, in which the initial inventor and a series of improvers must integrate their contributions, a pure anticommons involves not so much improvements as different, complementary technologies that must be aggregated to produce a useful whole. Aggregating such fragmented property rights entails high search and negotiation costs to locate and bargain with the many rights owners whose permissions are necessary to complete broader development. This type of licensing environment may quickly become dominated by "holdouts" that refuse to license their component unless paid to do so.[59] Because a given project will fail without their cooperation, "holdouts" may demand a bribe close to the value of the entire project.[60] Every property holder needed for the project is subject to this same incentive, and if everyone holds out, the cost of the project will rise substantially and probably prohibitively. This happens with real property, but it is even more likely with IP, because of the uncertain scope of patent rights and the large number of rights that may have to be aggregated.[61]

The "anticommons" problem is a particular species of a more general problem in economics—the issue of complementarity of products. Complementarity exists where two or more components must be combined into an integrated system. Economists have noted the problem of double (or triple or quadruple) marginalization that can occur when different companies own rights to complementary goods. This is the so-called Cournot Complements problem. The problem is this: If a product must include components A and B, and A and B are each covered by patents that grant different companies monopoly control over the components, each company will charge a monopoly price for its component. As a result, the price of the integrated product will be inefficiently high—and output inefficiently low—because it reflects an attempt to charge two different monopoly prices in the same downstream market.[62] The anticommons literature builds on this economic work, offering additional reasons to believe that the companies may not come to terms at all, and that even if they do those terms will not be efficient.

Complements or anticommons problems can arise either horizontally or vertically in an industry. The problem arises horizontally when two different companies hold rights at the same level of distribution—say, inputs into the finished product (the producer of the pencil and the producer of the eraser). It arises vertically if a product must be passed through a chain of independent companies (such as a monopoly manufacturer who must sell through an independent monopoly distributor), or if patents on research tools or upstream components must be integrated with downstream innovation in order to make a finished product.

The anticommons literature suggests that too many companies have patents on components or inputs into products.[63] The problem is not necessarily the scope of those patents but the number of rights with different owners that must be aggregated. Thus, this literature addresses a dimension of patent rights not considered in any of the theories discussed above. It is generally at odds with the divided entitlement proposals of cumulative innovation theory. Two ways to solve the anticommons problem exist: consolidate ownership of rights among fewer companies or grant fewer patents. Most legal scholars working in the anticommons literature have assumed that the solution is to grant fewer patents, particularly to developers of upstream products such as research tools or DNA sequences.[64] Economists, by contrast, tend to assume that the solution to vertical complementarity problems is to vertically integrate—that is, to consolidate rights in a single company. Alternatively, horizontal anticommons licensing rights can be consolidated into a collective rights organization such as the American Society of Composers, Authors and Publishers (ASCAP) or a patent pool, even if the rights themselves remain under separate ownership.[65] Obviously, these two solutions have very different implications for patent policy. As a result, the anticommons theory does not necessarily dictate particular policy results. It does, however, militate against the excessive division of property entitlements, and therefore points out the limits of cumulative innovation theory.

PATENT THICKETS

Closely related to the problem of complementarity is the problem of horizontal overlaps between patents. Just as vertical overlaps between sequential inventions or the need to integrate different complementary inventions may give rise to the "cumulative innovation" problem discussed above, patent claims may also frequently be broader than the products the inventors actually make. Multiple patents often cover the same ground. Sometimes this is an intentional result of the patent system in cases where a later-developed improvement fits within the broad scope of an earlier claim. At other times patent claims may overlap because patents are too broad or tread on prior art that should have been but was not identified. Because patent examiners spend very little time with each patent, patents regularly issue that would not withstand more searching scrutiny, and indeed nearly half of all litigated patents are held invalid.[66] Thus, whether by mistake or by design, various parties may be able to lay claim to the same technologies or to aspects of the same technology.

Carl Shapiro has termed this overlap of patent claims covering the same technology the "patent thicket."[67] Like the anticommons problem, the patent thicket has the potential to prevent all parties from making a final product that incorporates multiple inventions. Indeed, anticommons and patent thickets are close cousins. Nonetheless, we think it is worth distinguishing them. While the anticommons analysis focuses on the need to aggregate fragmentary property rights owned by many different players and the difficulty of assembling those fragments into a coherent product, the patent thicket analysis focuses on the overlap of existing rights. Those overlapping rights can be owned by a relatively small number of companies with large patent portfolios.[68] Particularly in areas such as the semiconductor industry, companies need some means for "clearing" the patent thicket, such as cross-licensing all the rights needed for their complex product. Thus, one implication of the patent thicket is that patent law must permit the quick and easy clearance of these overlapping rights. Even with such clearance, patent thickets create a private patent tax on new entrants who cannot bring their own patents to the table.[69] More generally, the patent thicket problem—unlike its anticommons cousin—suggests not that patents shouldn't issue on different inventions but that patents should be narrowed so that the problem of overlapping scope will not arise in the first instance.

The basic agreement on the utilitarian goals of the patent system, then, conceals a surprising amount of complexity. Scholars disagree about how the patent system promotes innovation, about what kinds of innovation we need to promote, about how strong patent rights need to be to encourage innovation, and about how we should allocate those rights. In the next chapter, we argue that these disagreements can be traced to the industry-specific character of the patent system we identified in chapters 4 and 5.

Parts of the Elephant
How Industry Perspective Drives Patent Theory

The patent theories described in chapter 6 seem to be fundamentally ir-reconcilable, because they appear to orient patent policy in contradictory directions. Their prescriptions run the gamut of possible policy options. According to these various theorists, patents should be broad, narrow, or should not exist at all. They should be granted to initial innovators but not improvers, to downstream but not upstream developers, to both or to nei-ther. Who is right?

The answer, curiously, is everyone. The key to understanding the wide range of theories for optimizing patent rules is recognizing the different industry contexts in which patents exist. The range of patent theories par-allels the range of ways in which the patent system affects companies in different industries. Like the proverbial blind men with the elephant, ev-ery theorist has focused on one aspect of the patent system, appropriate for one industry but irrelevant to or even harmful in others.[1] In this chapter, we integrate these various theories by relating them to the industries for which they seem most appropriate. We emphasize that this mapping pro-cess is highly stylized; none of the theories we discussed in the last chapter maps perfectly onto any particular industry. Indeed, even determining the precise contours of an "industry" for these purposes is a problematic exer-cise. But each of those theories has a paradigm technology in mind that fits the theory more or less well, and it is no accident that each of those different theories has a *different* paradigm invention in mind.

At the outset, we emphasize that this divergence is a feature of patent theories, not a bug. The diversity of economic models about patents is a vir-tue; it is analytically robust. We resist calls for a "grand unified theory" of the patent system. Indeed, one main point of this book is that the search for such a theory is fundamentally misguided: patents work differently in different industries, and we should not expect our analysis of patents in one industry to apply easily to another industry with radically different characteristics.

Prospect Theory

Prospect theory is based on the premise that strong rights should be given to a single coordinating entrepreneur. Thus, prospect theory necessarily envisions invention as something done by a single firm, rather than collectively; as the result of significant expenditure on research, rather than the result of serendipity or casual experimentation; and as only the first step in a long and expensive process of bringing a product to market, rather than as an activity close to a final product.[2] This view follows Joseph Schumpeter in distinguishing between the act of invention, which creates a new product or process, and the broader act of innovation, which includes the work necessary to revise, develop, and bring that new product or process to commercial fruition. As a result, prospect theory suggests that patents should be broad, stand alone, and confer almost total control over subsequent uses of the product.

The prospect vision of patents maps most closely onto invention in the pharmaceutical industry. Pharmaceutical innovation is notoriously expensive and time-consuming. The pharmaceutical industry reports that it spends as much as $800 million on research and development (R&D) (including product development) for each new drug produced.[3] That number is almost certainly inflated, including among other things substantial marketing expenditures, which should not count as part of R&D, but there is no doubt that R&D is extremely expensive in the pharmaceutical industry.[4] The industry spends over $30 billion a year in private R&D, more than the total budget of the National Institutes of Health.[5] Furthermore, inventing a new drug is only the beginning of the process, not the end. The Food and Drug Administration requires a lengthy and rigorous set of tests before companies can release drugs to the market.[6] The Pharmaceutical Research and Manufacturers of America estimates that the total time spent from the beginning of a research project to the marketing of a successful drug is twelve to fifteen years, 1.8 years of which is due to the FDA approval process. Although imitation of a drug is reasonably costly in absolute terms, a generic manufacturer that can prove bioequivalency can avoid the R&D cost entirely and can get FDA approval much more quickly than the original manufacturer. The ratio of inventor cost to imitator cost, therefore, is quite large in the absence of effective patent protection. As a result, it is likely that innovation would drop substantially in the pharmaceutical industry in the absence of effective patent protection.[7] And indeed a wealth of empirical evidence finds that patents are extremely important to innovation in pharmaceuticals.[8] James Bessen and Michael Meurer go so far as to argue that the evidence suggests that patents are worth the cost *only* in the pharmaceutical and chemical industries.[9]

Patents also map well onto products in the pharmaceutical industry. As a general rule, the scope of patents in the pharmaceutical industry tends to be coextensive with the products actually sold. Pharmaceutical patents do not merely cover small components that must be integrated into a marketable product, and this in turn means that a company that wishes to sell a pharmaceutical product generally won't need licenses for many different patents.[10] Chemicals are readily characterized using existing scientific terminology, so people can generally tell what a pharmaceutical patent covers, unlike patents in the information technology industries. Drugs generally have stable effects, meaning that significant improvement in a pharmaceutical product is likely to take the form of finding a new drug rather than somehow building on an existing one. And the fact that structurally related chemicals (called homologs) often have similar effects means that if patents do not cover a group of related products, imitators can easily design around the patent by employing a close chemical analog to the patented drug.

All of these factors suggest that patents in the pharmaceutical industry should look like those that prospect theory prescribes. In the pharmaceutical industry, there is no serious problem of either cumulative or complementary innovation. Strong patent rights are necessary to encourage drug companies to expend large sums of money on research years before the product can be released to the market. And because much of the work occurs after the drug is first identified, it is important to give patentees the right to coordinate downstream changes to the drug so they can recoup the costs of that additional work. Some empirical evidence supports this result. Patents in the chemical and pharmaceutical industries were more likely to be licensed ex ante—a central facet of prospect theory—than patents in any other field.[11] Prospect theory works in the pharmaceutical industry.

Competitive Innovation

The theory of competitive (or at least imperfectly competitive) innovation focuses on the incentives companies have to innovate even if they do not hold a monopoly position and are unlikely to acquire one through innovation. This approach emphasizes the fact that many inventions do not require substantial and sustained R&D expenditures; they may be relatively simple ideas or discoveries happened upon serendipitously. It is also premised on competition's role in improving products and on the existence of other incentives to innovate, such as lead time or government research funding.

Competitive innovation theory maps well onto a variety of industries that have experienced substantial innovation in the absence of patent protection. One notable example is business methods. Under long-standing precedent, business methods were excluded from patent protection.[12] That rule changed dramatically in 1998, when the Federal Circuit concluded that business methods were patentable and, indeed, always had been.[13] As many commentators have noted, however, companies have ample incentives to develop business methods even without patent protection, because the competitive marketplace rewards companies that use more efficient business methods.[14] Even if competitors copy these methods, first-mover advantages and branding can provide rewards to the innovator.[15] FedEx, for instance, has preserved substantial market share in the overnight package delivery market despite entry into the market by other companies that copied its business model. Because new business methods do not generally require substantial investment in R&D, the prospect of even a modest supracompetitive reward will provide sufficient incentive to innovate. This does not mean business methods can never be sufficiently innovative to deserve protection, but it does mean that patenting every new business practice is unnecessary and probably unwise.

Innovation has flourished in other industries in the absence of patent protection. The early history of the software industry is one in which innovators developed impressive new products at very little cost in the absence of patent protection.[16] Patent protection was not available for software until well into the 1980s. Copyright protection may have been available, though the applicability of copyright was not really settled until Congress amended the statute in 1980. Some have argued that software should not be patentable even today,[17] though that argument ignores some economic changes in the industry and in any event seems unlikely to prevail. More recently, the Internet developed without patent protection for its fundamental protocols, in part because it was based on government-funded work and in part because the academic developers simply did not seek patent protection. A number of scholars have argued that the open, nonproprietary nature of the Internet is directly responsible for the dramatic innovation it fostered in the 1990s. They point out that AT&T, which had a monopoly in telephony and therefore under prospect theory the right incentives to innovate in the field, did not engage in similar innovation.[18] Open protocols permitted competition, and competition drove innovation. This too is changing, not because of differences in the economic structure of the Internet but because patent owners have flocked in droves to try to control various aspects of the Internet.

Competitive innovation theory suggests that ownership is not a necessary prerequisite to innovation, and indeed that it is sometimes inimical to innovation. Patent protection is not always appropriate, particularly where expected R&D cost is small, where the ratio of innovator cost to imitator costs is small, or where first-mover advantages or network effects can provide the needed incentives. Under these conditions, patents should be rare and very modest in scope, in order to allow market forces their fullest latitude. Competitive innovation theory fits business methods, arguably fits the Internet, and—at least in the 1970s—fit software.

Cumulative Innovation

The theory of cumulative innovation starts by rejecting the proposition that invention is an activity engaged in by a single inventor or company acting in isolation. Rather, innovation is an ongoing, iterative process that requires the contributions of many different inventors, each building on the work of others.[19] Cumulative innovation theory questions the ability of any one inventor to identify and coordinate all the improvers needed to optimize a product over time. Rather, those who emphasize cumulative innovation argue that the law must divide property entitlements in order to provide incentives to each improver in the process.

Cumulative innovation maps very well onto the modern software industry. The computer industry is characterized by a large number of rapid, iterative improvements on existing products.[20] Computer programs normally build on preexisting ideas and often on prior code itself.[21] This incremental improvement is desirable for a variety of reasons. First, it responds to the hardware-based architectural constraints of the software industry. Following Moore's "law," the speed of microprocessors has historically doubled every eighteen months, and storage capacity and transmission rates have shown similarly exponential increases. Programs written during an older period therefore faced capacity constraints that disappear over time. It makes sense to improve those products progressively as the constraints that limit the functionality of the programs disappear. Second, incremental improvement of existing programs and ideas tends to render programs more stable. It is received wisdom in the industry that customers should avoid version 1.0 of any software product, because its maker is unlikely to have all the bugs worked out. Iterative programs built on a single base tend to solve these problems over time. This is most obviously true when actual computer code is reused,[22] but it is true even when tested algorithms or structures are replicated in new programs. Third, iterative improvement helps preserve interoperability, both among generations of the same program and across programs. For the same reason, reverse engineering has had a respected place as a legitimate means of creating interoperability. Virtually all recent copyright decisions have endorsed reverse engineering in some circumstances.[23]

The software industry also has relatively low fixed costs and a short time to market. The archetypal computer invention is one made by two people working in a garage—Hewlett and Packard and Jobs and Wozniak are the classic examples, but the story has taken on a life of its own.[24] Although the costs of writing software have increased substantially over time as programs have become more complex,[25] the costs of writing and manufacturing computer programs remain low relative to the fixed costs of development in many industries. More critically from the perspective of innovation policy, the ratio of innovation cost to the cost of follow-on competition is not particularly high. Although it does cost less to clone someone else's program than to design your own from scratch, the difference is not enormous.[26] (Simply copying someone else's code is much cheaper, of course, but doing so violates copyright law, so software developers don't need patent incentives to prevent exact duplication.) Furthermore, computer program life cycles are short. Unlike industries such as steel or aircraft, where new generations of products are infrequent and those products may last for decades, computer programs tend to be replaced every few years, often by new versions of the same program.

The implications of these economic characteristics for patent law are threefold. First, the need for strong patent protection is somewhat less for software inventions than it is in other industries. Copyright law is the predominant protection for software, and trade secret and contract law also provide protection. One factor militating in favor of stronger IP protection in software is the ease of duplication of digital information in the networked world. Copyright protection is much better suited to preventing exact duplication than is patent protection, however. Copyright law has also been modified to better prevent such copying in the computer context by allowing copyright owners to control access to copy-protected works.[27] Software patents are important, but the relatively low fixed costs associated with software development, coupled with other forms of overlapping IP protection for software, mean that innovation in software does not depend critically on strong, broad protection.

Second, the rapid incremental innovation crucial to the software industry may be retarded by older companies that own software patents based on prior generations of products. The danger is that a single patent covers not only a single product but several generations of products that reflect incremental improvements by a number of different companies. Julie Cohen and Mark Lemley offer several reasons to fear that patents in the software industry may be given too broad scope, allowing owners of old software patents to prevent the development of new generations of technology:

> The pattern of cumulative, sequential innovation and reuse that prevails in the software industry creates the risk that software patents will cast large shadows in infringement litigation. Specifically, we believe that because innovation is especially likely to proceed by building on existing code in other programs, the temptation for the trier of fact to find equivalence of improvements will be correspondingly greater.[28]

It is also worth noting, however, that the Federal Circuit decisions on this point are decidedly mixed—the court has restricted the doctrine of equivalents across the board, and this has translated into some narrow readings of software as well as other sorts of patents. Instead of the doctrine of equivalents, the problem Cohen and Lemley identified has come to pass in claim construction, as hundreds of patentees have argued in court that their patent—originally written with one invention in mind—should be applied to a very different technology that others later developed.

Finally, a culture of rapid-fire incremental improvements leads to a large number of low-level innovations in computer technology. Copyright is not capable of providing effective protection for such innovations because it does not protect functionality.[29] Some form of protection for such innovations is desirable. In the absence of other forms of protection, a large number of narrow software patents may be the best way of protecting these low-level innovations.[30] Some might object to a large number of software patents because they increase the transaction costs of inventing. Indeed, this very argument underlies the theory of the patent thicket. We are not persuaded, however, that *narrow* software patents will increase transaction costs much more than software copyrights do. The only relevant patents are those that are licensed or litigated—perhaps 5 percent of the total number—not the whole universe of patents.[31] If those patents are of modest scope, they do not present opportunities for their owners to impede largely unrelated technologies, and the transaction costs should be relatively modest. (Of course, if those patents are not of modest scope, or if the scope is unclear, software patents can create more problems. That is what appears to have happened in the last ten years as more and more "patent trolls" have sought to characterize their inventions as decidedly broader than what they originally conceived of).

These characteristics are precisely those suggested by cumulative innovation theory. Because innovation is relatively low cost but rapid, the need for patent protection is generally modest. Patent protection for such incremental software inventions should be relatively easy to acquire, but should be narrow. In particular, software patents should not generally extend across several product generations to cover technology not conceived of by the patent owner.[32] Cumulative innovation theory, which balances rights given to initial inventors with rights given to improvers, makes sense for the modern software industry.

Anticommons Theory

Anticommons theory emphasizes the problems of divided entitlements among complements. These problems can occur either horizontally or vertically—horizontally if patents cover different pieces that must be integrated into a product, and vertically if patents cover different steps in a cumulative innovation process. Anticommons theorists point to the risk of bargaining breakdown whenever the development of a product requires permission from the owners of two or more inputs. Different strands of anticommons theory suggest that the solution to this problem is either to consolidate ownership in a single owner—a result reminiscent of prospect theory—or to preclude patent protection altogether for certain types of inputs, particularly upstream research tools.

Anticommons theory maps well onto DNA sequence patents, a critical component of the biotechnology industry, at least in theory. The biotechnology industry has some of the characteristics of the pharmaceutical industry, with which it shares certain products.[33] In particular, the long development and testing lead time characteristic of pharmaceuticals is also evident in DNA-related innovation. These delays are due in part to the stringent regulatory oversight exercised over the safety of new drugs, foods, biologics, and over environmental release of new organisms. Another similarity between DNA and pharmaceuticals is that generic drug producers seeking to imitate an innovator's drug face substantially lower costs and uncertainty than do innovators in the industry. Although the FDA imposes regulatory hurdles even on second-comers, the process is substantially more streamlined than it is for innovators. Indeed, the primary regulatory hurdle a generic company faces is to show that its drug is bioequivalent to the innovator's drug.[34] Assuming bioequivalency, the FDA allows the generic to rely on the innovator's regulatory efforts. The uncertainty associated with developing and testing a new drug is also completely absent for generic competitors; they need only replicate the drug the innovator has identified and tested. Similarly, the hard work involved in producing a complementary DNA (cDNA) sequence coding for a human protein is in identifying and isolating the right sequence; once the sequence is known, a follow-on competitor can quite easily replicate it. (The same is not true of gene therapy, however; there is no FDA procedure for producing "generic biologics," which means that imitation of biologics as opposed to the proteins gene sequences might produce would be extremely expensive.) And the existence of numerous functional equivalents to a particular DNA sequence means that patent protection must be broad enough to effectively exclude simple design-arounds, just as pharmaceutical patents must be broad enough to cover chemical analogs.

Still, the total cost of sequencing a particular gene is significantly less than the cost of more traditional drug design, especially since computers have made it possible to automate much of the process.[35] Additionally, DNA sequencing, unlike pharmaceuticals, involves both vertical and horizontal complements. Patentees have acquired thousands of patents on DNA sequences that cover specific genes or in some cases fragments of genes.[36] Moreover, biotechnology companies have patented probes, sequencing methods, and other research tools. Any particular gene therapy is likely to require the simultaneous use of many of these research tool patents, leading to anticommons problems. The problem is exacerbated by "reach-through" licenses in which the owners of upstream research tools seek control of and royalties on the downstream uses of the tool.[37]

Scholars have proposed several different ways of solving these aggregation problems. First, vertical integration of companies may make much of the problem disappear.[38] If biotechnology companies are owned by, or allied with, pharmaceutical companies, the resulting company may own enough rights to research tools, gene sequences, and implementation methods to move from research through drug design and manufacture alone, although ironically this leads some to worry that such integration may result in any one company holding patent rights that are too broad.[39] Second, if the absolute cost of sequencing DNA is sufficiently low, or the existence of nonproprietary incentives sufficiently great, the anticommons problem could be solved by refusing to protect certain types of biotechnological inventions—such as expressed sequence tags (ESTs)—at all.[40] The fact that a publicly funded effort sequenced the human genome without the need for patent protection is instructive here. Finally, the problem might be solved if bargaining were easy enough. There is some literature that suggests that the owners of upstream DNA patents are releasing them into the public domain in a sort of open source genomic licensing,[41] perhaps because the relationship between DNA sequences and gene therapies has proven more elusive than first thought, so that the value of holding a patent on a particular gene sequence is reduced or at least less certain.[42] One empirical investigation by John Walsh suggests that the anticommons problem in biotechnology research tools is often overcome in practice.[43] Notably, this study does not deny the existence of the problem in biotechnology, but merely suggests that parties can sometimes get around the problem. For instance, the authors suggest that researchers have so far managed to overcome the anticommons problem in part by challenging the validity of patents or by simply ignoring them altogether.[44]

Although the predicted anticommons problems have only rarely materialized at the research stage in biotechnology, it is downstream that the real threat seems likely to emerge. As our understanding of genetics has advanced, it has become clear that a simple one-gene–one-disease relationship is the exception rather than the rule.[45] In fact, treatment of a disease using gene therapy—where it is effective at all—may require the aggregation of modifications to or proteins from dozens of different genes. And certain products, like Affymetrix's "gene on a chip," by their nature require the use of genes throughout the genome. Some, like David Adelman, have drawn from this the conclusion that an anticommons is unlikely at the research stage, because no one knows which genes might prove valuable in researching which diseases. Empirical evidence on this question is mixed, but there is evidence that scientific papers from which discoveries are patented are significantly less likely to be cited by subsequent scientific papers, suggesting that patents may be restricting the flow of scientific knowledge.[46] And in any event the anticommons risks are significantly greater when a company does identify an effective gene therapy, because that therapy is likely to require the use of a dozen or so different genes, and each of those genes may well be patented by a different company.[47] Like the fragmentary property rights Michael Heller identified in Moscow stores, the aggregation of these rights to make a single product may face debilitating holdup problems.

Anticommons risks may also affect segments of the biotechnology industry outside of human pharmaceuticals and biologics to a greater extent. Specifically, there is some evidence that an anticommons may be more likely in agricultural biotechnology, where the transgenic plants are not unitary inventions, but rather incorporate multiple patented technologies. The poster child for agricultural anticommons has been the celebrated "golden rice" that incorporates a beta-carotene pathway into a variety of japonica rice in order to supply Vitamin A to malnourished populations that depend on rice as a staple. The transgenic grain is the subject of over seventy patents held by diverse interests. As a practical matter, these patents are unlikely to be an impediment to deployment of golden rice in impoverished nations, as the patents, obtained in developed countries, do not extend to the countries where golden rice is most needed. But the licensing exercise necessary to deploy such a product in the developed world would be prohibitive.[48]

In short, the structure of the biotechnology industry seems likely to run high anticommons risks, though not necessarily the research-level risks originally suggested. Product development times from creation to market are long and costly, but DNA patents are numerous and narrow. Production of any given product may require bargaining with multiple patent holders who own the rights to different genes. The potential for divided patent entitlements to prevent efficient integration into downstream products is particularly high.[49] Anticommons theory was designed with DNA in mind, and seems to work most effectively there rather than in other aspects of biotechnology, though its most likely application will be to complicate the sale of downstream products rather than to prevent upstream research, and though there is some dispute as to whether the anticommons problems in biotechnology can be overcome in practice by licensing or by simply ignoring patents.

Patent Thickets

Closely related to the anticommons theory is the concept of patent thickets—accumulations of overlapping patents that cover the same products and choke out an industry. Those who talk about patent thickets emphasize both the complements problem—the fact that a product must include many different components, each of which may be patented—and the overlap between patent rights covering the same technology, which results from either improvidently granted patents or from the effect of the doctrine of equivalents. Nonetheless, we think that the anticommons and patent thickets, while related, are analytically distinct. Anticommons exist where several different technologies owned by different parties must be aggregated to make an integrated product. Patent thickets, by contrast, occur when multiple IP rights cover the same technology and therefore overlap. Although anticommons problems occur because of distributed ownership, thickets can occur even in relatively concentrated industries, if each of a small number of companies has large patent portfolios. The theory of patent thickets emphasizes the importance both of limiting the issuance and the scope of such overlapping patents and the need for bargaining mechanisms that permit the efficient clearance of patent rights.

The patent thickets problem maps well onto the semiconductor industry. As in the case of pharmaceuticals, developing a new microprocessor involves a substantial investment of time and resources in a range of different activities—designing the circuit layout, improving materials, changing packaging, and reconfiguring the manufacturing process. In the last decade, developing a new-generation microprocessor has meant building an entirely new fabrication facility using a different manufacturing process, at a cost of billions of dollars.[50] Unlike pharmaceuticals, however, semiconductor chips are not protected by a patent that covers the entire product. Rather, semiconductor companies obtain many different patents on components that individually represent only a minor part of the whole chip. Circuit designs, materials, packaging, and manufacturing processes are all the subject of different patents. Furthermore, because many different companies are attempting to do the same thing—that is, make chips smaller and faster—at about the same time, they will often obtain patents on similar inventions with overlapping claims.

The result is that a new microprocessor likely infringes hundreds or even thousands of different patents owned by dozens of different companies.[51] Semiconductor companies, therefore, exist in the advanced stages of a "patent arms race," in which many established companies each possess the power to exclude all others from the market. They rarely exercise this right, however, instead entering into broad cross-licensing deals that permit everyone to make their products without fear of being sued by other established members of the industry.[52] One study provides evidence that suggests that the rate of actual litigation of semiconductor patents is less than that of other types of patents.[53] Other evidence suggests that there is virtually no ex ante licensing of patents in the semiconductor industry: companies take licenses when they are threatened with suit on a product they have already made, not when they set out to improve on an existing invention.[54] This is not to say that semiconductor patents have no value; far from it. Rather, their value is primarily symmetrical, so that the patents tend to be used defensively, to prevent the company from being sued by other patent owners.

These cross-licensing deals depend on the existence of a symmetrical relationship between the parties. Where stakes are not symmetrical—either because the patentee does not participate in the industry or because the defendant does not have its own stable of patents—litigation is far more likely. Thus, David Teece observes that cross-licensing in the semiconductor industry doesn't necessarily favor large companies, as commonly supposed, but rather companies with large patent portfolios, regardless of firm size.[55] Patentees that want to license their patents for royalties also tend to be parties with asymmetric stakes. That is, they are individuals who do not sell products, "licensing shops" whose primary output is patents, or older companies that are no longer major players in the marketplace. Parties in these situations have no need to "trade" patents in the patent arms race described above. For example, independent inventor Jerome Lemelson is famous for having licensed his patents aggressively, and Texas Instruments is the most aggressive licensor of patents in the semiconductor industry. Lemelson did not make any products himself, and therefore did not need cross-licenses from anyone. TI, while still a player in many markets, litigated primarily in the area of large-scale integrated circuits, an area in which it did not have significant sales by the time of the lawsuits. And Rambus began its aggressive litigation strategy when it became clear that its RDRAM technology would not be adopted as an industry standard.

Semiconductors are the canonical example of an industry in which the value of patents lies not in protecting individual inventions but in accumulating massive patent portfolios. James Bessen has suggested that software too has evolved in this direction, though it is worth noting that the companies that have built sizeable software patent portfolios tend not to be software companies per se, but hardware or electronics companies whose software patent portfolio is an adjunct to a larger portfolio of hardware patents.[56] Scholars have only recently begun to study the effects of patent portfolios.[57] They find that portfolios tend to develop as industries mature, and that different companies within an industry may take more or less aggressive approaches to cross-licensing.[58]

There is some preliminary evidence suggesting that patent portfolios may favor incumbents.[59] If a new entrant without a patent portfolio wants to enter the semiconductor market, recent evidence suggests that they would have to pay $100–$200 million in patent licensing fees alone.[60] These are the classic characteristics of a patent thicket. Rather than promoting innovation, patents threaten to impede it or, at best, are deployed to counter the impeding patent rights of competitors. Overlapping patent claims covering complementary goods owned by many different parties threaten to paralyze the industry. Companies can make integrated products only if they can find a way to clear the patent thicket. Bargaining mechanisms and limiting patent scope are critical factors in finding such solutions. The theory of patent thickets works in the semiconductor industry.

⚬⚬

Existing patent theories, then, are not so much wrong as incomplete. Each tells a plausible story of how patents work or should work in a particular industry. Outside of that industry, however, their utility is limited. Prospect theory works well for the pharmaceutical industry, but its prescriptions are all wrong for software or for the Internet. The concept of patent thickets nicely captures the condition of IP in the semiconductor industry, but it does not adequately describe that of the software or pharmaceutical industries. Just as we have described the use of patents differing by industry, so too does patent theory. Matching the right model to the right industry allows us not only to make predictions about the use of patents in an industry but to begin the process of setting optimal patent policy for that industry.

Mapping theory to industry characteristics is a dynamic rather than a static process. Industries change over time. The software industry in 2009 looks rather different than it did in the 1970s, and what was appropriate patent policy then might not be so today. While we have identified the current software industry with cumulative innovation, one can imagine it becoming a patent thicket similar to semiconductors if and when markets for tradable software components become a reality.[61] Certain industries may also modulate between related innovation models; for example, the narrowness of biotechnology patents makes that industry look like an anticommons, but many commentators worry that biotechnology patents will overlap, creating a patent thicket as well as an anticommons.[62] The semiconductor industry may also be characterized by anticommons problems since integration of many different inputs is necessary to produce a commercial semiconductor product. The question then becomes whether we can accommodate the shifting landscape of innovation under a single patent system, or whether we need many, a question that we turn to in the next chapter.

PART THREE

The Solution

Why Courts and Not Congress Offer
a Way Out of the Crisis

The previous chapters provide a strong indictment of a unitary patent system, which simply cannot offer the range of proper incentives for the variety of technologies and industrial sectors it would need to serve. One obvious response to the different policy prescriptions described above would be to legislate different patent standards for different industries. If different industries acquire, value, and use patents differently, and if the optimal number, scope, and division of patent rights differ by industry, then it seems easy to conclude that we need different patent statutes for each industry. We resist that conclusion, however. Instead, we suggest that the unitary patent statute already gives substantial discretion to courts to build industry-sensitive policy analysis into their decisions, and that courts have latitude to create other such opportunities. These "policy levers"[1] permit patent law to take account of the technology-specific nature of the patent system without inviting the rent-seeking and balkanization that specialized statutes would engender. We will discuss those policy levers in the balance of this book. In this chapter, we discuss the dangers of legislating industry-specific statutes. We also defend the proposition that courts, rather than Congress or the PTO, are the right place to implement those policy levers.

Specialty Statutes

Although patent law has historically been uniform, with a single set of legal standards designed to cover "anything under the sun that is made by man,"[2] Congress has shown increased interest in tailoring patent law to the needs of particular industries. In the last twenty years, it has lengthened the patent term for most pharmaceutical patents (see 35 U.S.C. §§ 155, 156

[2000]), protected certain experimental uses of pharmaceuticals by generic suppliers from liability (see 35 U.S.C. § 271(e) [2000]), prohibited enforcing patents on medical procedures against doctors (see 35 U.S.C. § 287 [2000]), prohibited issuing patents for genetically modified humans (P.L. 108–199 § 634), relaxed the obviousness standard for biotechnological processes (see 35 U.S.C. § 103(b) [2000]), and created a new defense against business method patents (see 35 U.S.C. § 273(a)[3]). It has supplemented patent protection for semiconductors with a sui generis statute (see Semiconductor Chip Protection Act, 17 U.S.C. §§ 901–14 [2000]). It has enacted non-patent statutes granting patentlike exclusive rights in particular industries (see Plant Variety Protection Act, 7 U.S.C. §§ 2321–2583). It has even passed a "private" patent bill, lengthening the term of one narrow group of patents.[3] In each case, Congress reacted to particular complaints about the perceived unfairness of applying a general legal standard to a particular industry. Still other bills recently introduced in Congress, but not passed, would have changed the obviousness standards for business method patents, had the government "take" a particular financial services patent, or extended the patent for Claritin.[4]

These rather modest technology-specific changes to the patent statute are but the tip of the iceberg. There are any number of scholars, lawyers, and clients out there who want to revise the law further, in diverse and sometimes contradictory directions. Here are a few examples. A number of scholars suggest that patent law needs to be modified to take account of the particular needs of the software industry. Some suggest that software patents are inappropriate altogether,[5] some that only Internet business method patents are.[6] Others suggest that a form of sui generis patentlike protection is appropriate for software.[7] Still others who endorse the general framework of patent law argue that the courts should apply patent law to software in somewhat different ways than they do in other industries. Most commonly, scholars suggest that the rapid market cycles in software justify shorter terms of protection for software patents.[8] Similarly, some scholars have explored whether biotechnology deserves its own sui generis form of protection,[9] while others have suggested that biotechnology patent standards should deviate from the general patent law rules.[10] Some argue that certain types of biotechnological innovations should be entirely unpatentable.[11] Others suggest that the disclosure requirements should be loosened for biotechnology patents,[12] that the obviousness standard should be lowered,[13] or that the scope of DNA sequence patents should be restricted.[14] They have variously argued that the Federal Circuit should defer to the PTO,[15] or conversely that the PTO should defer to the Federal Circuit.[16]

Given what we have said so far in this book, the reader might be forgiven for expecting us to add our voices to the chorus calling for industry-specific statutory reform. Calls to modify patent law are a natural response to the different effects patent law has on different industries. The economic effects of patents are quite different in software and biotechnology, two of the industries in which the calls for specific legislation are loudest. It is hard to imagine that the same statute is in fact the best possible one for both of these very different industries. Thus, in a perfect world the patent system might well be tailored to give optimal incentives to each different industry.[17]

In the real world, however, a number of factors caution against explicitly tailoring the patent statute to the needs of particular industries.[18] The most obvious barrier is legal—the agreement on Trade-Related Aspects of Intellectual Property Rights (TRIPs) prohibits member states from discriminating in the grant of patents based on the type of technology at issue.[19] As we have noted elsewhere, however, the United States has not faithfully followed this treaty mandate.[20] Neither has the European Union, which has industry-specific rules for compulsory licensing of pharmaceuticals and for the patentability of software and business methods.[21] TRIPs seems to leave some leeway for industry-specific tailoring, or at the very least it has not been enforced so far against departures from the nondiscrimination norm. But more systematic departures might trigger complaints by other countries, and it is not clear that an industry-specific patent statute would survive the scrutiny of the World Trade Organization under TRIPs.

Even if industry-specific patent legislation is legal, we are not persuaded that it is a good idea, for several reasons. First, while economics can make useful policy suggestions as to how patents work in different industries, we are skeptical of the ability of a statute to translate those suggestions into detailed patent rules for each industry. Many of the predictions of economic theory are fact-specific—they suggest different factors that should bear on the outcome of particular cases, but that require case-by-case application that cannot easily be captured in a statute. Economic theory is more useful in making general suggestions about how the patent system can be adapted to particular factual contexts than it is dictating hard and fast statutory rules.

Second, rewriting the patent law for each industry would involve substantial administrative costs and uncertainty. Congress would have to write new statutes not just for biotechnology and software but for numerous different industries with special characteristics. Semiconductors, pharmaceuticals, chemicals, nanotechnology,[22] telecommunications, and other industries would all need separate statutes. District court judges, who already have enough trouble learning the arcane rules of patent law in the relatively few patent cases they hear, would have to learn a host of new statutes. The law supporting these statutes would be slow to develop, since fewer cases would come up involving each statute. The resulting uncertainty might enrich lawyers, but it surely would not be conducive to encouraging innovation.

Industry-specific legislation would also require a great deal of line drawing, as the boundaries between industries are vague and notoriously mutable. Semiconductor manufacturers and computer hardware companies patent and use software all the time. So, for that matter, do carmakers. Indeed, one study suggests that most software patents are obtained not by software companies but by hardware or electronics manufacturers. Drug delivery systems might be thought of as medical devices, pharmaceuticals, or biotechnology; presumably a different law would apply depending on how the invention was characterized. Even technologies that seem radically different, such as biotechnology and software, may unexpectedly converge, as recent developments in bioinformatics and proteomics have made clear.[23] Further, a significant percentage of inventions fall into more than one field. John Allison and Mark Lemley find that on average each patented invention fits into 1.5 different technology categories,[24] a number that is increasing with time.[25] And new fields arise regularly. Nanotechnology, for example, combines advances in semiconductors, biotechnology, materials science, and even optics. As a result, it would prove impossible to carve up innovation into static fields. Imagine trying to fit all modern inventions into categories created fifty or one hundred years ago. The result would likely be a combination of constant legislative tinkering with categories and a system that was nonetheless behind the times.

Past experience with such specialized statutes is also not encouraging. The history of industry-specific statutes suggests that many fail because they are drafted with then-current technology in mind and are not sufficiently general to accommodate the inevitable changes in technology. In the United States, the poster child for failed sui generis legislation has been the notoriously neglected Semiconductor Chip Protection Act, or SCPA (17 U.S.C. §§ 901–914 [2000]). Passed at the behest of the U.S. semiconductor industry after six years of legislative debate, the SCPA created a detailed set of rules designed to protect the "mask work" or circuit design pattern etched into semiconductor chips. The statute was tailored specifically to the purported needs of the industry, including special provisions on reverse engineering and other practices common to semiconductor circuit design. The ostensible reason was to protect American innovation from foreign competitors. But the statute has virtually never been used to enforce the rights it created, generating only two published judicial opinions in the quarter century since its enactment.[26] The most likely reason is that the particular focus of the SCPA (duplication of mask works) is obsolete because the nature of the semiconductor business changed to make the manufacturing process much more difficult and hence harder to imitate at low cost.[27] The foreign competition so feared by U.S. chip fabricators has not vanished, but it is not based on imitation of the sort the SCPA prohibits, and in any event the industry appears to be thriving without recourse to its specialized statute.

A similar fate befell some industry-specific patent statutes, such as the biotechnology-specific amendments to the U.S. patent statute's obviousness provisions (35 U.S.C. §103[b]). Like the SCPA, the biotechnology obviousness provisions were enacted after lobbying by the biotechnology industry, which claimed that the general standard for obviousness failed to meet the special process-based characteristics of their industry, requiring a sui generis standard. But the biotechnology amendment became irrelevant nearly as soon as it was enacted, in part because general patent standards now reach the same result[28] and lack the more onerous procedural requirements of the specialized provision. It has apparently never been litigated.

Preliminary studies of the U.S. Plant Patent Act and Plant Variety Protection Act, as well as studies of the European Union's relatively recent experiment in database protection, suggest that similar stories might be told in the case of those specialty statutes.[29] Indeed, the tenure of the EU directive, intended to foster a robust European database industry, has seen EU database publishing fall well behind that of the United States, where no specialized statute is available to database publishers.[30] And the U.S. plant protection statutes, while they have triggered litigation, are increasingly ignored in favor of obtaining ordinary patents on plant-related inventions.[31] The sorry history of such industry-specific statutes suggests that they typically turn out to be failures because they are drafted with the technology at the time of their passage in mind and are not sufficiently general to accommodate the inevitable changes in technology. This general problem with statutory obsolescence was identified by Guido Calabresi more than twenty years ago,[32] and it becomes particularly acute in the case of technologically oriented statutes.[33]

Finally, and of most concern, both public choice theory[34] and practical experience warn that each new amendment to the patent statute represents an opportunity for counterproductive special interest lobbying.[35] Industry-specific legislation is much more vulnerable than general legislation to industry capture, since only a few groups have an interest in the

outcome and that interest is quite concentrated. This has been the history of
the U.S. copyright statute, where industry-specific rules and exceptions have
led to a bloated, impenetrable statute that reads like the tax code, which is
itself the product of such special-interest rent-seeking.[36] It is no accident that
the industry-specific portions of the patent law are among the most complex and confusing sections: try reading section 103(b) on biotechnological processes, sections 155A and 156 extending pharmaceutical patent terms,
and section 287 restricting surgical process patents on a sleepless night
sometime.[37] Nor should it be surprising that these industry-specific statutes
have had some pernicious consequences—for example, the pharmaceutical-
specific Hatch-Waxman provisions have been gamed on numerous occasions as pharmaceutical patent owners have manipulated stay provisions or
colluded with putative generic entrants to prevent entry into the market.[38]
Patent law has some balance today in part because different industries have
different interests, making it difficult for one interest group to push through
changes to the statute. But each time the legislature reopens the patent statute to amendment the opportunity arises for lobbying by special interest
groups, not the least of which will be the industry at which the amendment
is directed. Technology-specific patent legislation encourages rent-seeking,
either by those who stand to benefit directly from favorable legislation or by
those who will seize each new legislative opportunity to hijack the amendment process for their own interests. It may therefore make the resulting
legislation less socially desirable.

The Object Lesson of Patent Reform

Congress has spent the last four years, from 2005 to 2008, in an ultimately
futile effort to reform the patent system. Reform proposals have come and
gone; advanced and retreated; merged and coalesced; multiplied, divided,
and vanished at every conceivable stage of the legislative process. The debates between proponents and opponents of various amendments have been
fierce and protracted. The story of that legislative effort is instructive for
future efforts to create industry-specific patent statutes.

Patent reform began with a number of reports in the early 2000s that
documented important failings in the patent system, including laxity in the
PTO examination process that let a number of bad patents issue and various
doctrines that encouraged abuse of the patent litigation system by so-called
patent trolls out to make a quick buck. Congressional leaders introduced
legislation in 2005 that would have cut back on abuses in the PTO and in
patent litigation. That legislation would, among other things, have given the

PTO the power to restrict continuation applications (which give applicants an unlimited number of "do-overs"), created a postgrant opposition system under which competitors could have challenged patents they believed were improperly issued, limited patent damages to bring them in line with the actual contribution made by the patentee, and given courts the discretion to deny injunctive relief. It would also have made other changes not aimed at abuse of the patent system, including giving patents to the first to file an application rather than the first to invent.

But the road to patent reform proved to be strewn with political land mines. The pharmaceutical and biotechnology industries opposed virtually all elements of patent reform directed at abuse. Universities objected to some of those provisions as well as the move to first-to-file. Individual inventors objected both to the first-to-file provisions and to the limitations directed at abuse of the patent system. On the other side, the software, electronics, Internet, and telecommunications industries generally lined up behind reform, but expressed skepticism toward those few reforms the pharmaceutical industry supported (such as restrictions on the defenses of inequitable conduct and best mode).

By early 2007, it seemed likely that patent reform would pass. The top Republicans and Democrats in both the House and the Senate cosponsored a compromise bill. And indeed the bill rapidly advanced, passing the House and being reported by the Judiciary Committee to the Senate floor in 2007. Along the way, it was watered down in a number of ways—postgrant opposition was rendered largely toothless by the imposition of time limits, for example, and implementation of first-to-file was delayed indefinitely. Further, various pet projects were added to the bill, including a requirement that patent searches be done by U.S. citizens and a provision that would immunize financial services companies from infringement of a specific patent by having the government effectively buy the patent. Notwithstanding this progress, the process stalled in early 2008 as even repeated weakening of the reform provisions failed to generate consensus among different industries. After four years of apparently fruitless struggle, it appears at this writing that patent reform is dead for the foreseeable future.

The patent reform process has three useful lessons for our story.

- First, it makes clear the industry-specific valence of patent debates. In the early years of this century, a number of people were skeptical of our argument that different industries in fact had different characteristics or viewed the patent system differently. It is no longer possible to make that argument with a straight face. On virtually every issue of patent reform, the IT industries lined up on one side and the biomedical industries on another. The latent stresses on the unitary patent system broke in this debate into obvious fault lines.

- Second, the changes in the patent bill as it progressed through Congress demonstrate some of the public choice worries we have articulated in this chapter. A bill that started out written with public policy in mind (good or bad policy, depending on one's perspective, but public policy nonetheless) ended up encumbered with private protections, just as the tax code ends up with exemptions designed to favor particular parties. Most notable is the exemption of financial services firms from liability for infringing a particular patent owned by Data Treasury, but the bill in its latest form also prevented the patenting of tax shelters and included a provision that favored particular U.S. search firms by requiring that patent searches be done by U.S. citizens.

- Finally, the failure of congressional patent reform doesn't represent the end of the story. During the period in which Congress tried and failed to reform the patent system, courts were actively involved in fixing many of the very same problems Congress was ultimately unable to resolve. Courts during this period reversed the rule that patentees were always entitled to injunctions after a finding of infringement,[39] made it easier to sue to challenge the validity of a patent,[40] made it harder to obtain a patent by strengthening the obviousness test,[41] and changed the standard for claiming that a defendant was a willful infringer and therefore owed punitive damages.[42] The PTO during that period also released rules that imposed some limits on abuse of continuation applications, though those rules were ultimately struck down in court.[43] The fact that courts proved capable of solving many of the problems on which Congress ultimately foundered suggests that policy levers, not industry-specific legislation, may be the most effective way of dealing with problems in the patent system going forward.

Rules and Standards

The difficulties we have identified with industry-specific legislation do not mean that we must abandon the idea of tailoring patent law to the needs of specific technologies. Where common-law rulemaking is available, the courts both can and should engage in deliberate modulation of a general patent statute.[44] Indeed, to a large extent they already do. The business of innovation is too dynamic for a patent statute to function in any other way. Not only do new technologies come into existence and old technologies fade into obscurity, but the innovation profile of industries varies from sector to sector, and from time to time. Broad disparities exist across economic sectors in the cost of research and development, the length of product cycles, the return on investment, and the cost of obtaining patents itself. The incentives necessary to promote innovation in the pharmaceutical industry are not those necessary to software or to semiconductors. The incentives necessary to a mature software industry are not those that were once necessary to nascent software developers. Only a dynamically interpreted statute can hope to meet the needs of so many disparate industries.

Statutes differ in the specificity with which they dictate the rules for judicial decision. They exist on a continuum. At one end lie the kind of tightly drafted, detailed rules that Grant Gilmore characterized as "aimed at an unearthly and superhuman precision."[45] As Gilmore noted, such statutes are drafted precisely to curtail judicial interpretation but are nearly impossible to adjust "to changing conditions without legislative revision."[46] At the other end of the continuum lie general delegations of authority to judges to make correct decisions. We might think of the tax code as a stylized example of the former type of statute, and the antitrust law as a (not-so-stylized) instance of the latter. In the case of the antitrust laws, the few sentences of sections 1 and 2 of the Sherman Act have spawned a vast set of judicially created standards for identifying and punishing anticompetitive behavior (15 U.S.C. §§ 1–2 [2000]). The tax laws, by contrast, fill several volumes of the United States Code and specify rules not only for a vast array of situations and industries but even for particular companies. On this statutory continuum, the Patent Act appears closer to antitrust law than to the tax code. Although the statute sets the basic parameters for patentability and infringement, and has some detailed provisions, it does not specify in detail how most of its basic principles are to be applied. Further, in many instances, such as application of the doctrine of equivalents or of inequitable conduct, there is no legislative guidance at all. Instead, judicially created doctrines play a major role in defining the scope of patent protection.[47]

The formulation of statutory discretion to administer patent law partakes to some extent in the long-running debate over the comparative merits of rules and standards.[48] Within this debate, "rules" have been characterized as bright-line and definite decisional criteria. Rules are cheap to administer because they are simple and straightforward, but due to their inflexibility they may lead to costly outcomes if they fit a given situation poorly. Standards, by contrast, are characterized as flexible case-by-case decisional criteria that can take situational variance into account. Standards are typically and intentionally stated indeterminately. As a result, they offer little guidance to expected behavior and so may impose costs associated with this uncertainty. Because of their flexibility and a priori indeterminacy, however, standards typically imbue courts or decision makers with greater discretion than would a rigid decisional rule, and so standards are favored where greater discretion is needed.

The need for industry-specific statutory tailoring implicates the broader question of legal generalization versus particularization, of which the issue of rule-based or standards-based decision making is, perhaps paradoxically, a particular instance.[49] Law necessarily contains general prescriptions for governing behavior, prescriptions that may fit particular instances well or poorly. Where the fit is poor, it may be sensible to equip decision makers with discretion to tailor the general prescription. The patent statute equips courts with precisely such discretion via a series of doctrinal policy levers. Adaptation of the patent statute to specific industries requires allowance for judicial discretion, but the adaptation process will not necessarily be standards based. Where commonalities within an industry can be identified, tailoring may sometimes be best accomplished via judicial application of a bright-line rule. At other times it may be best accomplished case by case, via application of a flexible standard. Additionally, the definitional line between rules and standards is not always pristine, and largely depends on the level of abstraction at which decisional discretion is viewed. Standards operationalize case-by-case determinations, but only by laying down a broad decisional criterion. The choice to decide certain types of cases under a standards regime is itself a decision that channels the discretion of future courts.

Institutional Competence

We suggest that, as a general principle, a flexible common-law approach of ongoing judicial oversight will best accommodate new and different technologies within the general framework of a patent statute. It may at first seem odd for us to endorse industry-specific judicial interpretation, given our emphasis above on the administrative costs of industry-specific legislation. But our endorsement of judicial tailoring is reconcilable with our concerns about legislative tailoring because judicial interpretation occurs in a particular factual context. The litigation process will provide judges with the information they need to decide cases. The incentives of the adversary system create a powerful engine for the development of relevant evidence by the parties, including expert testimony. The Federal Rules of Civil Procedure also provide for courts to appoint their own experts if necessary to advise them in complicated matters of litigation. Additionally, the money spent on litigation purchases not only resolution of a private dispute but the public good of judicial decision making. The costs of dispute resolution in effect subsidize statutory upkeep. So while there is an administrative cost to judicial as well as legislative determination of industry-specific factors, it is largely a cost society would be paying anyway to resolve the lawsuit.[50] Only if patent litigants would not have gone to court at all would society have saved these expenses. And we are skeptical that there are any rules of, say, patent validity sufficiently clear that a patentee will agree its patent is invalid or an accused infringer will agree that it is valid without a fight. Indeed, in decades of experience litigating and reading patent cases, we are unaware of a single one in which the defendant did not argue that the patent was invalid.

Skeptics of the judicial approach might rightly observe that litigation is not cost-free, that judicial expertise is bounded, and that appellate courts in particular are not entirely immune from problems of public choice. However, all advantages are comparative, and the question is not whether courts are the perfect statutory tailors, but whether we are better off with no tailoring at all, and, if not, whether given the risks of industry-specific statutes described above courts are better situated to engage in tailoring than are legislatures. The likelihood that a unitary, unvarying, and monolithic statute could supply the correct level of incentive to so many diverse industries with divergent incentives is essentially nil. The prospect of the legislature continually revisiting the circumstances of each industry and passing appropriate new legislation for each situation is equally bleak—as Grant Gilmore long ago observed, "[G]etting a statute enacted in the first place is much easier than getting the statute revised so that it will make sense in the light of changed conditions."[51] In democratically elected legislatures, an enormous commitment of political capital is typically required to draft, promulgate, and reach consensus on new IP legislation, especially if the legislation is to be supported by credible fact-finding and reliable expertise. The lessons of each of the last two rounds of patent reform—the American Inventors Protection Act of 1999 and the 2005–08 reform efforts—are that patent reform is surprisingly hard fought, divisive, takes a very long time, and rarely produces satisfying results. The issues involved are typically not magnets of populist sentiment and are more likely to be viewed as esoteric and obscure to voters. We can anticipate serious legislative investigation of, and response to, specialized industry needs to be relatively rare and potentially counterproductive when it does occur.

Thus, although legislatures are often characterized as having the better resources to investigate and develop factual evidence, this capability is often more theoretical than actual. At the same time, courts have substantial ability to profile an industry inductively, by hearing cases presenting recurrent themes, and to adapt intellectual property policy according to the profile within a reasonable time frame and at reasonable cost. Courts are routinely expected to fill the statutory tailoring function in areas such as antitrust. They can fulfill a similar role in patent law and in fact are already doing so with regard to a variety of patentability criteria, including obviousness and the doctrine of equivalents.[52]

Such tailoring necessarily vests a fair degree of discretion in the judiciary in order to adapt the general statute to the particular circumstance, and judicial discretion is not costless. Courts are not immune from the sorts of rent-seeking criticisms that have been leveled against Congress.[53] But the effects of special interest lobbying are blunted in the judicial context: federal judges have life tenure, they are not compensated based on anything litigants (and certainly not patent litigants) do or don't do, they have no supervisors, and they are less likely to engage in logrolling than large legislative bodies. In the specific context of patent law, capture could take the more subtle form of influence by parties who appear repeatedly before the courts. This seems less of a problem in patent law than in some other areas, however, because companies and law firms tend to be both plaintiffs and defendants in patent cases.[54]

In considering comparative advantage, courts and legislatures are not the only institutions available to address statutory upkeep; administrative agencies are a third option. There is an argument to be made that agencies offer the best of both institutional worlds, having greater expertise and investigatory resources than courts, without the special-interest rent-seeking of legislatures. But in reality, the middle road of administrative agencies to some extent partakes of the worst of both worlds.[55] Administrative agencies are by no means independent from legislative forces of public choice, and the same legislator who succumbs to the pressure of special interest groups likely controls the budget of the agency that deals with those groups.[56] But at the same time, neither is the staff of the administrative agency directly accountable to voters, removing even the threat that voters might overcome collective action problems to impost discipline on imprudent or improper actions. Additionally, the problem of direct capture may be greatly exacerbated in this context. To the extent that an administrative agency interacts repeatedly with a particular constituency, especially a constituency with whom it shares particular expertise, that constituency is likely to exercise undue influence on the agency's rulemaking process. That is a special risk with patents. The Patent and Trademark Office interacts regularly with those seeking patents, but very little with third parties affected by the patents they grant. It is little wonder, then, that the PTO in the 1990s stated its mission as "to help our customers get patents." That's capture.

Giving discretion to the PTO in particular has another problem as well. The PTO by design sees only one piece of the patent puzzle—the question of whether a patent should issue in the first place. It never sees infringement disputes, or licenses, or has to allocate remedies. As a result, even if we thought the PTO were best suited to setting industry-specific standards for determining patent validity, there is no reason to believe they have any comparative advantage in deciding many of the most important questions of patent law.

This is not to say that there cannot be a carefully modulated adjunct role for an agency, in this particular case the Patent Office, to play in statutory upkeep. The PTO may be best suited to creating rules that govern practice before the office itself, such as the information applicants must submit to the PTO or the ability of applicants to use continuation applications. Most particularly, there may be such a role if the agency can be held to what it does best, which is fact-finding, without becoming involved in setting legal standards, which is the strong suit of the courts. Something very like this has begun occurring between the Patent Office and the courts, in part as a response to the specialized patent jurisdiction of United States Court of Appeals for the Federal Circuit. Some commentators have suggested that the Federal Circuit has been too quick to second-guess the fact-finding of the Patent Office.[57] The Supreme Court has extended to the Patent Office a standard of review that grants it judicial deference in fact-finding, without (so far) granting deference in the Patent Office's views on statutory interpretation.[58] The legal standards for patentability have remained squarely with the court.[59] The separation of functions in the patent context may yield the best of both institutions; the expertise of the agency tempered by the independence of judicial review.[60] But it is a far cry from application of the PTO's fact-finding expertise to the sort of dynamic interpretation of legal rules with which courts have experience, and which we suggest the patent system needs.

Judicial Activism?

"Wait a minute!" scholars of a particular political stripe might object. "Aren't you arguing for judicial activism?" Not so. If judicial "activism" means anything beyond a conclusory label suggesting that the speaker disagrees with the court decision, it refers to courts usurping the role of Congress, generally by invoking the Constitution to strike down congressional statutes. We are suggesting something different. Within the framework created by Congress, there remain a large number of issues to be determined, and it is the proper job of the courts to resolve those disputes. That much has been uncontroversial since *Marbury v. Madison* was decided in 1803.[61] The question is how courts are to resolve those issues in the absence of congressional guidance and subject to legislative veto. We think it makes sense for courts in that position to take account of the realities of the modern patent system. And foremost among those realities is that our unitary patent law confronts an amazing diversity of industry needs and experience. For courts to ignore that diversity in setting the rules it necessarily must set strikes us as foolish.

Policy Levers in Existing Patent Cases

The great flexibility in the patent statute presents an opportunity for courts to take account of the needs and characteristics of different industries. Courts can, and should, apply the general rules of patent law with sensitivity to the characteristics of particular industries. This may sound like a radical proposal—judicial activism run amok. But if industry-specific judicial policy is a radical idea, it is not our idea. The Federal Circuit already does this, consciously or not. Indeed, both the patent statute and the common law of patents are chock-full of examples of judicially created, industry-specific rules. In this chapter, we identify a number of policy levers that already exist in patent jurisprudence to tailor the unitary patent system to the more complex realities of the world while avoiding the problems of industry-specific legislation. The levers we have identified are not, by any means, the only sources of judicial discretion in patent law. Indeed, we do not discuss one of the largest judicially created doctrines in patent law—the doctrine of inequitable conduct. Rather, we have concentrated on policy levers that seem to us to require, or at least permit, systematic variation in patent rules by industry.

Courts have not used all of these doctrines to achieve policy goals expressly, though they have sometimes done so accidentally or implicitly. Some of these policy levers operate on a "macro" level—that is, they expressly treat different industries differently. For example, the rules for obviousness and written description have been applied differently to biotechnology and software, and the utility rule announced in *Brenner v. Manson*[1] is applied only in biotechnology and chemical cases. These levers may require courts to differentiate between industries, defining certain inventions as "biotechnological," for example, in order to invoke a particular rule. Or they may apply not to whole industries but to particular technologies. For example, DNA is treated differently for certain purposes than other types of technology; that obviously has a significant effect on the biotechnology industry as a whole, but it is technology- rather than industry-specific, so it does not require industry definition. A more common set of levers operate on a "micro" level: they treat different inventions differently without express regard to industry, but in ways that have disproportionate impacts on different industries. Although they are not as obviously technology-specific, micro policy levers are just as important as macro policy levers in industry-specific tailoring because they permit the law to build up industry-specific treatment through case-by-case application. For example, the secondary considerations of nonobviousness will primarily benefit industries that patent inventions that translate directly into commercial products, and the pioneer patents doctrine will affect industries with major new inventions more than industries in which invention is cumulative.

Examples of Policy Levers

What follow are brief descriptions of a dozen policy levers courts already use to differentiate patent law in different industries. We break them into three basic categories—levers that affect whether an inventor can obtain a patent at all, and if so whether that patent is valid; those that affect the scope of the resulting patent; and those that affect the remedies for patent infringement. There is obviously some interplay between these groupings— the written description doctrine affects both validity and patent scope, for example—but they help to organize our thinking about policy levers.

PATENT ACQUISITION AND VALIDITY

Utility

Proof that an invention is useful has long been required for patent protection. This requirement arises in part under the subject matter provisions of the statue, which requires that an invention be "new and useful" in order to qualify for a patent. In addition, the statute requires disclosure of how to "make and use" the invention. Naturally, no use can be disclosed unless the invention has one. Courts traditionally interpreted the utility requirement to mandate three separate tests: whether the invention has any purpose other than idle amusement, whether the invention actually works for its intended purpose, and whether the purpose is one that society would consider beneficial.

In the last several decades, however, the utility requirement has lost much of its force. The courts have all but abandoned the requirement that an invention be morally beneficial,[2] permitting patents even on inventions that seem calculated to deceive.[3] Some have argued that we should revive the moral utility doctrine specifically in the field of biotechnology, making it a macro policy lever that we apply against the patenting of some forms of life.[4] But the law today does not treat morality as a significant restriction on patenting, and it seems unlikely that it will do so in the foreseeable future.[5] The PTO has also permitted patents on a wide variety of seemingly frivolous inventions, gutting the requirement that an invention have a purpose other than idle amusement.[6] Courts and commentators have even gone so far as to suggest that if people are willing to buy products (or infringe patents), they must be useful,[7] and that products meet the moral utility requirement as long as they are not actually illegal.[8]

The only exceptions to the effective elimination of the utility requirement in patent law are in the fields of biology and chemistry. Beginning with *Brenner v. Manson*,[9] the courts have required proof that a new chemical molecule or chemical process display some concrete and finished application before it can be patented. Further, that use must be "specific"—that is, the use identified for the molecule must be, if not unique, at least specially adapted to that molecule.[10] The rationale is that developing a new molecule without any particular use is not a completed innovation, but merely the opening stage of a long and complex research process. Permitting broad upstream patenting of such chemicals might discourage the downstream research necessary to find a market for those chemicals. And if we are to require an applicant to find the use associated with a chemical before patenting it, we must require that use to be specific to the chemical or applicants will simply allege minor incidental uses in order to circumvent the requirement.

In the case of pharmaceuticals, the PTO at one time applied this principle to require proof of therapeutic efficacy before a patent could issue.[11] That went too far; by the time the developer of a new drug could show efficacy, they would likely have lost patent protection under section 102(b). The Federal Circuit properly stepped back somewhat from this rule, holding that indirect indicators of therapeutic efficacy such as animal modeling or in vitro data can satisfy the utility requirement.[12] Still, even after *Brana* the PTO requires proof of specific, substantial and credible utility in chemical inventions. Although the Federal Circuit has not been as systematic in applying utility to inorganic chemistry, the requirement still has significant force there as well.[13]

Under these cases, the standard for utility in the chemical and life sciences is different—and substantially higher—than the standard in any other industry. This is similarly apparent in a related life sciences manifestation of the *Brenner* legacy: patents on DNA molecules, especially short or partial gene sequences such as expressed sequence tags (ESTs).[14] ESTs are fragments of genes that do not themselves produce a functional protein, but can be used as markers to identify a particular DNA sequence on a chromosome. The PTO's Utility Examination Guidelines for patents drawn to such molecules require a showing of "specific," "substantial," and "credible" applications for the technology, requirements not found in examination of other technologies.[15] The Federal Circuit ratified this view in *In re Fisher*.[16] Similarly, the Board of Patent Appeals applied the Utility Guidelines in *Ex parte Fisher* to reject a patent application claiming amino acid sequences for identifying plant compounds, demanding that a genus claim show specific, substantial, and credible utility for each species within the genus.[17] Although the Utility Guidelines are nominally technology-neutral, one will search in vain for applications of the guidelines to reject patents for lack of utility outside of the biotechnology and chemistry contexts.[18] This variance from other fields is not reflected in the statute, which after all is merely the word "useful." Rather, it is a creation of the PTO and derives ultimately from judicially created rules.

Thus, the utility doctrine constitutes an example of a macro policy lever: it creates a blanket rule for one set of cases that differs from the rule in others.[19] This rule is expressly framed in policy terms. In *Brenner,* the Supreme Court worried that if a patentee could patent a product before discovering its function, "a vast, unknown, and perhaps unknowable area" might fall within the patentee's control.[20] By giving patent protection too early—before the actual use of the product has been identified—patent law might deter research by others on the use of the product. This is a significant concern only in an industry in which downstream research is important to innovation. As we noted in chapter 5, the concern about upstream patenting is particularly significant in the context of biotechnology, and arguably those concerns are present in inorganic chemistry as well. The courts have indeed applied the utility doctrine more strictly in biotechnology cases than in others, though the application to pharmaceuticals may be more problematic.[21]

Experimental Use

Patent law has two different doctrines of experimental use, one entirely nonstatutory and the other partially so. Experimental use first arises as an exception to the rule that an invention cannot be patented if it was on sale or in public use more than one year prior to the filing of a patent application (35 U.S.C. § 102[b]). Although the statute seems to brook no exception for public uses made for some legitimate purpose, a long line of cases beginning with *City of Elizabeth v. Pavement Co.*[22] has held that patent applicants do not trigger the one-year statutory bar if their use or sale is part of a bona fide experiment.[23] The courts have looked to a variety of factors to determine whether a patentee's use is experimental, including whether the goods were sold, whether the patentee kept control over them, whether the patentee sought feedback, and whether the final product changed as a result.[24] The Federal Circuit case law is inconsistent in its application of this doctrine,[25] but the basic inquiry is focused on the patentee's purpose in releasing the product.

The second doctrine of experimental use arose as a defense to a claim of infringement. In an early opinion, Justice Story wrote that "it could never have been the intention of the legislature to punish a man, who constructed such a [patented] machine merely for philosophical experiments, or for the purpose of ascertaining the sufficiency of the machine to produce its described effects."[26] The Federal Circuit has construed this defense to infringement extremely narrowly, holding that any intent to make commercial use of the resulting product precludes reliance on the defense[27] and even that use in an academic lab is a commercial use because the university is a business.[28] The practical effect of this reading is that the defense may as well not exist; in any case worth litigating there will be sufficient commercial use to disentitle the defendant to invoke it. The defense was not always so narrow, however, and commentators have suggested that it could play an expanded role in permitting legitimate efforts to improve on or design around a patent.[29] Most of the rest of the world, for example, interprets experimental use more broadly than the Federal Circuit does.[30]

Both judicially created experimental use doctrines are micro policy levers. They do not expressly differ by industry, but for obvious reasons they are more likely to be applied in industries where reproduction and testing of products in the marketplace are a necessary part of the product development process. Experimental use as a defense to infringement is likely to be particularly important where it is difficult or impossible to evaluate a product or design around a patent without reproducing the product itself. Julie Cohen and Mark Lemley have argued that this is true in computer software but not in most other industries.[31] And as Katherine Strandburg explains, a proper distinction between experimentation on finished products and experimentation with research tools will cause the doctrine to apply primarily in circumstances where improvers can learn by experimenting with finished products, rather than by working with research tools.[32] Similarly, the experimental use exception to the section 102(b) statutory bar may benefit inventions whose design requires testing by a large segment of the public or inventions whose durability over a substantial period is at issue. Software is a good example of the former. Software companies tend to engage in extensive "beta-testing" of their products with consumers before— indeed, even after—releasing the first commercial version. The pavement at issue in *City of Elizabeth* is a good example of durability. By contrast, chemical process inventions may be tested in laboratories for years without release to the public. Pharmaceuticals are an intermediate case, since the composition and effects of the chemical can be determined in a laboratory, while its safety and efficacy in humans necessarily requires more public exposure. The experimental use doctrines can accommodate the general rules of patent law to the needs of iterative industries in which copying or open use of prototypes is a practical necessity—at least if they are generously interpreted.

The Level of Skill in the Art

A number of factual questions in patent law are answered from the perspective of the person having ordinary skill in the art (the PHOSITA). Much of the case law concerning the PHOSITA arises out of the consideration of the obviousness standard found in section 103 of the patent statute. Although originally developed as a common law doctrine, the nonobviousness criterion was codified in the 1952 Patent Act as a requirement that the claimed invention taken as a whole not be obvious to one of ordinary skill in the art at the time the invention was made (35 U.S.C. § 103). The PHOSITA is equally central to calibrating the legal standard for patent disclosure. In return for a period of exclusive rights over an invention, the inventor must fully disclose the invention to the public. The first paragraph of section 112 requires that this disclosure enable "any person skilled in the art" to make and use the claimed invention (35 U.S.C. § 112 ¶ 1). This same standard controls several other disclosure doctrines as well. First, the definition of enablement affects the patentability requirement of specific utility, as the invention must actually work as described in the specification if the inventor is to enable one of ordinary skill to use it.[33] Additionally, compliance with the independent requirements of adequate written description and best mode disclosure is measured with reference to the understanding of a person skilled in the art. Finally, the definiteness of patent claims, which must be written so as to warn members of the public what is covered by the patent, has traditionally been assessed with regard to the knowledge of one having ordinary skill in the art.[34] If the terms of the claims would not be comprehensible to such a person, they fail the requirements of section 112.

The PHOSITA also shows up as a convenient metric in other unexpected areas, including judicially created patent doctrines. Claim construction requires reference to how the PHOSITA would understand terms in the patent claims.[35] The PHOSITA reappears in some formulations of the standard for infringement by equivalents. In its germinal opinion on the doctrine of equivalents, *Graver Tank Manufacturing Co.* v. *Linde Air Products Co.,* the Supreme Court indicated that the equivalence between elements of an allegedly infringing device and those of a claimed invention might be tested by determining whether the elements were known in the art to be substitutes for one another.[36] The Federal Circuit strengthened this use of the PHOSITA by making the "known interchangeability" of elements—judged from the perspective of one of ordinary skill in the art—a fundamental test for equivalence.[37] A great deal of patent doctrine therefore rests upon the measurement of some legal parameter against the skill and knowledge of the PHOSITA. In many of these instances, the role of the PHOSITA is a judicial, rather than a statutory, creation.

As the name suggests, PHOSITA-based analysis is specific to the particular art in which the invention is made. Courts measure most significant patent law doctrines against a benchmark that varies by industry and within industry by technology. If the court concludes that an art is uncertain, and its practitioners not particularly skilled, it will be inclined to find even relatively modest improvements nonobvious to the PHOSITA. At the same time, the court will be inclined to require greater disclosure to satisfy the requirements of section 112, and correspondingly to narrow the scope of claims permissible from any given disclosure. If the art is predictable and the PHOSITA quite skilled, the reverse is also true. The result is to make the PHOSITA a potentially significant macro policy lever, awarding many narrow patents to some industries and a few broader patents to other industries.[38]

There is overwhelming evidence that the application of the PHOSITA standard varies by industry, leading for example to fewer, but broader, valid software patents and more, but narrower, biotechnology patents. It is less clear that the court is in fact using the PHOSITA explicitly as a policy lever, responding to the characteristics of particular industries, rather than merely trying to predict what those of skill in the art would think. But as we have observed elsewhere, if the court is trying to apply the PHOSITA standard neutrally, it is not doing a very good job. It is substituting constructs for detailed analysis, and failing to update those constructs as knowledge in the industry changes. In any event, because application of the PHOSITA standard causes nominally unitary patent rules to be applied very differently—indeed, in directly contradictory ways—in different industries, it does not matter whether or not the court explicitly uses the PHOSITA in setting policy. The use of the PHOSITA is a macro policy lever because it explicitly creates different standards for different technologies and different industries. Indeed, it is in some ways the most fundamental policy lever, because it makes so much turn on the knowledge of scientists in any given field. A PHOSITA-based patent law *must* be industry-specific.

APPLICATION: THE *KSR* CASE AND POLICY LEVERS

Obviousness is the most important test for patentability—both the argument that defendants make the most and the one that is most often responsible for invalidating patents.[39] The problem is that it is very difficult for a judge or jury to put themselves in the shoes of a scientist in the field ten years earlier and predict whether that scientist would have found the invention obvious. One reason is hindsight bias: simple ideas that no one thought of for some time will look obvious with the benefit of hindsight once someone actually does think of them. To combat the problem of hindsight bias, the Federal Circuit over the past twenty years created a rule that required anyone challenging a patent as obvious to prove that the existing prior art provided a teaching, suggestion, or motivation to do what the patentee ultimately did. This "TSM" test avoided hindsight, but it created a different problem. Scientists in the field aren't merely automatons who read the prior art and mechanically apply it. Requiring litigants to find a teaching or suggestion for every modification to the prior art, no matter how trivial, led to a number of cases in which straightforward modifications of existing technology were held patentable.

In 2007, the Supreme Court changed the standard of obviousness in the *KSR* case.[40] Rather than focus on the existence of a written suggestion in the prior art, the Court said, the test for obviousness must focus on the knowledge and abilities of the PHOSITA, including whatever creative or innovative tendencies the ordinary scientist in the field possessed. In one fell swoop, the Court turned obviousness from a search for written suggestions in the prior art, regardless of industry, to a question of what the PHOSITA in a particular field would know or could figure out. In so doing, *KSR* gave courts the power to use obviousness doctrine as a whole as a micro policy lever, one that will lead to more valid patents in industries in which the PHOSITA knows little or is uncreative and more invalid patents in industries with more sophisticated players.

Secondary Considerations of Nonobviousness

Section 103 of the Patent Act provides that obviousness shall be tested by reference to the differences between the invention and the prior art (35 U.S.C. § 103[a]). In *Graham v. John Deere Co.,*[41] the Court introduced a series of nonstatutory factors, called "secondary considerations" of nonobviousness, which the court said "may have relevancy." The Federal Circuit has elevated these secondary considerations to a required element of any obviousness analysis.[42] The considerations the court has endorsed include the commercial success of the invention, the failure of others to make the invention, existence of a long-felt need for the invention, unexpected results reached by the inventor, efforts by others to copy the invention, licensing or other acquiescence by the market treating the patentee as the inventor, and (in some but not all circumstances) simultaneous invention by others.[43] With the exception of simultaneous invention, all of these factors favor a finding of patentability, while their absence is not evidence that an invention is obvious.[44] These secondary considerations are policy-based; they result from the court's belief that the reaction of the market will show that certain inventions are more deserving of protection than others. They are also evidence based on hindsight, and therefore more susceptible to application by the courts in infringement proceedings than to use by the PTO. In the wake of the Supreme Court's decision in *KSR,*[45] which made it harder for patentees to survive the obviousness test, it is reasonable to expect that patentees will put more reliance on secondary considerations, since they may represent the strongest possible argument for patentability in the new regime.[46]

The standard secondary considerations of nonobviousness are micro policy levers. They nominally apply to every case in any industry. In fact, however, the secondary considerations are actually weighted toward inventions that are embodied in actual products, toward patents that cover entire products, and toward significant "leaps," rather than toward components of a product or incremental inventions. Commercial success, long-felt need, licensing, and copying all work best for actual products that are sold, rather than for upstream research tools or intermediary products. Commercial success depends on the connection between the patent and a product on the open market,[47] so it is more likely to be evident in products such as pharmaceuticals that are patented in their entirety rather than in a patent on one of the myriad components of a semiconductor chip. Factors such as commercial success, long-felt need, and acquiescence tend to favor inventions that are significant breaks with what came before, rather than incremental improvements. Thus, these factors are more likely to apply in a pharmaceutical or biotechnology case than in a software case. Although secondary considerations are nominally neutral, their application in fact favors inventions in certain industries.[48]

Written Description

One of the disclosure requirements in section 112 of the Patent Act is that the patentee provide an adequate "written description" of the invention (35 U.S.C. § 112, ¶1). Section 112 separately provides that the patent specification must enable the PHOSITA to make and use the invention; this "enablement requirement" is related to, but distinct from, the written description requirement.[49] The written description doctrine traces its origin to older versions of the patent statute that lacked a requirement for the inventor to provide claims. Thus, the written description once served the purpose now served by claims: to define the technology protected under the patent and to put the public on notice of the boundaries that would define infringement.

Because these purposes are now served by the claims, the written description criterion has evolved to serve a new purpose. The modern written description requirement is designed to ensure that at the time the patentee files a patent application, she actually has conceptual possession of the invention she is now claiming. In its modern incarnation, written description evolved as a highly technology-specific doctrine centered in the chemical arts. After remaining dormant for many years, the doctrine has more recently been applied in different ways in two different sets of cases. Its primary use in the last dozen years has been to bar patentees from changing their claims during prosecution to track a competitor's product that they did not themselves conceive of, even though their specification might have enabled one of skill in the art to make it.[50] That use has been applied in every industry, without obvious differentiation.[51]

In biotechnology, however, the doctrine has been applied as a sort of "super-enablement" requirement, forcing patentees to list particular gene sequences in order to obtain a patent covering those sequences.[52] For example, in *Fiers v. Revel*,[53] the court considered the decision of the Patent Office in a three-way interference over patent applications claiming the human DNA sequence that produces the protein fibroblast beta-interferon (β-IF).

(In biotechnology terms, we say that the DNA sequence in question "codes for" the protein.) One of the applicants, Revel, relied for priority upon his Israeli patent application, which disclosed methods for isolating a fragment of the DNA sequence coding for β-IF and for isolating messenger RNA coding for β-IF. The court considered whether the disclosure in Revel's Israeli application satisfied the U.S. written description requirement and could therefore support a U.S. application. The Federal Circuit upheld a determination by the Board of Patent Appeals and Interferences that Revel's disclosure was not an adequate description, largely because it failed to disclose the actual sequence of the DNA molecule at issue. According to the court's reasoning, disclosing a method for obtaining the molecule was not the same as disclosing the molecule itself:

> An adequate written description of a DNA requires more than a mere statement that it is part of the invention and reference to a potential method for isolating it; what is required is a description of the DNA itself. . . . A bare reference to a DNA with a statement that it can be obtained by reverse transcription is not a description; it does not indicate that Revel was in possession of the DNA.[54]

Since the Revel application did not disclose the sequence for the molecule claimed, the court characterized it as disclosing merely "a wish, or arguably a plan, for obtaining the DNA."[55] Under *Fiers,* an inventor does not conceive of a DNA invention until she actually creates it.[56] The court stopped short of creating an absolute rule, noting that "[t]here may be situations where an organism's performance of certain intracellular processes might be reasonably predictable, and evidence of such predictability might be sufficient to support a finding of conception prior to reduction to practice."[57] But the court's limiting language focuses on organic processes, not DNA sequences.

A similar conclusion was reached in a subsequent case, *Regents of the University of California v. Eli Lilly.*[58] The patent at issue covered a microorganism carrying the DNA sequence coding for human insulin. The patentee supported this claim by disclosing a method for obtaining the human cDNA,[59] as well as the amino acid sequences for the insulin protein and the corresponding insulin DNA sequence in rats. Relying on the *Fiers* opinion, the court concluded that the written description requirement again was not met: "Describing a method of preparing a cDNA or even describing the protein that the cDNA encodes, as the example does, does not necessarily describe the DNA itself."[60]

In reaching these results, the Federal Circuit has been adamant that the degree of specificity required for an adequate description of nucleic acids requires description of "structure, formula, chemical name, or physical properties."[61] In *Eli Lilly,* because "[n]o sequence information indicating which nucleotides constitute human cDNA appears in the patent . . . the specification does not provide a written description of the invention."[62] The court in such cases seems particularly incensed by applicants who designate a macromolecule by generic or functional terms, such as "vertebrate insulin cDNA":

> A definition by function . . . is only an indication of what the gene does, rather than what it is. It is only a definition of a useful result rather than a definition of what achieves that result. Many such genes may achieve that result. The description requirement of the patent statute requires a description of an invention, not an indication of a result that one might achieve if one made that invention. Accordingly, naming a type of material generally known to exist, in the absence of knowledge as to what that material consists of, is not a description of that material.[63]

Failure to describe more than one or two nucleotides is a particular problem where the patent claims are drawn to a broad class of nucleotides. For example, Revel's claim covered all DNA molecules that code for β-IF, but "[c]laiming all DNAs that achieve a result without defining what means will do so is not in compliance with the description requirement; it is an attempt to preempt the future before it has arrived."[64]

The two very different uses for the written description requirement have prompted one Federal Circuit judge to observe that we now have two distinct written description requirements, one that applies when patentees change claims and another that applies only to gene sequences.[65]

For software patents, by contrast, a series of Federal Circuit decisions has all but eliminated the Section 112 disclosure requirements.[66] In recent years, the Federal Circuit has held that software patentees need not disclose source or object code, flow charts, or detailed descriptions of the patented program. Rather, the court has found high-level functional descriptions sufficient to satisfy both the enablement and best mode doctrines.[67] For example, in *Northern Telecom, Inc. v. Datapoint Corp.,*[68] the patent claimed an improved method of entering, verifying, and storing (or "batching") data with a special data entry terminal. The district court invalidated certain claims of the patent on the grounds that they were inadequately disclosed under § 112.[69] The Federal Circuit reversed the lower court decision.[70] It held that when claims pertain to a computer program that implements a claimed device or method, the enablement requirement varies according to the nature of the claimed invention as well as the role and complexity of the computer program needed to implement it.[71] Under the facts in this case, the court reasoned, the core of the claimed invention was the combination of components or steps, rather than the details of the program the applicant actually used.[72] The court noted expert testimony that various programs could be used to implement the invention, and that it would be "relatively straightforward [in light of the specification] for a skilled computer programmer to design a program to carry out the claimed invention."[73] The court continued:

> The computer language is not a conjuration of some black art, it is simply a highly structured language. . . . The conversion of a complete thought (as expressed in English and mathematics, i.e. the known input, the desired output, the mathematical expressions needed and the methods of using those expressions) into a language a machine understands is necessarily a mere clerical function to a skilled programmer.[74]

And in *Fonar Corp. v. General Electric Co.,*[75] involving the best mode requirement, the Court explained:

> As a general rule, where software constitutes part of a best mode of carrying out an invention, description of such a best mode is satisfied by a disclosure of the functions of the software. This is because, normally, writing code for such software is within the skill of the art, not requiring undue experimentation, once its functions have been disclosed. It is well established that what is within the skill of the art need not be disclosed to satisfy the best mode requirement as long as that mode is described. Stating the functions of the best mode software satisfies that description test. We have so held previously and we so hold today. Thus, flow charts or source code listings are not a requirement for adequately disclosing the functions of software.[76]

Indeed, in a few cases the Federal Circuit has gone so far as to hold that patentees can satisfy the written description and best mode requirements for inventions implemented in software even though they do not use the terms "computer" or "software" anywhere in the specification![77] To be sure, in these latter cases it would probably be obvious to one skilled in the art that the particular feature in question should be implemented in software, though it would not necessarily be obvious *how* to do so. One more recent case suggests limits on this conclusion, holding that an oil drilling company failed to enable its method for calculating the location of a borehole when it kept all information about the computer programs used to perform the calculation secret.[78] However, even in that case the court made it clear that only the general nature of the program, not the program itself, need be disclosed.[79] It is remarkable that the Federal Circuit is

willing to find the enablement requirement satisfied by a patent specification that provides *no* guidance whatsoever on how the software should be
written.[80]

The second application of written description doctrine—to gene
sequences—is a macro policy lever. The Federal Circuit has applied the doctrine to biotechnology cases in a way that would be inconceivable in other
industries, such as software. The effect is to narrow the scope of biotechnology patents—or at least DNA patents—rather dramatically. (The court
has proven less willing to apply the written description doctrine to other
biotechnology inventions, such as monoclonal antibodies, at least in the
absence of some effort to change the claims in prosecution.)[81] Application
of the enablement requirement through the intermediary of the PHOSITA
has the same narrowing effect. In certain industries, such as software, the
enablement requirement is easily satisfied and therefore plays virtually no
role in limiting the scope of claims. In other industries, such as biotechnology, the doctrine has been applied with much more vigor. Whether courts
intend the differences they have created as macro policy levers, or whether
they result from the court's highly stylized views of the level of skill in the
software and biotechnology arts, the effect is the same—Section 112 doctrines significantly limit the scope and validity of patents in some industries
but not in others.

PATENT SCOPE

Abstract Ideas

Section 101 of the Patent Act defines the range of subject matter that is potentially patentable (35 U.S.C. § 101). Patentable subject matter has been defined quite broadly, as encompassing "anything under the sun that is made
by man."[82] Read literally in light of this definition, it is hard to think of
any new idea in any field of human endeavor that would not qualify for
patent protection. There are, however, a few judicially created exemptions
from the scope of patent protection,[83] including the rule against the patenting of abstract ideas. The rule originated in the case of *O'Reilly v. Morse,*
which involved Morse's patent on the telegraph.[84] Samuel Morse, of "Morse
code" fame, was allowed a broad patent for a process using electromagne-
tism to produce discernable signals over telegraph wires. The *O'Reilly* Court
denied Morse's eighth claim, in which Morse claimed the use of "electro-
magnetism, however developed for marking or printing intelligible charac-

ters, signs, or letters, at any distances." As the Supreme Court, in disallow-
ing the patent claim in *O'Reilly*, said:

> If this claim can be maintained, it matters not by what process or machin-
> ery the result is accomplished. For aught that we now know some future
> inventor, in the onward march of science, may discover a mode of writing
> or printing at a distance by means of the electric or galvanic current, with-
> out using any part of the process or combination set forth in the plaintiff's
> specification. His invention may be less complicated—less liable to get out
> of order—less expensive in construction, and in its operation. But yet if it is
> covered by this patent, the inventor could not use it nor the public have the
> benefit of it without the permission of this patentee.[85]

The rule against patenting abstract ideas, while couched in terms of patentable subject matter, is really a judicial effort to restrict the permissible
scope of patents and to channel patent protection toward finished products.
As the Court explained in *Chakrabarty*, laws of nature and abstract mathematical principles like $E=mc^2$ are simply not eligible for patent protection,
no matter how inventive they are.[86] The Court worried that patenting an
abstract idea or concept, rather than the particular device or process used
to implement that concept, would permit the patentee to "engross a vast,
unknown, and perhaps unknowable area."[87]

This abstract ideas rule is a "micro" policy lever: it applies to inventions
in all industries, but has particular significance for certain industries. This
policy lever has two potential effects that differ from industry to industry.
First, it prevents patents from covering entire concepts, limiting them instead to particular implementations. This gives room for subsequent innovators to work out new implementations of the abstract idea without fear
of patent liability. Indeed, the Court in *O'Reilly* was prescient in suggesting
that the development of the telegraph did not justify giving Morse a patent on all possible uses of electricity to communicate information: much
modern communication relies on the nontelegraphic use of electricity. To
borrow from the language of copyright, this lever limits the control an initial inventor has over derivative works. Such a prohibition is particularly
significant in software and telecommunications, where it would be unwise
to give the first person to think of an idea the exclusive right to control all
implementations of the idea. It may serve a particularly important role in
nascent industries, by preventing the owner of a broad foundational patent
from stifling the early development of an industry.

Second, and relatedly, the abstract ideas doctrine prevents those who
discover abstract ideas or natural rules—$E=mc^2$ is the example most com-

monly cited—from asserting control over the entire idea, rather than concrete implementations of that idea. It therefore forces patents downstream,
away from unfinished research and toward completed products or processes
more suitable for the market. In Schumpeter's taxonomy, it channels patents toward innovations rather than merely inventions.[88] This result may
have particular importance in biotechnology, where the patenting of upstream research ideas and tools threatens to stifle downstream innovation.[89]
The abstract ideas doctrine therefore works hand in hand with the utility
requirement.

The abstract ideas doctrine has not been applied much (if at all) by the
Federal Circuit. So it's a bit odd to speak of it as an existing policy lever; it
is a lever that exists in the case law but never seems to be pulled. But in a
recent decision, *In re Bilski*, the Federal Circuit set new standards for deciding whether claims to ideas that do not require physical implementation
are patentable subject matter. *Bilski*'s more stringent limits on patentable
subject matter will disproportionately affect patents in the financial services
and software industries. We are skeptical that it is wise to carve swaths out
of patentable subject matter, but there is no question that a reinvigorated
doctrine would be a micro policy lever.

Reasonable Interchangeability

The doctrine of equivalents in patent law permits a court to find infringement in some circumstances even though the accused product does not fall
within the literal scope of the patent claims. For the doctrine of equivalents
to apply, the differences between a particular claim limitation and the accused product must be "insubstantial."[90] Courts have formulated a variety of tests to determine whether the differences in question are substantial. One major test—adopted by the Supreme Court in *Graver Tank*—asks
whether the accused element performs substantially the same function in
substantially the same way to achieve substantially the same result.[91] This
tripartite function-way-result test has been criticized on the grounds that it
doesn't work well in all circumstances, particularly for composition of matter claims.[92] The most significant alternative is the "reasonable interchangeability" test, which asks whether one of ordinary skill in the art would
consider the accused element to be reasonably interchangeable with the
limitation described in the patent.[93]

It is not clear how the two tests interact, and what a court would do if it
found one test but not the other satisfied. We believe the better view is that
function-way-result is the dominant test in cases in which it can be applied,

and that reasonable interchangeability is merely evidence shedding light on the application of the tripartite test. In other words, if two elements work in a substantially different way, a court would likely find them not equivalent even if those of skill in the art would find those two different ways reasonably interchangeable for most purposes as of the time of infringement. Some evidence for this proposition comes from *Key Manufacturing Group v. Microdot*, in which the court noted that "an interchangeable device is not necessarily an equivalent device,"[94] suggesting that there is some broader test of which reasonable interchangeability is merely a part.

A separate question is how function, way, and result are to be tested. To the extent that they are measured by reference to the knowledge of a PHOSITA, the tripartite test may collapse into reasonable interchangeability. In either event, reasonable interchangeability remains important both as evidence bearing on the tripartite test and because in many cases the tripartite test simply will not work.

Reasonable interchangeability is a micro policy lever in two different senses. First, the tripartite test works well for inventions in certain industries, such as mechanics and, arguably, software—industries in which patents tend to cover devices or processes. It works far less well for industries such as organic chemistry, pharmaceuticals, and biotechnology, in which patents tend to cover compositions of matter. Thus, reasonable interchangeability is likely to take on greater importance as a test in some industries than others. Second, because reasonable interchangeability relies on the PHOSITA, it is technology-specific for the same reasons that the obviousness and enablement PHOSITAs are technology-specific. The less certain the court perceives a field to be, the less scope it will give to patents under the doctrine of equivalents. These two principles reinforce each other. The court has concluded that chemistry, pharmaceutical research, and biotechnology are inherently uncertain disciplines,[95] meaning that in those disciplines—the very ones in which the reasonable interchangeability test will be most important—the test is likely to lead to narrow interpretations of the doctrine of equivalents. Finally, some commentators have argued that reasonable interchangeability should be adopted as the explicit rule in biotechnology,[96] suggesting that it could serve as a macro policy lever as well.

Element-by-Element Analysis

It is well established that the doctrine of equivalents is tested not with respect to the invention as a whole, but on an element-by-element basis.[97] Only if each element of the patent claim is present in the accused device, either literally or by equivalents, will there be infringement under the doctrine of equivalents. The idea behind this approach is to cabin the power of juries to expand the scope of patents under the doctrine, ensuring that accused devices found equivalent are in fact only insubstantially different from the patent claims.

Applying the doctrine of equivalents on an element-by-element basis begs the question "what is an element?" As we have explained elsewhere, there is no good answer to this question. Courts have in the past defined an element to be as small as a word and as large as the entire claim.[98] More important, and more problematic, there are no standards in the law by which to make the "right" decision as to either the size of the element or the level of abstraction at which it will be evaluated. Indeed, the indeterminacy is so acute that courts generally don't acknowledge that they are even engaging in either inquiry. They define an element almost arbitrarily, and even when judges disagree as to the proper definition they can offer no principled basis for doing so. They argue over the procedures to be used and sources to consult in deciding what particular elements mean, but rarely look through to the underlying question of how broadly a particular term should be understood.

Although there are no clear standards for choosing the "right" size of an element, there is good reason to believe that the structure of claims in some industries will be broken into fewer quanta than in other industries.[99] Mechanical and electronic devices often have a number of parts; at a minimum each part will be a different element, though courts have sometimes gone further and found that each word defining or limiting a part is itself a separate element.[100] By contrast, the structure of claims to DNA or chemicals is inherently less susceptible to division into many different elements, because those claims will usually be written by identifying either a generic or a specific chemical structure. Although it is conceivable that a court would break an identified DNA sequence or chemical structure into pieces, perhaps by concluding that each codon was a separate element, it seems unlikely.[101] A single chemical is likely to be treated as a single element, while a single machine will likely be treated as involving several different elements. As we have explained elsewhere, the effect of this division will be that chemical and biotechnology claims will get somewhat more use out of the doctrine of equivalents than other types of claims, since multi-element claims are easier to avoid altogether by making a single change to the device. The result is that the element-by-element analysis is a micro policy lever.

Pioneering Patents

It is a venerable (some might say decrepit) principle of patent law that pioneering patents—important patents that open up a new field—should be entitled to a broader range of protection than more modest inventions or improvements on existing ideas.[102] The Wright brothers, for example, won their patent infringement suit against Glenn Curtis in 1914 because they were pioneering inventors, and the court accordingly afforded them broad protection even against the somewhat different Curtis plane.[103] The Court of Customs and Patent Appeals, the predecessor to the Federal Circuit, applied the pioneer patent doctrine,[104] and the Supreme Court continues to talk about patent scope under the doctrine of equivalents as a function of how pioneering the patent is.[105] To some extent broadened claim scope follows naturally from the situation of a pioneering patent: there is little prior art in a newly opened field that would prevent the inventor from claiming broadly. Broad literal claims may not anticipate later-invented technologies that could be substituted for elements of the claim, however; such substitutions may instead be captured under the doctrine of equivalents, if applied broadly. The pioneer patent rule has not been invoked by the Federal Circuit in recent years, leading some to consider it moribund,[106] but it provides at least one factor to consider in deciding how broadly to apply the doctrine of equivalents. Some scholars have argued that it should play a greater role in doctrine of equivalents cases than it does today.[107]

The pioneering patent rule is a micro policy lever. The rationale for the rule is expressly policy-based: if we do not give broad equivalents protection to pioneers in new fields, they will be unable to capture adequate returns from their invention, as subsequent improvers figure out commercial applications of the new idea that avoid the literal scope of the patent.[108] The power of the doctrine is tied to the nature of innovation in a particular industry. In some industries, such as pharmaceuticals, innovation is likely to take the form of discrete new inventions that in many cases open up entire fields of inquiry. Not all pharmaceutical inventions will take this form, of course. Pharmaceutical companies increasingly engage in the creation of safer, "copycat" drugs. Those inventions would be less likely to qualify for pioneer status. But the canonical pharmaceutical invention will open up a new market for treatment of an illness or disease. By contrast, industries such as software and most semiconductor inventions are characterized by more incremental improvements. These incremental improvements will not be entitled to a broader range of equivalents under the pioneering patents

rule. Thus, application of the rule, while nominally neutral, is likely to result in broader protection under the doctrine of equivalents in some industries than others.

Reverse Doctrine of Equivalents

The reverse doctrine of equivalents is in some sense the contrapositive of
the pioneer patents rule. The reverse doctrine of equivalents permits an accused infringer to escape literal infringement by demonstrating that the device, while falling literally within the scope of the claims, is so far changed
in principle from the patented invention that it would be inequitable to hold
the infringer liable.[109] The doctrine is rarely applied, and the Federal Circuit
in *Tate Access Floors v. Interface Architectural Resources*[110] suggested that
the doctrine had no continued meaning after the passage of the 1952 Patent
Act. The court also (misleadingly) suggested the Federal Circuit had never
applied the doctrine.[111] The Federal Circuit has since backed off from this
crabbed and ahistorical reading.[112] In the rare cases in which it is applied,
the reverse doctrine of equivalents serves as a vital release valve, preventing
patent owners from stifling radical improvements.[113]

The reverse doctrine of equivalents is a micro policy lever. The doctrine
can apply to radical improvements in any area of technology, and indeed
has been used to cover technological paradigm shifts within an industry.[114]
Radical improvements are more likely in some industries than others. Software, for example, tends to progress through iterative steps, and software
inventions are therefore less likely to be the sort of radical improvements
that qualify under the reverse doctrine of equivalents. Recent applications
of the reverse doctrine of equivalents have focused on significant changes in
the biotechnology industry, where the development of genetic engineering
has permitted quantum leaps in the production of certain proteins. Indeed,
the one Federal Circuit case applying the doctrine involved biotechnology,[115]
and commentators have suggested the doctrine might fairly be applied
there.[116]

REMEDIES: REASONABLE ROYALTY

A patent is protected by a property rule, and the ordinary remedy for patent
infringement is an injunction. But patentees are also entitled to damages
"adequate to compensate" for infringement that occurred before the injunction took effect (35 U.S.C. § 284) or in those cases in which the court denies

injunctive relief. Although patentees can prove entitlement to lost profits in a narrow set of circumstances, the fallback remedy is a reasonable royalty. The courts define a reasonable royalty as one that would have been negotiated by hypothetical willing buyers and sellers at the time infringement first began, though they bias the royalty rate upward to avoid undercompensation by having those hypothetical bargainers assume that the patent is valid and infringed.[117] But of course there was no such negotiation, and the fact that the parties just spent $8 to $10 million on average to litigate the patent dispute suggests they were unlikely to readily come to terms. To help determine the proper royalty rate, courts turn to a multifactor test that includes questions such as the importance of the invention, the possibility of designing around, the profit margins in the industry, and the customary royalty rates for similar inventions.[118]

The multifactor reasonable royalty test is both a macro and a micro policy lever. At the macro level, the courts look expressly at the conditions of the relevant industry to determine such facts as the profit margin that a company might expect and the royalty rate common in licenses in that industry. There is some empirical evidence suggesting that licensing royalty rates differ significantly by industry.[119] If so, those differences are expressly taken into account in setting royalty rates. At the micro level, many of the characteristics in the royalty inquiry that aren't expressly industry-specific are nonetheless factors that vary systematically by industry. Industries in which inventions cover components, not whole products, should have systematically lower royalty rates, for example, at least if courts correctly apply the principles of apportionment to assign to the patentee only the value of its contribution to the overall product. And designing around a patent may be easier in some industries than others.

Finally, because the reasonable royalty remedy applies only when lost profits are unavailable, the application of the remedy at all may vary systematically by industry. Patent "trolls"— nonmanufacturing patent owners who seek royalties on the basis of patents written with a different invention in mind—will not be entitled to lost profits, because they weren't in a position to make the sales the infringer did. They will therefore be entitled only to a reasonable royalty. Industries in which most of the patent suits are brought by nonmanufacturing patent owners will therefore rely more on the reasonable royalty rate than the (generally larger) lost profit awards.

The result is a rather powerful policy lever. The application of the reasonable royalty remedy will compensate patent owners for infringement at systematically different rates in different industries. These differences have the potential to mediate many of the problems arising from the application of patent law in such patent-intensive, component-specific industries as semiconductors, telecommunications, and software. If—as seems reasonable given the law—royalty rates are systematically lower in those industries than in industries such as pharmaceuticals and chemistry, that fact may help mediate the dangers of royalty stacking and double marginalization in those patent-thicket industries. (Of course, if the reverse is true—if plaintiffs can win as much or more in a reasonable royalty inquiry, as some recent decisions have mistakenly held[120]—the policy lever won't work.)

This list of doctrines highlights twelve industry-specific policy levers, already present and being used in patent law, that evidence the substantial discretion already built in to patent jurisprudence. The list provides ample evidence that despite general rules that are nominally unitary, in practice patent law is already technology-specific. Courts are making decisions in a wide variety of areas that depend on the characteristics of particular industries. Further, none of the policy levers we have discussed in this chapter result from industry-specific legislation. Instead, they are evidence that the courts can and do apply a nominally unitary patent system with sensitivity to the needs and characteristics of different industries. The doctrines we have discussed in this chapter all implicate the technology-specific potential of patent law, and they are all capable of being used to bring patent law in line with optimal patent policy. But we suspect that a variety of other doctrines could also be used by the courts to achieve such policy goals, and it is to these nascent policy levers that we turn in the next chapter.

More We Can Do
Potential New Policy Levers

In all of the instances we have just discussed, courts not only have discretion granted to them in the patent statute (or assumed as part of the common law process) but they have also used that discretion (wittingly or not) to tailor patent law to individualized circumstances in different industries. The discretion granted to courts in patent law, however, does not end there. Various other doctrines *could* be used as policy levers within the discretion granted in the statute. Yet other doctrines could become policy levers but would require congressional action. In this chapter we consider several such potential policy levers. We emphasize that there are costs as well as benefits to the use of these policy levers, and that it may not make sense to use all of them. Rather, we throw them out as suggestions for consideration, and as examples of how the courts could make more use than they do of the policy levers built into patent law.

Patent Acquisition and Validity

NEW SECONDARY CONSIDERATIONS OF NONOBVIOUSNESS

The classic economic framework pioneered primarily by Robert Merges views obviousness as a function of uncertainty.[1] Where uncertainty is higher, the theory goes, courts should lower the standard of patentability to compensate for the risk of failure and therefore compensate for the attendant lower expected reward per dollar invested. Although courts have traditionally focused on the uncertainty, and hence the obviousness, of the act of invention itself, invention is rewarded in the marketplace only to the

extent it is embodied in a successful commercial product that can be sold at
a price above marginal cost. Getting from an invention to a successful product requires many more steps: developing the product, testing it, producing
it, marketing it, and in many cases developing complementary products or
even whole new industries that can take advantage of the invention in the
most efficient way. The entire process of research, development, and turning
an idea into a finished product can be described as innovation. *Invention* is
thus a subset of—a first step in—*innovation*.[2]

IP law assumes that absent legal protection, the costs and risks of innovating are systematically higher than the costs of imitation. As a result,
no one will invest in research and development if the costs of doing so fall
exclusively on the innovator, but the benefits of that research can be freely
appropriated by all. High costs will tend to correlate with higher risks, as
the larger investment increases the opportunity for loss at any probability of
success. The greater variance in outcomes might be expected to deter the rational entrepreneur from investing in such high-cost projects unless the expected reward is correspondingly greater. Where research and development
costs are especially high relative to the costs of imitation, Merges argues,
lowering the standard for patentability may increase the incentive to invest
in innovation by increasing the likelihood of financial reward.

Courts might extend Merges's theory beyond the cost and uncertainty
of invention to account for the cost and uncertainty of innovation as well.
On this approach, the Federal Circuit could take account of the cost and
uncertainty of postinvention development in the same way it takes account
of other economic indicia of the importance of an invention: by creating a
new secondary consideration of nonobviousness that measures the cost of
innovation. Proof that an invention was merely the first step in a long and
uncertain road would be evidence that supported patentability, not because
it was direct proof of nonobviousness but because it increased the need for
a patent reward to encourage that innovation. As we suggest in chapter 11,
obviousness may not be the most reasonable way to take account of the cost
and uncertainty of innovation. But it is one possible way.

We have already suggested that secondary considerations are typically
micro policy levers. Cost and uncertainty of innovation, incorporated into a
new secondary consideration, could be conceived either as a macro or a micro policy lever. Courts could inquire into the cost and uncertainty of each
given innovation, in which case the rule would be facially neutral, though
it would apply more often in industries such as pharmaceuticals than in industries where barriers to market entry were lower and the path to prof-
itability was more clearly defined. A more efficient approach would be to

inquire more generally into the cost and uncertainty of innovation in an industry as a whole and to set rules that apply to a given industry. Uncertainty is difficult to measure with respect to a specific invention. Indeed, it may not even make sense to measure uncertainty only in the subset of inventions that are successful enough to be the subject of patent protection without considering the research and development efforts that did not produce patentable inventions. It is uncertainty across many inventions—the number of inventions that do not pan out and consequently do not result in patent applications—that the test is designed to measure. That measurement can only be done in the aggregate, rather than in individual terms. On this more general approach, uncertainty of innovation as a nonobviousness factor would be a macro policy lever.

We emphasize that there are problems with this approach; we address them in chapter 11. It is not clear that obviousness is the best way to address the cost of postinvention development. But it is *a* way, one that courts could adopt on their own within the existing obviousness framework to address a market failure.

PRESUMPTION OF VALIDITY

The patent statute provides that issued patents are presumed valid.[3] The Federal Circuit has interpreted this provision to require an accused infringer to prove by clear and convincing evidence that a patent is invalid.[4] Doug Lichtman and Mark Lemley, among others, have argued that such a strong presumption of validity is unwarranted, given the minuscule amount of time that the PTO spends actually examining patents and the number of bad patents that slip through the system.[5] The arguments against a strong presumption of validity are compounded by the rather startling fact that the patentee never has the burden of proving to the PTO that it should be entitled to a patent; rather, it is the PTO that carries the burden of showing that an application is not deserving of a patent.[6] Although abolishing the presumption of validity outright would require legislative change, the Federal Circuit has substantial control over the strength of the presumption and the cases in which it applies. It could, if it wished, make the presumption one that could be overcome by the preponderance of the evidence, rather than by clear and convincing evidence. Alternatively, the Federal Circuit could change its rule so that the presumption did not apply to prior art that was not considered by the PTO. The Federal Circuit expanded the presumption of validity to encompass prior art the examiner did not consider,[7] a rule that makes little sense. Before the Federal Circuit was created, a majority of circuits held that the presumption was strong if the PTO had considered the art, but weak otherwise,[8] and the Supreme Court recently suggested in dictum that the old rule made more sense than the uniformly strong presumption of validity.[9] Yet another approach would be to presume valid only those patents whose owners had conducted a diligent prior art search during the application process. There is no such requirement now,[10] and many sophisticated entities refuse to search for prior art out of concern with what they might find.[11]

The Federal Circuit could use the presumption of validity as a policy lever. It is possible to envision it as a macro policy lever, granting stronger presumptions in some industries than others based on either historical experience with patents or on the policies favoring stronger or weaker patent protection. For example, commentators have long criticized the quality of patents that issue in the software industry.[12] A court that agreed with this assessment might conclude that software patents were less deserving of the presumption of validity than other types of patents. At the other extreme, the PTO now provides a special two-step review to business method patents, despite the fact that the office was already rejecting more business-method-patent applications than other kinds of applications.[13] A court might take this fact into account in strengthening the presumption of validity for business-method patents, since evidence suggests that the two-stage review lets very few applications issue,[14] though John Allison has shown that the two-stage review is easily evaded.[15]

The problem with this macro approach is that it requires strong evidence about the validity of particular types of patents—not only evidence of how serious the PTO scrutiny of those patents is but also evidence of how many applications *should be* rejected in each industry. That evidence is impossible to come by. For instance, despite widespread complaints about the quality of software patents, empirical evidence shows that software patent applications are more likely to be rejected than any other type of application.[16] So a first-order industry-specific validity rule would give software patents the *strongest,* not the weakest, presumption of validity. But to know whether that is the right result, we would also need to know how many software patent applications deserved to be issued in some Platonic sense. If only 10 percent of software patent applications are objectively valid, the fact that the PTO grants patents to 50 percent of the software patent applications would mean that scrutiny of those applications was not strict enough.

These problems lead us to believe that the presumption of validity won't work terribly well as a macro policy lever. A more plausible approach would be to use the presumption of validity as a micro policy lever. If the Federal Circuit were to apply the presumption only to cited prior art, for example, the effect would be to give stronger protection to patents that cite more prior art. Because the empirical evidence is clear that patents in some industries, notably pharmaceuticals, biotechnology, and chemistry, cite more prior art than patents in industries such as electronics,[17] the effect of such a general rule would be to strengthen patent protection in those industries. Or if Congress were to adopt a postgrant opposition or a gold-plated-patents approach,[18] giving some patents additional scrutiny at the request of either the patent applicant or a competitor, it would seem reasonable to link that additional scrutiny to a higher presumption of validity. Because those opt-in systems would likely be used more in some industries than others, the result would be a micro policy lever, one that quite logically gave a stronger presumption of validity to stronger patents, those that have survived a more searching examination process.

Patent Scope: Patent Misuse

Under a long-standing common law doctrine, patents are unenforceable if they have been misused by their owner.[19] Patent misuse can take one of two basic forms. First and most commonly, a patent is misused if it is employed to violate the antitrust laws.[20] Because the patent laws themselves permit certain types of anticompetitive conduct that might otherwise be illegal,[21] the test is normally stated as whether a patentee seeks to expand the patent beyond its scope with anticompetitive effect.[22] Second, even absent anticompetitive effect, a patentee may commit misuse by expanding the patent beyond its lawful scope in certain ways that are deemed illegal on their face. Most notable among these is a license agreement that purports to extend the patent beyond its expiration or invalidity.[23]

Although misuse claims have been on the wane in patent law, they have experienced something of a renaissance in the context of copyright. Copyright misuse provides an excellent example of a policy lever at work in another legal field. Misuse claims are unknown in most copyright industries. Successful misuse claims have been made mostly with respect to computer software.[24] In addition, digital music and movie cases are increasingly fertile ground for copyright misuse.[25] Patent misuse similarly has the potential to serve as a powerful micro policy lever in a variety of contexts. The concept of misuse necessarily contains within it an implicit definition of the scope of permissible control over an invention; it is only the expansion beyond that lawful scope that can trigger misuse. Thus, in one sense, the content of misuse will necessarily vary from patent to patent. For example, the Fifth Circuit found misuse in *DGI* and *Alcatel* where the copyright owner argued that the defendant committed copyright infringement by testing the compatibility of its product with the copyrighted one, because such testing necessarily made a temporary copy of the plaintiff's work in RAM memory.[26] The court concluded that the plaintiff had attempted to extend the copyright beyond its scope. In so doing, it necessarily concluded that plaintiff's copyright claim failed on the merits, as otherwise it would not have extended the copyright beyond its proper scope.[27]

This use of misuse in copyright may be instructive for patent law. In copyright the doctrine has been applied primarily in cases relating to computer software in which the copyright holder has attempted to suppress competition in some fashion. Most significantly, misuse has been employed by courts to preserve a right of reverse engineering access by competitors seeking to create interoperable products.[28] As we explain in chapter 12, reverse engineering is critically important to progress in the software industry, but patent law lacks any explicit reverse engineering provision. If patent misuse were to develop in a parallel fashion to misuse in the software copyright cases, it might provide a basis for reverse engineering of patented software.

More generally, whether conduct gives rise to misuse is likely to vary from industry to industry, depending on a number of factors. First, the concentration of market power in an industry will determine whether certain licensing practices, such as exclusive deals, have anticompetitive effect. Highly concentrated industries or those dominated by a single firm are more amenable to patent misuse claims. Second, the importance of interconnection between different products and the need to cross-license different patents will determine the prevalence of such potentially anticompetitive practices as tying one product to another, patent pooling, and cross-licensing. Industries with overlapping and conflicting patents, such as software and semiconductors, are more likely to see efforts to use a patent to gain control of an adjacent product market. Third, the rate of change in an industry will determine whether patentees have much to gain by seeking to extend patents beyond their temporal scope. Pharmaceutical companies have strong incentives to extend the life of their patents, which are most valuable years after the invention, and indeed they have engaged in a variety of strategies designed to restrict generic competition by extending the effective life of their patents.[29] Software companies, by contrast, generally have no similar incentive. More generally, the courts could use patent misuse to enforce a conception of the proper scope of a patent in a given industry in the face of efforts by patentees in different industries to change that scope.

Although patent misuse has the potential to serve as a policy lever, its use by the Federal Circuit to date has been minimal and seems to have diminished over time. The court has seemed more concerned with strictly cabining patent misuse and its cousin antitrust than it has with engaging in detailed determinations of the facts and characteristics of given industries.[30] We do not intend to suggest that the court is necessarily wrong to do so. Patent misuse has its share of problems, including an irrational set of rules for standing and remedy.[31] The antitrust/misuse inquiry into competitive effects is necessarily industry-specific, however, and regardless of its significance, it could serve as a policy lever designed to ensure that patents are given no more than their appropriate scope.

Patent Remedies

INJUNCTIONS

Patent rights are exclusive rights that fit the classic formulation of a "property rule."[32] Indeed, the patent right to exclude was regarded by the Federal Circuit as a nearly absolute property rule, and the assumption that a finding of patent infringement would be accompanied by an injunction was almost universal from the mid-1980s until 2006.[33] In fact, however, the patent statute provides only that courts may grant injunctive relief, not that they must (35 U.S.C. § 283 [2000]). The legal standard for *preliminary* injunctive relief has vacillated over time. Preliminary injunctions were virtually impossible to obtain before the creation of the Federal Circuit.[34] The Federal Circuit substantially liberalized the standard for granting such injunctions in the 1980s,[35] but then tightened up the standard considerably in the 1990s, to the point where today preliminary injunctions are quite rare.[36] The court has the discretion under the statute to do something similar with permanent injunctive relief. Indeed, in copyright, as opposed to patent, cases, the Supreme Court has on several recent occasions encouraged the lower courts not to grant injunctive relief as a matter of course.[37]

On rare occasions before 2006, courts in patent cases refused to grant permanent injunctive relief. The most significant examples are *Foster v.*

American Machine & Foundry Co.,[38] in which the court was influenced
by the fact that the patentee did not practice the invention,[39] and *Vitamin
Technologists, Inc. v. Wisconsin Alumni Research Foundation,*[40] in which
the court was swayed by the health-related nature of the invention, finding
a strong public policy interest in continued access to the invention.[41] The
rare other cases in which patentees are denied injunctions generally also
involve health and safety—judges have been unwilling to enjoin operation
of a sewage treatment plant and let sewage flow into Lake Michigan,[42] or
to prevent the operation of brakes on railroad cars,[43] for example. Most recently, Judge Richard Posner, sitting by designation in the district court in
SmithKline Beecham v. Apotex,[44] found that SmithKline's patent on Paxil
was not infringed and that, even if it were infringed, injunctive relief would
be improper. (The Federal Circuit refused to accept Judge Posner's decision
on this ground, however). Beyond these cases, most classic refusals to grant
injunctive relief involve compulsory licensing of patents as a remedy for antitrust violations.[45]

Injunctive relief can serve as a policy lever at either the macro or micro level. Courts could deny injunctive relief in some industries altogether.
Some consumer advocates suggest that life-saving drugs ought to fit into
this category, for example. Alternatively, courts could deny injunctive relief
on a case-by-case basis depending on other characteristics that differ by industry, such as whether the plaintiff actually practices the invention. This is
the way the courts have gone in the wake of *eBay v. MercExchange.*

EBAY AND THE CREATION OF A NEW POLICY LEVER

As we write this book, we have the opportunity to witness the creation of a
policy lever in real time. In its 2006 decision in *eBay v. MercExchange,* the
Supreme Court rejected the long-standing rule that patentees who won their
cases were automatically entitled to an injunction shutting down the infringing product. Relying on the statutory language and common-law principles
of equity from outside patent law, the Court held that the decision whether
to enjoin a defendant's product must be made on a case-by-case basis after
consideration of four (really three) factors—whether the plaintiff will suffer
irreparable injury without an injunction, or whether it has an adequate remedy at law; whether the hardship to the defendant from granting an injunction outweighs the hardship to the plaintiff from denying the injunction; and
where the public interest lies.[46] The Court emphasized that this determination should be on the basis of individual facts, not rigid rules or tests.

Dozens of district courts have applied these standards in the past two years. Despite the case-by-case nature of the inquiry, the district court opinions have established some general rules. Patentees who compete in the market essentially always get injunctions under the four-factor test, because it is extremely difficult to determine what would have happened in a counterfactual world in which the patentee actually had market exclusivity, so damages are unlikely to be adequate as a remedy for the lost market share that infringement causes. By contrast, patentees that do not participate in the market, but merely seek to license their patent to those who do, can almost never satisfy the four-factor test, because by definition what they want is money damages in the form of a reasonable royalty. Further, almost all of those nonpracticing entity cases arise in complex technology industries in which the patent covers only a small component of the larger product. In those cases, the balance of the hardships strongly favors the defendant, because an injunction will shut down not merely the infringing technology but a much larger set of noninfringing technologies attached to it.[47] There is only one exception so far to this general rule that practicing entities get injunctions and nonpracticing entities don't: an aberrational Texas district court, reversed on other opinion grounds, that held that special rules should apply to nonprofit entities.[48]

This developing distinction operates as a micro policy lever. While practicing and nonpracticing entities exist in every industry, in some industries, such as pharmaceuticals, the patentees are almost all practicing entities, while in IT industries a high percentage of patent plaintiffs are nonpracticing entities, sometimes called "trolls" for the practice of hiding under a bridge and popping up to demand a toll from surprised passersby. A rule that practicing entities generally get injunctions while nonpracticing entities generally do not has dramatically different effects in the pharmaceutical and IT industries. Coupled with apportionment of patent damages, a rule that limits injunctions to plaintiffs that really need them might help solve the problems with abuse of the patent system we identified in chapter 3, while preserving a strong property rule entitlement for those who really need it.

Whether injunctive relief can fulfill this promise as a policy lever remains to be seen. Although the results in the district courts are encouraging, the Federal Circuit has not yet spoken definitively on the entitlement of nonpracticing entities to injunctive relief. If the court undoes the line the district courts have drawn, or if it allows patentees denied injunctions to collect punitive damage awards that effectively serve as the equivalent of an injunction, we may lose our best chance at efficient patent reform.

PROPERTY RULES AND POLICY LEVERS

As a general matter, courts are correct to treat patents as a property rule regime. The difficulty of valuing the unique assets common in patent cases and the possible variation in the licenses that might be granted make compulsory licensing difficult, and many have accordingly suggested that it is unwise as a general matter,[49] though the empirical evidence may not bear out this concern.[50] Denying injunctive relief may be appropriate in certain circumstances, however. First, if patents are being used to violate the antitrust laws, compulsory licensing of those patents is often a legitimate antitrust remedy designed to open a market to competition. For reasons noted above, these antitrust issues are likely to arise in some industries with more frequency than in others, so denying injunctive relief on antitrust grounds should similarly be industry-specific in effect. Second, injunctive relief may be inappropriate where patent rights are asserted primarily as hold-ups rather than as part of an effort to protect a legitimate invention. Injunctive relief may not be appropriate where the patentee does not practice the invention,[51] just as lost profits damages are unavailable in such a case.[52] Those holdup cases (and indeed enforcement by nonpracticing patent owners more generally) occur primarily in the IT industries, and are not generally a problem in the pharmaceutical industry. These applications would use injunctive relief as a micro policy lever.

Alternatively, injunctive relief could be used as a macro lever. Injunctive relief seems most problematic in industries characterized by anticommons problems, because individual patentees clear the rights necessary to sell products downstream. Indeed, the anticommons itself was originally defined with reference to this problem. Michael Heller observed that valuable property was going unused in Moscow because too many people held conflicting rights to the property and would not release them to a single user.[53] Such an industry may benefit from compulsory licensing.[54] Finally, some have suggested that patents covering products important to society, such as pharmaceuticals and perhaps some food products, should be available at less than the price a patentee could command if they could shut down alternative suppliers—in effect a subsidized, compulsory license.[55] All of these potential rules represent possible industry-specific policy levers, either by singling out particular industries for different treatment or by applying standards that would disproportionately affect patents in certain fields. We are skeptical, however, that using injunctive relief as a macro rather than a micro policy lever is either a good idea or consistent with international treaty obligations. It is better, we think, to confirm the discretion the statute vests in the courts to consider injunctive relief on a case-by-case basis, secure in the knowledge that the facts of individual cases will be quite different in the pharmaceutical industry than in the software or semiconductor industries.

⚘

We view this chapter as the opening thread in a continuing conversation. Clearly, there is more work to be done here. There will likely be other possible policy levers besides the ones we have identified. Chris Cotropia has interesting work suggesting various other common law patent rules that could be used as policy levers.[56] Not all judicial discretion can or should be applied in an industry-specific fashion, of course. But recognizing that courts are already doing this in many cases, consciously or not, should lead us to think more clearly about whether it makes sense to use other rules as policy levers and about the positive effects those levers can have on our fragmenting patent system.

Our preference in most specific cases for micro rather than macro policy levers is also instructive; courts may be better positioned to apply rules differentially in specific cases than they are to make the coarser industry-specific judgments. Put another way, courts may do better in applying standards than in creating rules.

Thinking about patent law in terms of policy levers can also help to design an optimal agenda for legislative reform. Our preference for case-by-case judicial tailoring does not mean that Congress has no role to play in adapting the patent system to the needs of different industries. Instead, we think that Congress can facilitate the use of policy levers. Rather than enacting industry-specific statutes or choosing one side or the other in the legislative debate over the future course of the patent system, we believe Congress should consider passing statutes that are nominally unitary but that permit courts to apply them in a case and industry-specific way. Proposed legislative reform confirming judicial discretion to decide when to issue injunctions would have fit well within this category, though the decision in *eBay* rendered it unnecessary. So too do proposed damages reforms that would deal specifically with calculation of damages for patents that cover only a small component of a larger product, since multicomponent products are a feature of some industries but not others. Even postgrant opposition or gold-plated patents can create needed industry-specific flexibility without legislating specifically for particular industries. In short, Congress, too, can and should facilitate judicial use of policy levers by giving courts the flexibility to take industry-specific differences into account.

11

Levers in a Specific Industry—Biotechnology

Having explored the characteristics of industries that map onto different theories of innovation, and having then described the legal and institutional architecture that matches legal incentives to different industries, we offer in this chapter a detailed discussion of the use of policy levers in a particular industry that provides a compelling example of the need for patent tailoring. Taking the biotechnology industry as our case study, we examine the use—and perhaps the misuse—of patent tailoring by the courts. We choose biotechnology because it has characteristics that distinguish it from many other industries, and because courts have already done a great deal of industry tailoring in that industry.

Because biotechnology has already been the subject of patent tailoring, we have used it in previous chapters as illustrative of certain policy levers. We suggest here how tailoring might be better fitted to biotechnology, focusing primarily on the levers that courts are already using. For example, we discuss use of obviousness and disclosure doctrines to modulate the scope and frequency of patents, as might be necessary where anticommons or patent thicket theories are applicable. These levers may also be employed to manage temporal sequencing of patent rights, particularly in industries where cumulative or follow-on innovation is present. We also suggest some cases where the use of new levers might be appropriate.

In doing so, we particularly want to emphasize the dynamic nature of any innovative technology. Industries change over time. This means that the fit of patent law to the industry must change over time. We have already described how the economic profile of the early software industry was quite different than that of the more recent, maturing software industry; the incentives needed in each phase of the industry's growth were different.

Consequently, the policy levers appropriate to patent tailoring for that industry have been different.

So, too, with biotechnology. Modern biotechnology is not monolithic, not built around a single product or technique. It includes a set of related technologies arising from methods for manipulation of biological characteristics at the molecular level. Some of these technologies were commercialized earlier than others; some have yet to reach their commercial potential. The innovation needs of the industry have changed as new technologies have become available, as some have required far greater investment than others. Although we cannot say what the precise economic profile of biotechnology will or should look like in the future, we can review the past and present use of policy levers in the industry, the fit of those levers to the developing innovation profile of the industry, and the appropriate application of those levers to the foreseeable trajectory of the industry.

Biotechnology's Profile

To date, commercial biotechnology has been mostly directed to the production of human pharmaceuticals and biologics. These pharmaceutical applications lend themselves in large part to prospect theory, but also in part to anticommons theory to the extent that the industry is directed to DNA research. In addition, there is some indication that portions of the biotechnology industry, notably agricultural biotechnology, may be developing characteristics that lean markedly toward anticommons theory.

If any technology fits the criteria of high-cost, high-risk innovation, it is certainly biotechnology. Development of biotechnology products, particularly in the pharmaceutical sector, has been characterized by extremely long development times and high development costs. These delays are due in part to the stringent regulatory oversight exercised over the safety of new drugs, foods, biologics, and the environmental release of new organisms.[1] Yet the onerous regulatory requirements to which biotechnology is subject may obscure a more fundamental uncertainty that justifies such oversight. Biotechnology products arise out of living systems and are typically intended to interact with other human or nonhuman living systems. These interactions, whether physiological or ecological, are enormously complex and the systems involved are poorly characterized. As a consequence, it is often hard to foresee how biotechnology products work, and their use can involve a high degree of uncertainty and risk.[2] Thus, while we have argued that the Federal Circuit has been wrong to suggest that identifying and making biotechnological products—*invention*—is always difficult and uncertain, it is also true that turning those research tools into medicines that can safely be sold in the market—*innovation*—is time-consuming, complex, and risky.

At the same time, generic manufacturers that wish to imitate an innovator's biotechnology-generated drugs face substantially lower costs and uncertainty than do innovators in the pharmaceutical industry. Although the FDA does impose regulatory hurdles on second-comers,[3] the process is substantially more streamlined than it is for innovators. Indeed, the primary regulatory hurdle a generic company faces is to show that its drug is bioequivalent to the innovator's drug.[4] Assuming bioequivalency, the FDA allows the generic to rely on the innovator's regulatory efforts. The uncertainty associated with developing and testing a new drug is largely absent for generic competitors; they need only replicate the drug the innovator has identified and tested. Similarly, the hard work involved in producing a cDNA sequence coding for a human protein is in identifying and isolating the right sequence; once the sequence is known, a follow-on competitor can easily replicate it. Notably, however, there is no statutory provision for generic biologics, so biotechnological pharmaceuticals may need less protection from infringement than do small-molecule pharmaceutical companies, since second-comers in the biotechnology industry cannot take advantage of the abbreviated drug application process on which generic pharmaceutical companies rely.

Early Biotechnology Tailoring

Early in the development of this industry, the Federal Circuit appeared to recognize these features and adapt the applicable patent law to them. Among the earliest commercial products of biotechnology were diagnostic tests based on the use of monoclonal antibodies. Monoclonal antibodies are proteins that will recognize and adhere to very specific molecular targets. In the body, a wide array of such antibodies is produced to attack foreign substances; one specific type of antibody is produced by identical cells from a particular "clone" of cells. There are many such clones of cells in the body. In the laboratory, uniform, specific "monoclonal" antibodies may be produced by identifying antibody-producing cells and inducing them to grow outside the body under artificial conditions. The development of such artificially grown cells, called hybridomas, was the technological breakthrough that allowed monoclonal antibodies to be produced. Hybridomas are produced by the artificial fusion of antibody-producing cells derived from mice or other mammals and cancerous cells that will grow continuously outside the body. The resulting fusion grows continuously under laboratory conditions, producing uniform batches of antibody all the while. Those uniform antibodies in turn can be used to uniformly bind to, identify, and quantify specific substances (called "antigens") present in the human body. Because the scientists creating the hybridomas are usually looking for a specific type of antibody among the myriad produced in an animal, hundreds or even thousands of antibody-producing cells typically have to be harvested, fused, and screened in order to find a desired monoclonal antibody.

This labor-intensive approach to antibody production was a critical consideration in the patentability of this early biotechnology. For example, in *In re Wands*,[5] the patentee claimed a method of using a specific type of monoclonal antibody in a diagnostic test. The patentee revealed that a very large number of cell fusions were performed in order to produce the type of antibodies needed to practice the claimed invention. The Patent Office rejected the application on enablement grounds, stating that methods disclosed by the applicant for producing the desired antibodies had a success rate too low to meet the requirements for a patent. However, on appeal to the Federal Circuit, the court held that such labor-intensive searches were routine in the art, and those of skill in the art would be able to screen a large number of hybridoma fusions to locate the desired type of antibody. In effect, the patent disclosed what to look for and a method to find it, and the level of skill in the art of creating hybridomas was sufficient to supply any other needed knowledge.

Other cases established monoclonal diagnostic kits as meeting the nonobviousness standard, for example the opinion in *Hybritech, Inc. v. Monoclonal Antibodies, Inc.*[6] This case involved one of the earliest commercial applications of monoclonal antibody technology, in the form of laboratory kits for medical diagnostics. The diagnostic kits produced by the patent holder, Hybritech, used monoclonal antibodies in what the industry dubbed a "sandwich assay," to test for a variety of clinical targets such as the hepatitis virus. The patent covering the kits was directed to the use of highly specific types of monoclonal antibodies in such a sandwich assay that would "sandwich" the clinical target between two types of antibody. The kits were enormously successful, effectively revolutionizing clinical testing. Competing kits also began to appear on the market, and when Hybritech sued producers of allegedly infringing kits, the defendants claimed that the Hybritech patent was invalid for obviousness.

The obviousness argument against the kits was based upon a wide spectrum of technical literature discussing aspects of clinical testing, use of antibodies in clinical assays, monoclonal antibodies, and sandwich assays. The references cited included articles on the use of an older technology, involving nonuniform or "polyclonal" antibodies in sandwich assays, articles on the use of monoclonal antibodies in other types of assays, articles predicting that the development of monoclonal antibodies, and even articles on the use of monoclonal antibodies in nondiagnostic sandwich assays. But the court held that none of the references revealed the combination of features that had made the Hybritech kits successful, and that one of ordinary skill would not have pieced the kits' features together from the available references. In reaching this result, the court relied heavily on the so-called secondary factors that indicate nonobviousness, such as commercial success and long-felt need. The fact that the monoclonal antibody diagnostic kits sold well when available and were not available sooner to meet commercial demand indicated to the court that if the invention were obvious it would have been developed more quickly.

These early biotechnology opinions deploy the PHOSITA standard in very different ways. *In re Wands* effectively sets the ordinary skill in the art at a very high level. The gist of the opinion is that the PHOSITA in immunology and monoclonal antibody technology is extremely knowledgeable and is able, with only a little guidance from the patent, to select among inoperative or nonfunctional antibodies to find the ones that will work in the invention. Information not supplied in the patent will be provided for already in the extensive knowledge of the PHOSITA. At the same time, the *Hybritech* opinion seems to view the PHOSITA in monoclonal antibody technology as a bit of a dullard. *Hybritech* suggests that the PHOSITA will be unable to put the pieces of the puzzle together, that despite a variety of references in the prior art pointing toward the use of monoclonal antibodies in a clinical testing kit, the PHOSITA would be unable to see this as obvious.

It may seem paradoxical that the person of skill in the art for monoclonal antibodies could be both so skilled as to need little help from the patent disclosure, and yet so dim-witted as to not be able to piece together prior art clues that would make the technology obvious. Part of the answer may be that although they share the same acronym, the PHOSITA for purposes of disclosure and the PHOSITA for purposes of obviousness are not the same construct. They have different imagined purposes and may be thought of as performing different imagined tasks. One PHOSITA is performing a technical task with known technology: sorting through the monoclonal antibodies produced in the laboratory in order to find the right ones to practice the invention. The other PHOSITA is engaged in a more imaginative predictive task: envisioning what future applications of monoclonal technology might emerge from the combination of presently available technologies. The obviousness PHOSITA might be thought of as a more creative or contemplative individual than his disclosure analog. One PHOSITA may be more skilled at his task than the other.

More importantly, these two PHOSITAs are performing different *doctrinal* tasks. The two PHOSITAs represent legal standards, not actual people, nor even representative people. One sets the standard as to how broadly an inventor can claim in relation to his own disclosure; the other sets the standard as to how broadly the inventor can claim in relation to the prior art. In each case the standard must be calibrated to a different patentability criterion in a given technology: to disclosure or to obviousness. Envisioning that standard as a kind of person is purely a legal fiction. The key consideration is that the standard be properly calibrated to allow for the right frequency and scope of patenting in a given industry.

This suggests that one should conceptually decouple the two PHOSITAs; despite the common title, each represents a separate policy lever for a given industry. And this is effectively the outcome from the early monoclonal antibody cases, separately setting the disclosure and nonobviousness standards to allow patents on early commercial products. *In re Wands* sets the requirements for disclosure in monoclonal antibody patents quite low; the inventor need not describe the invention in great detail in order to enable one of ordinary skill to practice the invention nor to demonstrate to one of ordinary skill that the inventor had possession of the invention. The case effectively views the PHOSITA in monoclonal antibody technology as knowing enough to fill in the details. The corollary is that the inventor could claim somewhat more broadly in relation to the disclosure; a minimal disclosure will support the claims. At the same time, these cases made it relatively easier to get a patent by setting a high standard for obviousness; only a very explicit prior art recommendation or prediction regarding a monoclonal invention would render that invention obvious.

These early cases may have the two PHOSITAs backwards. If the PHOSITA for obviousness purposes is more inventive than the ordinary user of the invention, the cases should have gone in precisely the opposite direction as a purely doctrinal matter—the quantum of invention needed to show nonobviousness should be higher if the obviousness PHOSITA is more creative, and the disclosure required of the patentee should be higher if the enablement PHOSITA is less skilled. Regardless, the effect of the court's early decisions was to strengthen patents in the early biotechnology industry by making them easier to acquire and uphold. Doing so may have encouraged development of the industry in its infancy. In short, the courts in the monoclonal antibody cases made implicit policy judgments designed to

encourage patenting, tweaking the legal doctrines to achieve what seemed
to be desirable results for innovation.

Recent Biotechnology Tailoring

As the biotechnology industry developed and matured, antibody products
remained important, but a new emphasis emerged on the use of recombinant DNA (gene-splicing techniques that could move genetic material into
new host organisms). In some cases the result of such gene transfers is an
organism with new commercial characteristics, such as crops that are resis-
tant to drought or insect pests. But perhaps the most touted and profitable
use of this technology has been to move genes for valuable pharmaceutical
proteins, such as insulin or human growth hormone, into microorganisms
that could be grown to produce large quantities of the otherwise rare protein. In most cases, the protein produced was well-known, and so unpatentable, having been isolated and characterized by classical biochemistry many
decades before production of a recombinant version. Consequently, since
the products of the technology were unpatentable, the industry focused on
patents directed to the precursor materials, to the genes and genetic constructs used to produce the proteins.

But although the emphasis on product and materials changed, the regulatory and innovation features of biotechnology remained much the same.
Consistent with the high innovation costs of the industry and Rob Merges's
standard economic model, the current Federal Circuit jurisprudence main-
tains a low obviousness barrier for biotechnology.[7] This lower barrier might
seem at odds with the modern science of biotechnology. The availability of
research tools has made the isolation and characterization of DNA and related biological macromolecules routine. As a result, there has been considerable criticism of the Federal Circuit's biotechnology obviousness cases.[8]
Given modern research tools, the outcome of a search for a particular nucleotide or protein seems relatively certain and hence obvious. If patents are to
drive innovation in biotechnology, rather than merely invention, however,
courts must take account of the cost and uncertainty of postinvention testing and development.[9] The ready availability of tools for finding a new biotechnology product does not change the high cost and uncertainty entailed
in developing a marketable product using that macromolecule. Hence, under Merges's framework, a lowered standard of obviousness might seem
to make sense from a policy standpoint not so much to encourage invention as to encourage the development of marketable products from those
inventions—what we have termed innovation.[10]

Yet, in its recent jurisprudence, what the Federal Circuit gives bio-technology with one hand it takes away with the other. In the more recent DNA cases, unlike the early monoclonal antibody cases, the court has not treated the PHOSITAs for enablement and obviousness purposes differently. Instead, although DNA-related patents are relatively easy to obtain under the obviousness standard, the accompanying enablement and written description standards dramatically narrow the scope of the resulting patents. By requiring disclosure of the particular structure or sequence in order to claim biological macromolecules, the Federal Circuit effectively limits the scope of a patent on those molecules to the structure or sequence disclosed.[11] This standard dictates that the inventor have the molecule "in hand" (so to speak) before being able to claim it. In other words, the inventor can have patent protection for any given molecule only after a substantial investment has already been made in isolating and characterizing the molecule. The result is that everyone who invests in discovering a new molecule will receive a patent, but one that is trivial to avoid infringing, at least literally. Under this standard, no one is likely to receive a patent broad enough to support the further costs of development.[12] Indeed, some promising lines of inquiry, such as the development of drugs custom-tailored to individual DNA, may be foreclosed entirely if a biotechnology patent is not broad enough to cover the small structural variations that inhere in custom drugs.

Unfortunately, this proliferation of narrow biotechnology patents may be nearly impossible to avoid if the courts adhere to the reciprocal structure of obviousness and enablement in current PHOSITA patent doctrine.[13] In order for the invention to avoid obviousness, it must be deemed beyond the skill of the PHOSITA to construct given the level of disclosure in the prior art. Yet this means that in disclosing the invention, the inventor must tell those of ordinary skill a good deal more about how to make and use it, effectively raising the standard for enablement and written description. The Federal Circuit's insistence that the results of biotechnology research are unforeseeable or unpredictable avoids the problem of obviousness but results in an extremely stringent standard for disclosure and description. The result is not optimal from the perspective of economic policy. As the early monoclonal antibody cases suggest, the doctrinal solution to this particular problem is to treat the PHOSITA standards in obviousness and disclosure as separate policy-based questions, rather than as a common standard.[14] Decoupling the PHOSITAs in this way allows courts to make decisions about the proper strength of the obviousness and enablement requirement in biotechnology.

Even given such doctrinal tools, however, courts must confront the policy question of the proper scope of patents in the biotechnology industry. The proper focus of biotechnology patent policy is a matter of some dispute. Merges's classic economic framework suggests that the standard of nonobviousness should be low to compensate for the high cost of innovation in the industry.[15] Both the need for effective protection and the anticommons literature suggest that the disclosure requirement should be less strict than it currently is, lest property rights be too disintegrated to permit effective licensing.[16] Yet if both the nonobviousness and disclosure requirements are lessened, the result will be more patents with broader scope. This increase, in turn, will produce a large number of blocking patents, potentially giving rise to a patent thicket.[17] Blocking patents are not necessarily bad, particularly when they are coupled with mechanisms for rights clearance and legal doctrines such as the reverse doctrine of equivalents that will relieve bargaining pressures in extreme cases.[18] They will certainly give biotechnology companies incentives to innovate, at least initially. But blocking patents do raise the specter of overlapping first-generation patents choking out downstream innovation, particularly where those first-generation patents are granted on upstream research tools, or where the maker of a particular product must aggregate many different complements, each of which is patented.[19] This is a particular concern for agricultural biotechnology products that combine multiple inventions.

A New Prescription for Biotechnology

We suggest instead that courts should modify Merges's classic theory. Lowering the obviousness threshold is only one way to encourage investment in uncertain technologies. An alternative is to broaden the scope of the patents that do issue by reducing the disclosure requirement or by strengthening the doctrine of equivalents for a particular industry. Doing either will encourage innovation in uncertain industries not by increasing the chance of getting a patent, but by increasing the value of the patent once it is granted. In fact, we believe that while Merges is correct to suggest that the standard of patentability should be responsive to the cost and uncertainty of innovation, obviousness is the wrong lever to use in biotechnology.[20] Lowering the obviousness threshold makes it more likely that marginal inventions will be patented, but does nothing to further encourage inventions that would have met the (already rather modest) obviousness standard anyway. If getting from invention to market is the costly and uncertain part of the endeavor, it is these more significant inventions that we need to worry about rewarding.[21]

There is some indication that the Supreme Court is already moving the obviousness standard in the direction that we have recommended. The Supreme Court opinion in *KSR* held that a suggestion to combine aspects of the prior art need not be explicit in the prior art in order for the combination to be obvious. *KSR* holds that some inventions may be obvious based upon the common knowledge in the art, even unwritten common knowledge. Effectively, *KSR* suggests that the PHOSITA is in general cannier and more perceptive, having a higher level of skill in the art, than the Federal Circuit has tended to define her. The *KSR* opinion also suggests that, contrary to Federal Circuit jurisprudence, trying out obvious combinations from the prior art is likely to produce an unpatentably obvious result. The Federal Circuit had long claimed that a combination of prior art that was "obvious to try" was not legally obvious, that more motivation or expectation of success was needed to meet the patent law obviousness standard. This trend was especially apparent in cases involving DNA sequences, where it was often routine to extract targeted DNA from biological samples. But, as we have seen, the Federal Circuit held that applying routine laboratory techniques was not obvious in biotechnology; rather, knowing the actual structure of the molecule seemed to be required for obviousness.

It would seem, then, that if the *KSR* opinion is read as reversing the Federal Circuit's stance toward "obvious to try" as a measure of obviousness, then it might be read more broadly as reversing the Federal Circuit's stance toward structure as the measure of obviousness in biotechnology. Patent Office decisions subsequent to *KSR* suggest that, given proven laboratory techniques and understanding of molecular genetics, "routine extraction of homologous DNA sequences might be the kind of invention" that would be obvious to try based on common knowledge in biotechnology, and so unpatentable.[22] There is some indication that the Federal Circuit's biotechnology and pharmaceutical opinions following *KSR* may have begun to raise the obviousness threshold.[23] However, there is also some reason to believe that the Federal Circuit may continue to hew to its mantra of biotechnology as an "unpredictable art" in which nearly everything is nonobvious.[24] How this tension plays out remains to be seen.

Our alternative approach—a fairly high obviousness threshold coupled with a fairly low disclosure requirement—will produce a few very powerful patents in uncertain industries. It will therefore solve the anticommons problem often identified with DNA while at the same time boosting incentives to innovate by giving stronger protection to significant inventions.[25] Although this approach will reduce the protection given to minor inventions—those that barely cleared the low obviousness threshold and will not clear a higher one—we think that is a cost worth paying. Inventors don't invent in hopes of barely winning a narrow patent on a modest improvement. If the patent system drives invention, it is because of the prospect of hitting it big with a strong patent on a major new invention.[26] Thus, we think that a few strong patents better fits the economic characteristics of the biotechnology industry than a morass of weak patents.

Some commentators, notably David Adelman, have questioned the concern over anticommons in biotechnology and might (or might not) accordingly question our conclusion here. The argument against an anticommons is based largely upon an ethnographic study of biotechnology managers that revealed little concern over an anticommons effect. But other empirical studies suggest the presence of an anticommons effect, and even follow-on studies by the ethnographic researchers suggest that the lack of an anticommons is due to a tacit agreement in the industry for researchers to ignore one another's overlapping patents.[27] A shift in the economy or normative practice could bring this fragile détente to an end at any time, resulting in the predicted anticommons effect. Semiconductor firms, which survived with similar deals for many years, have recently seen their patent bargain unravel as so-called patent trolls began to assert patents against them. Biotechnology has yet to see many patent trolls, but there is no reason to think they won't develop in the future.

Adelman's explanation for the lack of an anticommons is that the number of potential drug targets is so large that human pharmaceutical research is effectively "unbounded" and "uncongested." We think he confuses the average case with individual ones. Adelman's argument is essentially equivalent to claiming that New York and San Francisco will not become congested or experience soaring property values because of all the open space available in Montana and the Dakotas. But while it is true that the less congested spaces may at the margins absorb some uses from more congested areas, powerful incentives persist for remaining in Manhattan or near the Bay. So too we expect that certain targets will be the subject of multiple patents and concentrated research. Even if the landscape of drug targets is unbounded, rationality is not, and researchers will tend to focus on those targets that appear most promising: those with which they are most familiar, those for which models are readily available, and those with a wealth of established research on which the next researcher can build.

Thus we suggest that the risk of anticommons in biotechnology patents remains a concern, and can be best avoided by proper modulation of obviousness and disclosure. Under our approach, because there will be relatively few patents, the problem of patent thickets should not arise. This calibration of patent frequency and scope seems to be the proper response to the anti-commons concern found in much of the biotechnology literature. We worry that the alternate solution—favoring greater governmental control of inventions supported by public funds over unfettered intellectual property rights[28]—might unacceptably reduce the incentive for biotechnology companies to move beyond invention to innovation and product development.

Recalibrating patent scope through disclosure would seem to require a much more fundamental rethinking of the Federal Circuit's section 112 jurisprudence. The court currently requires *more* disclosure from patentees in uncertain arts, while our proposal would require *less*. The key to understanding this seeming puzzle is the difference between uncertainty about invention ex ante and the uncertainty about innovation (getting the product to market) ex post. The court repeatedly intones the maxim that biotechnology is an "uncertain art."[29] We think, however, that it is not so much invention as product development, production, and regulatory approval that are uncertain in the biotechnology industry. From a policy perspective, the result is the same: Biotechnological inventions need more incentive than other types of inventions if they are actually to make it to market. From a disclosure perspective, however, the difference is quite significant: There is no reason to require heightened disclosure of an invention—and correspondingly narrow its scope—if invention itself is not uncertain or particularly difficult to understand or replicate. And doing so will have significant benefits to biotechnology patent owners, who will get effective protection rather than a patent that is trivial to evade.

Future Directions

We expect that as the biotechnology industry continues to evolve, new policy levers may become appropriate to allow the proper scope of innovation and reward. We cannot predict the future. But based on current trends, we offer an example of how new policy levers may rise to prominence in tailoring patent law to this industry.

One of the most profound developments in biotechnology has been the so-called -omics revolution, referring to large-scale projects in genomics, proteomics, metabolomics, and so on. This remarkable development in biological research entails the combination of laboratory research with computational tools that allow the collection, search, and correlation of large collections of biological data. Such "bioinformatics" projects began with genomics, the mapping and sequencing of the genetic material of various organisms. The same techniques have quickly moved into proteomics, the collection of information on the sequence, structure, and function of proteins. Research on other types of biological materials is following the same path.

These vast warehouses of biological information are not simply being stored; they are being put to innovative use. Increased understanding of protein structure is allowing the design of biological molecules with specifically desired properties. For example, biologically active proteins are composed of structural "domains," only some of which catalyze chemical reactions. Understanding the nature of protein domains allows scientists to modify proteins, removing or downscaling inactive domains to produce smaller proteins with the same biological activity as their natural counterparts. Such smaller proteins may be easier to administer as pharmaceuticals or have enhanced industrial applications. Knowing the conformations of protein active sites also makes it possible to modify the catalytic properties of those sites, in order, for example, to enhance their rates of reactivity.

In a similar vein, increased understanding of nucleotide functions is facilitating a move toward so-called synthetic biology.[30] Recombinant DNA techniques are based upon the disassembly and reassembly of existing genetic components, but synthetic biology seeks to build genetic elements from scratch. This allows the de novo construction of new genetic structures, and possibly even new organisms, rather than the rearrangement of existing materials.

The new molecules being developed from proteomic and other biological information are being introduced into an innovation environment that is already rife with biotechnology patents. Many of these new molecules are modifications on, improvements on, or substitutes for known and possibly patented molecules. Consequently, although the new molecules may not be those claimed in existing patents, they will be close cousins. Early cases in the protein design area suggest that the infringement of existing molecular patents by these new substitutes will become an issue under the doctrine of equivalents.[31] We have already discussed how the doctrine of equivalents may be employed as a policy lever to allow greater or lesser latitude for new technology in areas where there are established patents. We expect that the doctrine of equivalents will be deployed to meet the innovation needs of proteomics and synthetic biology as these new areas of biotechnology develop. How that lever is applied remains to be seen, though we worry that work in these potentially important fields will be stifled if patentees with rights over existing molecules can exercise too much control over substantial new developments in proteomics or synthetic biology.

Other Policy Levers in Biotechnology

Biotechnology is properly described in part by the anticommons theory (too many narrow patents must be aggregated to produce a viable product) and in part by prospect theory (a long and uncertain postinvention development process justifies strong control over inventions). A rational patent policy for DNA would seek to minimize the anticommons problems and give inventors sufficient control to induce them to walk the uncertain path toward commercial development. A variety of policy levers might be employed to this end. The utility and abstract ideas doctrines can restrict the anticommons problem in a few cases by preventing unnecessary upstream patents (for example on ESTs) that threaten to hold up downstream innovation. The written description and enablement doctrines need to be recalibrated to permit broader claiming of inventions. The doctrine of equivalents can play a similar role, perhaps by rejuvenating the doctrine of pioneer patents or by applying the notion of known interchangeability with an eye toward function instead of structure. Experimental use may also play a role by ensuring that the long development time necessary in the biotechnology industry does not interfere with an inventor's ability to patent the ultimate product. As biotechnology changes and develops, the availability of such additional policy levers will be important to tailor patent law to its changing innovation profile.

12

Levers at Work—the IT Industry

As we have seen, the most dramatic differences between industries are between the biomedical industry, which we discussed in the last chapter, and the information technology industries. It is the IT industries that are the poster child for the claims of a patent crisis that we reported in chapter 3, while for most of the companies in the biomedical industry the patent system is working just fine. It should not be surprising, therefore, that the appropriate policy levers for the IT industry differ rather dramatically from those that were appropriate in the biotechnology or pharmaceutical industries. In this chapter, we focus on the software industry, though we also offer some more preliminary thoughts on similar problems in the semiconductor industry.

Software

CHARACTERISTICS OF THE INDUSTRY

While most biotechnological and chemical inventions require broad patent protection because of their high cost and uncertain development process, the opposite is true in the case of software development. Software inventions tend to have a quick, cheap, and fairly straightforward postinvention development cycle. Most of the work in software development occurs in the initial coding, not in development or production. The lead time to market in the software industry tends to be short, and so do product generations. The capital investment requirement for software development is relatively low—mostly consisting of hiring personnel, not building laboratories or manufacturing infrastructure. Debugging and test marketing is tedious and potentially time consuming, but it does not rival the cost of stringent safety testing and agency oversight that is necessary in the biotechnology and pharmaceutical industries.

The other significant attribute of software is the cumulative nature of invention. A common adage among those in the know is that to buy version 1.0 of any software product is to take a big risk. Software companies are continuously refining and improving their products with new releases, and adding new features as computer processing speed and data storage improve. And new companies are developing new and improved products in the same vein; it is quite common for new companies to displace older ones with improved software products.

As we have seen, the IT industry, and the software industry in particular, have arguably suffered the most from the crisis in the patent system. The cycles of improvement across quick product generations, coupled with the difficulty courts have had in defining the scope of software patents and the lax standards for issuing those patents in the last century, have led to a flood of software patent lawsuits, a large number of them filed by companies that either made no products or that once made products but that are no longer competitive in the marketplace. IT firms claim that their ability to grow and innovate is stifled by the pervasive threat of such suits.

As a result, a number of people (both inside the industry and in academia) have argued that we should abolish software patents. We find that argument unpersuasive. First, as John Allison has shown, it is virtually impossible to determine what a software patent is.[1] Courts have repeatedly sought to draw lines between software inventions that involved physical transformation and those that represented merely mental steps or mathematical algorithms. At each turn, those lines quickly eroded or had to be abandoned as unworkable. Worse, they were readily gamed, leading to what Julie Cohen and Mark Lemley have called "the doctrine of the magic words," in which software could be easily patented by those "in the know" merely by utilizing certain claim language to describe an invention indistinguishable in substance from a second claim that would be rejected.[2] To see this, ask yourself whether a patent covering a hybrid automobile engine is a "software" patent, considering that the engine could not run without software and that the software controlling the switch from gasoline to battery power and back is arguably the key to the success of the engine.

If the problem were merely that limiting patentable subject matter required the drawing of arbitrary lines, that fact alone might not be enough to conclude that the effort should be abandoned. But the problem is worse than that. Arbitrary limits on the patentability of particular types of inventions can interfere with the purposes of the patent system. New and nonobvious ideas do not arise only in fields of endeavor classically denominated "technological." Nor do they always involve the physical transformation of material. And even when they do, the new and nonobvious invention often resides not in the transformation but in the mental insight that a particular transformation would have an unexpected value. Limiting patent protection to classical physical transformations and excluding inventions based on mental steps or discoveries of natural phenomena might have problematic consequences for a variety of industries, including not only computer software but industries such as pharmaceuticals and biotechnology for whom patent protection is critical. Instead, patent protection should be available for new and nonobvious advances in any field, provided they involve the practical application of a new idea or discovery.

We do not intend to suggest that business method and software patents present no problems for society. Patents are sometimes wrongly issued in these fields, and those patents can have pernicious consequences. But the solution to the problem of bad patents in the software and business method fields is not the creation of absolute rules against patentability, but the application of existing doctrines designed to weed out bad patents, and if necessary the reform of other doctrines that encourage litigation abuse. Policy levers, in other words, can substitute for excluding software entirely from patentable subject matter. In the sections that follow, we discuss some policy levers that can and should apply to software.

OBVIOUSNESS AND THE LEVEL OF SKILL IN THE ART

Because innovation is less uncertain in software than in such industries as biotechnology, Merges's economic framework suggests that the nonobviousness bar should be rather high.[3] A few broad software patents are indeed what the current Federal Circuit jurisprudence will likely produce. Although the claim that there are few software patents would surprise many people, our claim is actually that there are few *valid* software patents under the Federal Circuit's approach. By relaxing the enablement requirement and permitting software inventions to be defined in broad terms, supported by very little in the way of detailed disclosure, the Federal Circuit has encouraged software patents to be drafted broadly and to be applied to allegedly infringing devices that are far removed from the original patented invention.[4] By implication, the Federal Circuit's standard also seems to suggest that many narrower software patents on low-level incremental improvements will be invalid for obviousness in view of earlier, more general disclosures.

They may also be invalidated under the on-sale bar, because the Supreme Court's view that a software invention is "ready for patenting"[5] when it is the subject of a commercial order and when the inventor has described its broad functions, even if it is not clear how the code will be written or that it will work for its intended purpose,[6] means that any patentee who waits until the code is written to file a patent application risks being time-barred for not filing earlier.

Unfortunately, the Federal Circuit's current standard seems to be precisely backwards. Software is an industry characterized, at least to a limited extent, by competition theory[7] and to a greater extent by cumulative innovation. Cumulative innovation theory suggests that patent protection for incremental software inventions should be relatively easy to acquire in order to reward incremental improvements, implying a somewhat lower obviousness threshold. It also suggests that the resulting patents should be narrow and, in particular, that they should not generally extend across several product generations for fear of stifling subsequent incremental improvements. This in turn means that software patents should be limited in scope.[8]

Implementing a rational software policy obviously requires some significant changes to existing case law. A number of policy levers might be brought to bear on this problem.

Obviousness

First, obviousness doctrine needs to be reformed, preferably by way of a more informed application of the level of skill in the art[9] or, alternatively, by application of new secondary considerations of nonobviousness.[10] The *KSR* decision offers a way out of the current Federal Circuit case law. By focusing on what people in the software industry actually do, a court that faithfully applies *KSR* will be able to find the inventiveness in improved or more stable computer programs.

Doctrines Directed at Patent Scope

A willingness to protect the invention inherent in cumulative innovation must be coupled with tight limits on the scope of the resulting inventions, lest we end up making the current morass of overlapping patent claims worse. Courts that recognize that refinement can be inventive must be particularly careful to limit the scope of the resulting patent to what was actually invented. A failure to do this in the PTO, coupled with rules of claim construction that permitted and even encouraged overclaiming of patent scope, has led to a large number of patentees claiming to own something much broader than what they actually contributed to the world. To solve this problem, the scope of a patent claim needs to be tied much more explicitly to the scope of the patentee's actual invention. Rejuvenating the pioneer patents doctrine is a first step toward addressing this problem, but ultimately more radical surgery might be in order, including the possibility of abandoning the effort to define the boundaries of a patent right through claims altogether. A stronger disclosure requirement—something that may be emerging in recent cases—will also help reduce patent scope.[11] So will strict limits on the doctrine of equivalents, something that has definitely happened in the last ten years.[12]

Patent Holdup and Patent Remedies

Because software is characterized by cumulative innovation, software companies are vulnerable to the sorts of patent holdup problems Mark Lemley and Carl Shapiro have documented.[13] Patentees in the software industry can use the threat of injunctive relief and the very real prospect of "reasonable" royalties that far exceed the value of the patentee's contribution to demand settlement payments no matter how weak their patent or their argument that it reaches as broadly as they claim. Companies can't risk punitive injunctive relief or damages awards, and so they pay patent owners to go away rather than benefiting society by invalidating bad patents or narrowing overbroad claims. Policy levers directed at making sure that patent owners can capture no more than the value actually attributable to their invention, such as discretion to deny injunctive relief and apportionment of reasonable royalties in complex industries, are particularly well suited to the software industry. Fortunately, the *eBay* case has proven to be a big help in tackling one of these problems—injunctions. But if courts continue to award supracompensatory damages, particularly in cases where they have denied injunctive relief, the benefits of the flexible *eBay* rule will be lost. The injunctive relief and reasonable royalty levers are ones that must work in combination to properly calibrate patent remedies.

Reverse Engineering

Finally, we think that software patents are the ideal candidate for a new policy lever: reverse engineering. Many commentators have explained the importance of permitting competitors to reverse engineer a product in order to see how it works and to discover ways to design around it.[14] In the case of copyright, courts have adapted the doctrine of fair use, sometimes together with copyright misuse, to allow competitors to engage in reverse engineering of computer software. Patent law includes no express provision allowing reverse engineering, nor is there any judicially developed exception akin to copyright's fair use doctrine that might permit it. Indeed, patent law generally lacks provisions akin to fair use or other exceptions that might readily be pressed into the service of reverse engineering, although commentators have suggested that patent law may need such exceptions for precisely this reason.[15]

This does not mean that reverse engineering a patented product is necessarily illegal under patent law. Some inventions, such as the paper clip, are readily apparent once embodied in a product.[16] Improvers do not need to reverse engineer the paper clip and determine how it works in order to improve it—they just need to look at it. Additionally, in many cases, the patentee has done all the work necessary for a competitor to reverse engineer a patented invention by disclosing how to make and use the claimed invention in the patent specification. In theory, an express provision authorizing reverse engineering would be superfluous if the enabling disclosures required to secure a patent were sufficiently strong—someone who wanted to learn how a patented device worked would only need to read the patent specification (35 U.S.C. § 112 [2000]).

Patentable inventions in software, however, generally do not have these characteristics.[17] Software devices typically cannot be readily understood by casual inspection, and particularly not without access to human-readable source code or other documentation. Examination of the patent itself is unlikely to yield information equivalent to a reverse engineered inspection because the Federal Circuit does not require would-be patentees of software inventions to disclose the implementing source code or, for that matter, very much at all about their inventions. Accordingly, software patents present unique obstacles to consummation of the patent law's traditional rights-for-disclosure bargain with the public.

The specific reverse engineering techniques commonly used for software, in turn, raise infringement problems that are unique to software. The definition of infringement in the patent statute is extremely broad, encompassing anyone who "makes, uses, offers to sell, . . . sells . . . , or imports" a patented product (35 U.S.C. § 271(a) [2000]). Reverse engineering a patented computer program by decompiling it likely fits within this broad category of prohibited conduct, at least where the program itself is claimed as an apparatus. Reverse engineering clearly constitutes a "use" of the patented software, though owners of a particular copy of the program surely have the right to use it.[18] More significantly, decompilation may also constitute "making" the patented program by generating a temporary yet functional copy of it in RAM memory[19] and, in certain instances, a longer-term (though still "intermediate") copy in more permanent memory.[20] Those copies probably constitute patent infringement unless protected by some defense.[21] The result of all of this is that the nominally neutral patent law rule—no defense for reverse engineering—affects software more than other industries.

The need for a reverse engineering exception in patent law militates in favor of adapting the existing doctrines of exhaustion or experimental use to that end.[22] The Supreme Court took a step toward reinvigorating the exhaustion doctrine in *LG v. Quanta,* but the significance of that step remains to be seen.[23] Patent misuse might also be adapted, as it has been in the copyright arena, to prevent patent holders from deterring or prohibiting reverse engineering related to their inventions. The exception might even be created by reinterpreting the infringement provisions of section 271(a). The resulting patent doctrine would constitute a macro policy lever. As Cohen and Lemley observe, in most industries there is either no need to reverse engineer an invention or reverse engineering can be done without infringing the patent.[24] Only in software is there a need for a particular doctrine to protect the right to reverse engineer—and therefore the ability of improvers to innovate. Thus, a judicially created reverse engineering defense would make sense across the board in software cases but not in other patent cases.[25]

Semiconductors

The semiconductor industry also displays unique characteristics that require incentive tailoring. Design and fabrication of microprocessors has become increasingly complex and expensive as a result of increasing miniaturization. Microprocessor innovation requires the coordinated and extended effort of large teams of skilled engineers, as well as the development and construction of production processes and facilities, at a cost of billions of dollars. This high R&D cost is matched, however, by a relatively high imitation cost. The days in which an imitator could copy a chip design by copying the "mask works" used in etching the chip and cheaply make identical chips overseas are long gone.[26] Imitators must build their own fabrication facilities, and much of the innovation in the industry lies in processes that are hard to identify and duplicate.

These characteristics suggest that patents could play an important role in encouraging semiconductor device innovation. Costs of development are extremely high, and patent incentives might serve to attract needed capital.[27] At the same time, the disclosure function of patents might be important in order to prevent expensive duplication of effort in wasteful patent "races."[28] These specific criteria militate in favor of relaxed standards for obtaining patents; as in the case of biotechnology, high development costs might be offset by heightened rewards.

Broadening the scope of patents might satisfy the need for increased patentability in the semiconductor industry, as it does in the pharmaceutical industry, were it not that the proliferation of patents in this setting might quickly develop into an innovation-obstructing patent thicket. Rather than being covered by a single patent, semiconductor chips are composite devices, comprised of multiple inventions, each of which may be covered by a separate patent. Different companies may hold patents to circuit designs, materials, and manufacturing processes that go into fabricating a single chip. Competing companies in the industry, working along parallel research lines to produce faster and smaller chips, will often obtain patents on similar inventions with overlapping claims. Thus, a new microprocessor may need to incorporate technology covered by hundreds or even thousands of different patents under the control of dozens of different companies.[29]

Thus, despite high development costs, the semiconductor industry does not need a "prospect" for broad rights. Placing broad rights in the hands of a developer might actually hinder creation of a device incorporating many inventions, particularly given the strong evidence that the patent system permits patent owners to capture more than the intrinsic value of their invention in many cases. Optimally, then, semiconductor patents should be calibrated either to avoid, to whatever extent possible, the creation of a patent thicket or to facilitate "clearing" of the thicket through quick and easy cross-licensing of overlapping rights. Unlike biotechnology, where broad patents are needed, we believe that the classic Merges analysis favoring a lowered obviousness bar[30] would work well in this setting. Indeed, there is some evidence that it already does so—semiconductor patent applications are more likely to issue as patents than any other type of invention.[31]

Granting many semiconductor patents will work, however, only if coupled with measures designed to reduce the scope of patents that issue. Patents in the semiconductor industry ought to be narrow, so that overlapping coverage is minimized and potential hindrances can be invented around or avoided. The written description and level-of-skill-in-the-art policy levers might be tailored to this end, just as we suggested they could be with software. As with software, something will have to be done about the problem of claim construction, though the indeterminacy of words defining inventions is less of a problem in semiconductors than it was in software. In addition, application of the doctrine of equivalents to semiconductors must be tightly disciplined. Such discipline might come from stringent readings of the "function, way, result" and "known interchangeability" tests under the doctrine of equivalents or from the logical converse of the pioneer patents rule—that minor improvements deserve only narrow protection.

While narrowing the scope of patents will help semiconductor companies avoid some of the frivolous claims that have plagued the software industry, the fact that semiconductors are complex, multicomponent inventions means that any chip on the market likely infringes a large number of patents even if they are construed narrowly. So merely limiting the scope of semiconductor patents won't avoid the patent thicket altogether.

Alternatively, patent thickets might be cleared by more drastic means. For example, we have identified injunctive power as a policy lever that courts have occasionally used to avoid holdup in compelling cases. Refusing to grant injunctions for the infringement of semiconductor patents at all could make the patented material more accessible, even in the face of extensive patent overlap, holdout behavior, and bargaining breakdown. This is not a course that we necessarily recommend, as we believe this type of policy lever should be used sparingly. The *eBay* approach—a case-by-case analysis of the need for an injunction and the harm it might cause—seems preferable to us. Nonetheless, we mention the possibility as an illustration of alternative levers that might accomplish the needed tailoring should "clearing" of the thicket by private means prove unworkable. And application of the *eBay* policy lever is likely to find more hardship and less need for an injunction in semiconductor cases than in any other industry. At a minimum, and at the same time, courts should encourage private ordering mechanisms such as standard-setting organizations and patent pools that seek to clear interfering rights.[32]

Future Directions

The applications of the policy levers we have described in the last two chapters are of necessity highly stylized. Inventions are not monolithic even within specific industries; whether a particular DNA patent satisfies the obviousness requirement, or a particular semiconductor invention is deserving of injunctive relief, is something that will depend to a large extent on the facts of any given case. Further, we have no pretensions to perfect knowledge of the industries we have described; others can and will disagree with the particular descriptions of conditions in those industries or with our prescriptions for how patents can best work under those conditions.

Finally, we are well aware that industry characteristics—and even industry categories—are not static. The biggest challenge for the courts in the next ten years might turn out to be determining optimal patent policy for nanotechnology rather than for software patents. We have some thoughts along those lines, too—nanotechnology seems like an interesting combination of prospect theory, with long lead times and significant development cost in many cases, and patent thickets, as many different patent owners jump in with overlapping rights[33]—but they are very preliminary and subject to revision. And in the end, that's our point. Optimal patent policy depends on assessments of industry characteristics that will always be preliminary and subject to revision. Only courts have the institutional competence and doctrinal flexibility to adapt to those revised assessments and apply them to the industries that drive innovation not just today but in the future. We can't tell courts what they should do with technologies that haven't yet been developed. All we can do is start the discussion by pointing to the tools courts have at hand and the importance of using those tools.

Conclusion

New Directions

Both innovation and patent law unquestionably work differently in different industries. The law can either take account of those differences or seek to ignore them. Ignoring them would require major changes in existing law, and would leave the law ill-equipped to deal with the fundamentally different ways in which innovation works in different industries. Indeed, given the crisis of confidence the system currently faces, it is not much of an exaggeration to say that the patent system must bend or break: a patent system that is not flexible enough to account for these industry differences is unlikely to survive.

If the law is to take account of industry differences, three different institutions might do so. First, we could leave the task to Congress. But doing so may not take sufficient account of the dynamic nature of both innovation and industry structure. Congress is likely to act only infrequently, and the rules they create will be set in stone for some time, whether or not they reflect the needs of the existing industry. Reliance on industry-specific patent legislation also runs into rather serious public choice problems. Our experience with those few statutory intellectual property provisions that are expressly industry-specific, and with recent efforts at patent reform, has not been encouraging. Congress is better suited to creating general rules, and we think it can and should aim at enacting rules that give courts the flexibility to apply policy levers.

An alternative to Congress is to give the task of tailoring to the PTO. This has some surface appeal, since the PTO employs scientists and engineers who might be thought to know the characteristics of particular industries better than either Congress or generalist judges. In practice, however, there are two significant problems with relying on the PTO to tailor patent law to different industries. First, the PTO as currently constituted is simply not equipped for the task. Examiners are overworked, and spend only a tiny amount of time evaluating each application—far less time than judges and their clerks spend on a patent case. Further, the PTO has virtually no policy staff and—at least until recently—little experience or apparent inclination to take a leadership role in setting patent policy. Although it is possible to imagine an agency with the confidence and expertise to take on the role, the PTO is not yet that agency. Further, a PTO with real policy-making power would face many of the same public choice problems Congress does. Indeed, when PTO Director Jon Dudas began to take seriously the agency's role in setting patent policy around 2005, he became the target of a firestorm of criticism from vested interests who just want the PTO to issue patents. It is not clear that even a reconstituted PTO could withstand those political pressures over the long term.

Second, and more systematic, is the problem that the PTO sees only validity and not infringement or remedial issues. Because the PTO looks only at applications, it will miss the subsequent development of the industry and in particular has no occasion to consider the effects of scope determinations. As a result, periodic suggestions that the PTO should engage in claim construction or weigh in on the scope of infringement are likely to fall flat, and for good reason: the PTO doesn't see those issues in the context that is required to make the right decision.

That leaves the courts. Courts have their problems. They are confined to hearing the cases before them, and in an adversarial system they can do very little independent fact investigation. But courts also have significant advantages. First, judicial decision making actually benefits from the adversarial process; we can expect the parties to come forward with the evidence that will allow courts to make the right decisions. Second, the process of common-law development permits both incremental improvement over time and responsiveness to changing conditions. Finally, the fact that we have a unified national patent court is a significant advantage because it gives courts a reservoir of domain-specific knowledge that they don't have in other legal fields. The Federal Circuit has come under fire in the past for inconsistent decisions, but in the last several years it has clearly begun to get its house in order, taking a number of significant issues en banc in order to provide consistent precedent. As the court hits its stride in its third decade, it is well positioned to consider the industry and policy implications of the many rules it has discretion to set.

If we are right that courts should continue and indeed expand their use of policy levers, where do we go from here? We think there are at least

NEW DIRECTIONS

three aspects of this approach that could profit from further exploration. First, scholars and courts will need to think carefully about what legal rules should be policy levers. We have identified twelve existing policy levers, and several more common law doctrines that could serve as policy levers. But it may be that not all of these rules should in fact serve this purpose. Similarly, it may be that there are other doctrines that can profitably be tailored to the needs of particular industries. Some exciting recent work has already been done in filling out the framework we have established. Chris Cotropia has identified a new policy lever in the doctrine of equivalents, for example.[1] Richard Gruner has suggested that obviousness could serve as a policy lever in industries such as software and business methods, in which a large majority of patents seem to consist of taking existing ideas and applying them in a new context.[2] And others have suggested that the foreseeability doctrine should be applied in different ways in the biotechnology industry.[3] Deciding which policy levers should and should not be used will require further work by a lot of people.

Second, courts and scholars will have to pay attention to the characteristics of the particular industries for which courts are setting rules. We don't claim any monopoly on knowledge about the proper patent law rules for any given industry, and others can and have disagreed with the suggestions we have made in this book. This disagreement is healthy; devoting serious scholarly attention to the needs of particular industries will help better tailor the law to those industries. Further, the scientific characteristics of industries and particular technologies within each industry change over time, and the law needs to adapt to those changes. The nature of the software industry as we have described it today looks very different than it did in the 1970s, and the legal rules that made sense then seem rather archaic today. Some have argued that biotechnology is undergoing a similar evolution, reducing the anticommons risks at the research stage[4] but heightening concerns at the downstream products stage. And surely it is true, as we suggested in chapter 11, that the biotechnology industry itself is not monolithic; the rules appropriate for DNA patents may not be the same ones that fit monoclonal antibody patents. Courts are better suited than Congress to take account of these changes, but to do so they will have to remain open to considering evidence of those changes. Put another way, legal rules will have to evolve in the common law tradition.

Finally, the industries themselves will come and go over time. If we had written this book 120 years ago, we would likely have focused significant attention on the railroad industry, which faced significant patent issues that previous industries had not had to deal with.[5] Ninety years ago we would

have discussed the problematic issues that arose in the nascent airline industry. Both industries still exist today, but their characteristics have changed.
As they have become more mature, the role of patents in both industries has
declined, to the point where it no longer makes sense to tailor patent rules
for those industries. By contrast, software and biotechnology—two of the
most important industries in the modern economy, and ones that occupy a
significant part of this book—were not even on the radar screen of the patent system forty years ago. New industries—nanotechnology, perhaps, or
synthetic biology—will doubtless challenge the courts in years to come.

   In short, our aim here is not to have the final word on the tailoring of
patent law. Rather, we offer the first word in what we hope will become a
long conversation. Getting patent law right is not easy, and getting it exactly
right may not even be possible. But getting it right is enormously important,
and we will never get it right if we refuse to even try.

Notes

Chapter Two

1. *Diamond v. Chakrabarty*, 447 U.S. 303, 309 (1980) (quoting S. Rep. No. 1979, 82nd Cong., 2nd Sess. 5 (1952); H.R. Rep. No. 1923, 82nd Cong., 2nd Sess. 6 (1952).

2. *See* Mark A. Lemley & Bhaven Sampat, *Is the Patent Office a Rubber Stamp?* 58 Emory L.J., forthcoming 2008 (studying patent applications and finding these results).

3. *Markman v. Westview Instruments, Inc.*, 517 U.S. 370 (1996).

4. *Graver Tank & Mfg Co. v. Linde Air Products Co.*, 339 U.S. 605 (1950).

5. *Dickinson v. Zurko*, 527 U.S. 150 (1999).

6. *Holmes Group, Inc. v. Vornado Air Circulation Systems, Inc.*, 535 U.S. 826 (2002).

7. Patent Cooperation Treaty, 28 U.S.T. 7645, T.I.A.S. No 8733 (opened for signature June 19, 1970; entered into force Jan. 24, 1978).

8. Final Act Embodying the Results of the Uruguay Round of Multilateral Trade Negotiations, Annex 1C: Agreement on Trade Related Aspects of Intellectual Property Rights, 33 I.L.M. 1197 (1994).

Chapter Three

1. These are only "utility" patents; they exclude design patents, plant patents, and reissue patents.

2. http://www1.uspto.gov/go/taf/us_stat.pdf (reporting PTO data).

3. In practice, many patent owners let their patents lapse for failure to pay maintenance fees, so the number of patents that could actually be enforced is somewhat less; a good guess might be 1.5 million, though the math is complicated. *See* Kimberly A. Moore, *Worthless Patents,* 20 Berkeley Tech. L.J. 1521 (2005) (calculating percentages of patents abandoned for failure to pay maintenance fees).

4. The PTO issued approximately thirteen thousand patents a year in the 1870s. Thomas Edison's lightbulb patent, issued in January 1880, was patent number 223,898; Alexander Graham Bell's telephone patent, issued nearly four years earlier in March 1876, was patent number 174,465.

5. Allison & Lemley found an average of 2.77 years in the late 1990s; *see* John R. Alli-

son & Mark A. Lemley, *Who's Patenting What? An Empirical Exploration of Patent Prosecution,* 53 Vand. L. Rev. 2099 (2000), and delay seems to have increased significantly since that time.

6. *See* Mark A. Lemley & Bhaven Sampat, *Is the Patent Office a Rubber Stamp?* 58 Emory L.J. (forthcoming 2008).

7. *See* U.S. Patent & Trademark Office, *Performance and Accountability Report for Fiscal Year, 2002,* at 21 (reporting that the mean time from when the patent application is filed to when the examiner issues her first office action on the application was 16.7 months in 2002), available at http://www.uspto.gov/web/offices/com/annual/2002/1-58.pdf.

8. The patent law was recently amended to provide for third-party participation in the reexamination of patents that the PTO has already issued. 35 U.S.C. §§311–318. However, virtually no one uses this system, because doing so precludes you from challenging the validity of a patent in later litigation. 35 U.S.C. § 315(c). *See* Mark D. Janis, *Inter Partes Patent Reexamination,* 10 Fordham Intell. Prop., Med. & Ent. L.J. 481 (2000).

9. 37 C.F.R. §1.56.

10. *See, e.g.,* Brenda Sandburg, *Speed over Substance?* Intell. Prop. Mag. (Mar. 1999) (eighteen hours on average; examiners may spend more time on complex technologies); John R. Thomas, *Collusion and Collective Action in the Patent System: A Proposal for Patent Bounties,* 2001 U. Ill. L. Rev. 305, 324 (sixteen to seventeen hours); author's conversation with Q. Todd Dickinson, director of the U.S. PTO, April 2000. *Cf. Patent Nonsense: The Knowledge Monopolies,* Economist, April 8, 2000 ("patent Examiners spend only eight hours on a patent, on average").

We should make it clear that this is an average across all industries, and that there may be substantial variation in the hours spent from one industry to another. *See* Dickinson, *supra* (hours spent range from eight per patent in some art units to thirty-two in other art units).

11. For a full discussion of the difficulties with the examiner incentive system, *see* Robert P. Merges et al., *Intellectual Property in the New Technological Age,* at 600–603 (4th ed. 2006) (discussing the PTO's examination budget); Arti K. Rai, *Addressing the Patent Gold Rush: The Role of Deference to PTO Patent Denials,* 2 Wash. U. J.L. & Pol'y 199, 218 (2000) (arguing for a change in the current patent examiners' incentive system to encourage them to grant patents); John R. Thomas, *Collusion and Collective Action in the Patent System: A Proposal for Patent Bounties,* 2001 U. Ill. L. Rev. 305, 324 (discussing the lack of trained patent examiners in high-tech fields).

12. Lemley & Sampat, *supra.*

13. Traditional continuation applications are governed by 35 U.S.C. § 120 (2000). In the last several years, the PTO has added the Request for Continued Examination (RCE), which has some different characteristics than traditional continuations but shares the basic characteristic that the applicant is allowed an unlimited number of "do-overs." *See* Request for Continued Examination Practice and Changes to Provisional Application Practice, 65 Fed. Reg. 50092, 50093 (Aug. 16, 2000) (to be codified at 37 C.F.R. pt. 1).

14. U.S. Patent No. 5,443,036.

15. U.S. Patent No. 6,368,227.

16. U.S. Patent No. 6,025,810.

17. Lemley & Sampat, *supra.*

18. Jean O. Lanjouw & Mark Schankerman, *Characteristics of Patent Litigation: A Window on Competition,* 32 RAND J. Econ. 129 (2001).

19. Deepak Somaya, *My Strategy Says "See You in Court": Determinants of Decisions Not to Settle Patent Litigation in Computers and Research Medicines,* http://bmgt3-notes.umd.edu/faculty/km/papers.nsf/6de61a84f4107c9d852567f2006c7c0e/1584f21fcdc94bbb85256abe0076fe09?OpenDocument (2001); John R. Allison et al., *Valuable Patents,* 92 Geo. L.J. 435 (2004).

20. Bronwyn H. Hall & Dietmar Harhoff, *Post-Grant Reviews in the U.S. Patent System—Design Choices and Expected Results,* 19 Berkeley Tech L.J. 989 (2004).

21. Robert P. Merges, *As Many as Six Impossible Patents before Breakfast: Property Rights for Business Concepts and Patent System Reform,* 14 Berkeley Tech. L.J. 577, 585 (1999).

22. James Bessen and Michael Meurer describe the problem colorfully: "If you can't tell the boundaries, it ain't property." James Bessen & Michael Meurer, *Patent Failure: How Judges, Bureaucrats and Lawyers Put Innovators At Risk* (2008).

23. Dan L. Burk & Mark A. Lemley, *Quantum Patent Mechanics,* 9 Lewis & Clark L. Rev. 29, 29–30 (2005).

24. Kimberly A. Moore, *Markman Eight Years Later: Is Claim Construction More Predictable?* 9 Lewis & Clark L. Rev. 231 (2005).

25. Christopher A. Cotropia & Mark A. Lemley, *Copying in Patent Law,* N.C. L. Rev. (forthcoming 2009).

26. Gordon Tullock, *Trials on Trial: The Pure Theory of Legal Procedure,* 50–51 (1980).

27. Mark A. Lemley & Carl Shapiro, *Patent Holdup and Royalty Stacking,* 85 Tex. L. Rev. 1991 (2007).

28. *Id.*

29. Mark A. Lemley, *Distinguishing Lost Profits from Reasonable Royalties* (working paper 2008). Available at http://www.ssrn.com.

30. Lemley & Shapiro, *supra.*

31. It is worth noting that the $1.52 billion verdict against Microsoft in the Alcatel case was vacated because it included worldwide damages. On retrial the jury awarded $348 million, quite a bit less but still not a paltry sum for one of several patents covering one technology that was used to implement one feature of Microsoft Windows.

32. *Amado v. Microsoft,* 517 F.3d 1353 (Fed. Cir. 2008). The court did not decide on the right license fee, but rejected a conclusion that it was simply the same as the damages the court had awarded for prejudgment infringement, and said that the logical range of possible fees was between that damages number and the plaintiff's desired royalty, fifty times greater.

33. Bessen & Meurer, *supra,* at 10–16.

34. Michele Boldrin and David K. Levine, *Against Intellectual Monopoly* (2008).

35. Although empirical evidence on this question is hard to come by, the 2003 IPO survey of IP managers found that only 22 percent said that competitor patents played an important role in companies deciding to abandon later-stage development of otherwise promising technologies. Iain M. Cockburn & Rebecca Henderson, *The 2003 Intellectual Property Owners Association Survey on Strategic Management of Intellectual Property* D2 (working paper 2004).

36. More than four thousand of those genes are patented. Stefan Lovgren, *One-Fifth of Human Genes Have Been Patented, Study Reveals,* National Geographic News, Oct. 13, 2005. *But cf.* David E. Adelman & Kathryn L. DeAngelis, *Patent Metrics: The Mismeasure of Innovation in the Biotech Patent Debate,* 85 Tex. L. Rev. 1677 (2007) (mapping the density of patents in biotechnology fields and finding relatively little concentration).

37. *Madey v. Duke University*, 307 F.3d 1351 (Fed. Cir. 2002).

38. John P. Walsh et al., *Effects of Research Tool Patenting and Licensing on Biomedical Innovation, in Patents in the Knowledge-Based Economy* (Stephen Merrill, ed., 2001); *see also* John P. Walsh et al., *Where Excludability Matters: Material v. Intellectual Property in Academic Biomedical Research* (working paper Jan. 9, 2007), available at http://www.ssrn.com (finding that even after *Madey*, patents didn't deter academic researchers).

39. Walsh et al., *supra*. Empirical research suggests that scientists don't in fact gain much of their knowledge from patents, turning instead to other sources. *See, e.g.,* Wesley M. Cohen et al., *R&D Spillovers, Patents and the Incentives to Innovate in Japan and the United States,* 31 Res. Pol. 1349, 1362–64 (2002).

40. Iain M. Cockburn & Rebecca Henderson, *The 2003 Intellectual Property Owners Association Survey on Strategic Management of Intellectual Property* F6 (working paper 2004) (a survey of IP managers found that 67 percent disagreed with the statement "we always do a patent search before initiating any R&D or product development effort").

41. In several high-profile patent cases in 2006, the adjudged infringer asserted that it had developed a noninfringing alternative but did not implement it pending final resolution of the case, instead either settling or fighting the injunction. *See eBay, Inc. v. MercExchange LLC,* 126 S. Ct. 1837 (2006); *NTP, Inc. v. Research in Motion, Ltd.,* 418 F.3d 1282 (Fed. Cir. 2005).

42. 21 U.S.C. §§ 355(b)(1) and (c)(2) (1994).

43. 21 U.S.C. §§ 355(j)(2)(A)(vii)(I)–(IV) (certification and disclosure requirements); 21 U.S.C. § 355(j)(5)(B)(iii) (thirty-month stay).

44. *See* Dan L. Burk & Mark A. Lemley, *Policy Levers in Patent Law,* 89 Va. L. Rev. 1575 (2003) (providing estimates of the cost and delay associated with regulatory approval, and arguing that they justify stronger patent protection in pharmaceuticals than in other industries).

45. This stands to reason, since patent owners who do not participate in the market would be unable to get revenue without licensing the patent up-front to someone who would invest the time and effort of obtaining FDA approval.

For a discussion of how FDA approval creates rents alongside the patent system, *see* William E. Ridgway, *Realizing Two-Tiered Innovation Policy through Drug Regulation,* 58 Stan. L. Rev. 121 (2006).

46. *See, e.g.,* 21 U.S.C. § 355a (providing for additional exclusivity to encourage clinical investigation of the safety of already approved drugs for use by children).

Chapter Four

1. *See, e.g.,* Gerald J. Mossinghoff & Vivian S. Kuo, *World Patent System Circa 20XX, A.D.,* 38 Idea 529, 529 (1998).

2. *See, e.g.,* John H. Barton, *Reforming the Patent System,* 287 Sci. 5460 (2000).

3. *See, e.g.,* Staff of Subcomm. on Patents, Trademarks, and Copyrights of the Senate Comm. on the Judiciary, 85th Cong., *An Economic Review of the Patent System: Study No. 15,* at 76–80 (Comm. Print 1958) (prepared by Fritz Machlup; *cf.* George L. Priest, *What Economists Can Tell Lawyers about Intellectual Property: Comment on Cheung,* 8 Res. L. & Econ. 19, 24 (1986) (concluding that economists can tell lawyers essentially nothing about IP).

4. Machlup, *supra*.

5. Priest, *supra*.

6. *See generally* Brett Frischmann, *Innovation and Institutions: Rethinking the Economics of U.S. Science and Technology Policy*, 24 Vt. L. Rev. 347, 351 (2000) (arguing that innovation is more complicated than traditionally understood by policymakers).

7. *See* Stephen M. Maurer & Suzanne Scotchmer, *Procuring Knowledge, in Intellectual Property and Entrepreneurship* 1, 2 (Gary D. Libecap ed. 2004) (noting that the diversity of innovation in different industries means that the logic of IP and other incentive schemes must be evaluated on an industry-by-industry basis).

8. Robert P. Merges, *As Many as Six Impossible Patents before Breakfast: Property Rights for Business Concepts and Patent System Reform*, 14 Berkeley Tech. L.J. 577, 585 (1999).

9. On the history of railroad patents and their unique character, *see* Steven W. Usselman, *Regulating Railroad Innovation* (2002).

10. U.S. Patent No. 5,153,041 (1992).

11. *See, e.g.*, Katherine Derbyshire, *Building a Fab—It's All about Trade-offs*, 3 Semiconductor Mag., (June 2002), at http://www.semi.org/web/wmagazine.nsf /4f55b97743-c2d02e882565bf006c2459/e0137dd2c4442ff988256bce007eecca!OpenDocument (time); Mark LaPedus, *Leading-Edge Fab Costs Soar to $4 Billion*, http://www.siliconstrategies.com/story/OEG20030310S0067 (Mar. 10, 2003) (cost); *see also* Steve Lohr, *World-Class Chip, but a Fragile Business*, N.Y. Times, Aug. 4, 2003, at C1 (noting that fabs cost two to three billion dollars each).

12. Bronwyn H. Hall & Rosemarie Ziedonis, *The Determinants of Patenting in the U.S. Semiconductor Industry, 1980–1994*, 32 RAND J. Econ. 101 (2001).

13. *See* Michael S. Dell & Patricia R. Olsen, *Executive Life: The Boss; More Fun Than School*, N.Y. Times, Mar. 9, 2003, at B12.

14. *Cf.* Mark A. Lemley & David W. O'Brien, *Encouraging Software Reuse*, 49 Stan. L. Rev. 255 (1997) (arguing that this is not always the case).

15. *See Griffith v. Kanamaru*, 816 F.2d 624 (Fed. Cir. 1987).

16. John R. Allison & Mark A. Lemley, *Who's Patenting What? An Empirical Exploration of Patent Prosecution*, 53 Vand. L. Rev. 2099 (2000).

17. *See* James Bessen & Michael Meurer, *Lessons for Patent Policy From Empirical Research on Patent Litigation*, 9 Lewis & Clark L. Rev. 1 (2005).

18. *See, e.g.*, John R. Allison & Mark A. Lemley, *Who's Patenting What? An Empirical Exploration of Patent Prosecution*, 53 Vand. L. Rev. 2099, 2117, 2128–30 (2000) (finding that the number of patents owned by individuals and small entities, and the number of inventors on each patent, varied significantly from industry to industry).

19. *See* Richard J. Rosen, *Research and Development with Asymmetric Firm Sizes*, 22 RAND J. Econ. 411 (1991); P. R. Beije & J. Groenewegen, *A Network Analysis of Markets*, 26 U. Econ. Issues 87, 101–02 (1992).

20. *See, e.g.*, Zoltan J. Acs & David B. Audretsch, *R&D, Firm Size, and Innovative Activity, in Innovation and Technological Change: An International Comparison* (Acs & Audretsch eds., 1991); K. Pavitt et al., *The Size Distribution of Innovating Firms in the U.K.: 1945–1983*, 35 J. Ind. Econ. 297, 307–08 (1992) (finding that in the United Kingdom, small firms spent only 3.3 percent of the R&D budget in the 1970s but produced 34.9 percent of the significant innovations during that period).

21. *See* Edwin Mansfield, *Some Empirical Findings, in R&D, Patents and Productivity* 128–29, 150–51 (Zvi Griliches ed., 1987).

22. Pavitt et al., *supra* note 21, at 301–2.

23. Jonathan M. Barnett, *Private Protection of Patentable Goods,* 25 Cardozo L. Rev. 1251 (2004).

24. Katherine Strandburg distinguishes between "self-disclosing" and "non-self-disclosing" inventions. Katherine J. Strandburg, *What Does the Public Get? Experimental Use and the Patent Bargain,* 2004 Wisc. L. Rev. 81.

25. The paper clip was once patented. Indeed, there were many different claimed inventors and even substantial litigation over ownership of the exclusive rights to the paper clip. *See, e.g., Cushman Denison Mfg. Co. v. Denny,* 147 F. 734, 734–35 (S.D.N.Y. 1906). And plastic paper clips are still under patent. U.S. Patent No. 5,179,765 (issued Jan. 19, 1993) (granting patent to a "Plastic Paper Clip").

26. *See, e.g.,* Pamela Samuelson et al., *A Manifesto concerning the Legal Protection of Computer Programs,* 94 Colum. L. Rev. 2308 (1994).

27. *E. I. DuPont de Neomours & Co. v. Christopher,* 431 F.2d 1012 (5th Cir. 1970).

28. Richard C. Levin et al., *Appropriating the Returns from Industrial Research and Development,* 1987 Brookings Papers on Economic Activity 783, 794–95.

29. Gary L. Lilien & Eunsang Moon, *The Timing of Competitive Market Entry: An Exploratory Study of New Industrial Products,* 36 Mgmt. Sci. 568, 569 (1990) (pioneers generally maintain their market share despite later imitation).

30. Levin et al., *supra* note 29, at 815–16 (concluding that the patent system and related institutions "*improve* the appropriability of returns from innovation," but "are not the only nor necessarily the primary barriers that prevent general access to what would otherwise be pure public goods"). *See also* Edwin Mansfield, *Patents and Innovation: An Empirical Study,* 32 Mgmt. Sci. 173, 176–77 (1986) (examining the extent to which various firms and industries rely on the patent system to protect their innovations). In fact, Nancy Dorfman argues that the first-mover advantage has been the primary reason for innovation in the computer hardware and semiconductor industries. *See* Nancy S. Dorfman, *Innovation and Market Structure: Lessons from the Computer and Semiconductor Industries,* 235–39 (1987).

31. We should make it clear that by "imitation" of a software invention we mean the development of similar products by computer programmers, not mere copying of the object code itself. Exact copying of software violates copyright law. If it didn't, imitation would be instantaneous and costless, and software inventors wouldn't be able to recoup even modest R&D investments.

32. *State Street Bank & Trust Co. v. Signature Fin. Servs.,* 149 F.3d 1368 (Fed. Cir. 1998).

33. Gideon Parchomovsky & Peter Siegelman, *Towards an Integrated Theory of Intellectual Property,* 88 Va. L. Rev. 1455 (2002).

34. *See also* Michael W. Carroll, *One for All: The Problem of Uniformity Cost in Intellectual Property Law,* 55 Am. U. L. Rev. 845 (2006) (adopting a similar measure).

35. For literature on network effects, *see* generally Joseph Farrell & Garth Saloner, *Standardization, Compatibility, and Innovation,* 16 RAND J. Econ. 70, 70 (1985) (discussing "whether . . . standardization benefits can 'trap' an industry in an obsolete or inferior standard"); Michael L. Katz & Carl Shapiro, *Network Externalities, Competition, and Compatibility,* 75 Am. Econ. Rev. 424 (1985) (using oligopoly models to understand markets with network externalities); Michael L. Katz & Carl Shapiro, *Systems Competition and Network Effects,* 8 J. Econ. Persp. 93 (1994) (examining behavior and performance of public and private institutions in systems markets); Mark A. Lemley & David McGowan, *Legal Implications of Network Economic Effects,* 86 Cal. L. Rev. 479, 479 (1998) (examining network theory

in the context of "antitrust law, intellectual property law, telecommunications law, Internet law, corporate law, and contract law") S. J. Liebowitz & Stephen E. Margolis, *Network Externality: An Uncommon Tragedy*, 8 J. Econ. Persp. 133 (1994) (arguing that the concept of network externalities as market failures is questionable).

36. *See, e.g.*, Robert P. Merges et al., *Intellectual Property in the New Technological Age* 10–18 (3d ed. 2003) (discussing such incentives).

37. *See, e.g.*, Michael Abramowicz, *Perfecting Patent Prizes*, 56 Vand. L. Rev. 115 (2003) (advocating a reward system to complement existing IP protection); Steven Shavell & Tanguy van Ypersele, *Rewards versus Intellectual Property Rights*, 44 J.L. & Econ. 525 (2001) (concluding that an optimal reward system is more effective than IP rights).

38. *See* Eric Schiff, *Industrialization without National Patents: The Netherlands 1869–1912, Switzerland 1850–1907*, at 40–41 (1971); Fritz Machlup & Edith Penrose, *The Patent Controversy in the Nineteenth Century*, 10 J. Econ. Hist. 1, 1–6 (1950). For a discussion of the history of arguments for patent abolition, *see* Mark D. Janis, *Patent Abolitionism*, 17 Berkeley Tech. L.J. 899 (2002).

39. Jonathan M. Barnett, *Private Protection of Patentable Goods*, 25 Cardozo L. Rev. 1251, 1252 (2004).

40. *See* Nat'l Inst. of Health, *Summary of the FY 2004 President's Budget*, Feb. 3, 2003, available at http://www.nih.gov/news/budgetfy2004/fy2004presidentsbudget.pdf. The 93 percent statistic is based on Nat'l Inst. of Health, *Setting Research Priorities at the National Institutes of Health*, figure 1 at http://www.nih.gov/about/researchpriorities.htm (June 18, 2003).

41. *See* Science and Engineering Indicators—2002, at app. tbl.4-4, http://www.nsf.gov/sbe/srs/seind02/append/c4/at04-01xls (Apr. 2002).

42. *See* Elias G. Carayannis & Jeffery Alexander, *Revisiting SEMATECH: Profiling Public and Private Sector Cooperation*, 12 Eng. Mgmt. J. 3342 (2000) (discussing the resurgence of the U.S. semiconductor industry and noting that "it is still difficult to identify any ways in which SEMATECH may have supported the renewal of the U.S. semiconductor industry").

43. *See* Rebecca S. Eisenberg, *Proprietary Rights and the Norms of Science in Biotechnology Research*, 97 Yale L.J. 177 (1987); Arti K. Rai, *Regulating Scientific Research: Intellectual Property Rights and the Norms of Science*, 94 Nw. U. L. Rev. 77 (1999).

44. William Ridgway, *Realizing Two-Tiered Innovation Policy through Drug Regulation*, 58 Stan. L. Rev. 1221 (2006).

45. *See* Morton I. Kamien & Nancy L. Schwartz, *Market Structure and Innovation* (1982).

46. *See* Brett Frischmann & Mark A. Lemley, *Spillovers*, 107 Colum. L. Rev. 257 (2007).

47. Dietmar Harhoff, *R&D Spillovers, Technological Proximity, and Productivity Growth—Evidence from German Panel Data*, 52 Schmalenbach Bus. Rev. 238 (2000); accord Ruslan Lukach & Joseph Plasmans, *Measuring Knowledge Spillovers Using Patent Citations: Evidence from the Belgian Firm's Data* (CESifo Working Paper No. 754, Munich, Germany 2002).

48. Harhoff, *supra*, at 238.

49. Ashish Arora et al., *R&D and the Patent Premium* 1, 33 tbl. 4 (2002).

50. *See* Bessen & Meurer, *Patent Failure*.

51. *See, e.g.*, David Dranove & Neil Gandal, *The DVD v. DIVX Standard War: Empirical Evidence of Network Effects and Preannouncement Effects*, 12 J. Econ. & Mgmt. Strategy 363 (2004) (fall 2003) (providing evidence that consumers delayed purchasing digital video players because of a standards competition).

52. Stavroula Malla, Richard Gray, & Peter Phillips, *Gains to Research in the Presence of Intellectual Property Rights and Research Subsidies*, 26 Rev. Ag. Econ. 63 (2004).

Chapter Five

1. Robert W. Hahn, *The Economics of Patent Protection: Policy Implications for the Literature*, 1 (working paper 2004), available at http://www.ssrn.com/abstract=467489.

2. F. M. Scherer et al., *Patents and the Corporation* (1959); E. Brower & A. Kleinknecht, *Innovative Output and a Firm's Propensity to Patent: An Exploration of CIS Micro Data*, 28 Res. Pol. 615 (1999).

3. Jean O. Lanjouw & Iain Cockburn, *Do Patents Matter? Empirical Evidence after GATT*, Nat'l Bureau of Econ. Res. Working Paper No. 7495 (2000).

4. *See* Wesley M. Cohen et al., *Protecting Their Intellectual Assets: Appropriability Conditions and Why U.S. Manufacturing Firms Patent (or Not)* (Nat'l Bureau of Econ. Res., Working Paper No. W7552, 2000); Levin et al., *supra*, at 784–86. *See also* Michael A. Carrier, *Unraveling the Patent-Antitrust Paradox*, 150 U. Pa. L. Rev. 761, 826–27 (2002) (arguing that weakening patents would damage some industries but not others).

5. *See* Orton Huang et al., *Biotechnology Patents and Start-ups*, para. 1 (2003) ("[P]atents are absolutely essential to the success of traditional biotech startups.").

6. Bronwyn H. Hall, *Exploring the Patent Explosion*, 30 J. Tech. Transfer 35 (2004); James Bessen & Robert M. Hunt, *An Empirical Look at Software Patents*, 16 J. Econ & Mgmt. Strategy 157 (2007).

7. Mark A. Lemley & Bhaven Sampat, *Is the Patent Office a Rubber Stamp?* 58 Emory L.J. (forthcoming 2008).

8. Allison & Lemley, *Who's Patenting What? supra*, at 2124–32.

9. *Id.* at 2146–47.

10. Douglas Lichtman, *Rethinking Prosecution History Estoppel*, 71 U. Chi. L. Rev. 151, 155 (2004).

11. *See* John R. Allison & Mark A. Lemley, *The Growing Complexity of the United States Patent System*, 82 B.U. L. Rev. 77, 78–81 (2002) [hereinafter Allison & Lemley, *Complexity*].

12. Allison & Lemley, *Who's Patenting What? supra* (documenting that most prior art citations are to other U.S. patents).

13. Julie E. Cohen, *Reverse Engineering and the Rise of Electronic Vigilantism: Intellectual Property Implications of "Lock-Out" Technologies*, 68 S. Cal. L. Rev. 1091, 1179 (1995).

14. Lichtman, *supra* note 10, at 155.

15. Mark A. Lemley & Bhaven Sampat, *Examiner Characteristics and the Patent Grant Rate* (working paper 2008, available from authors).

16. John R. Allison & Mark A. Lemley, *Empirical Evidence on the Validity of Litigated Patents*, 26 AIPLA Q.J. 185 (1998).

17. As a result of changes in patent law, we can now determine for the first time who cites prior art—the applicant or the examiner. For early studies, *see* Juan Alcacer & Michelle Gittelman, *How Do I Know What You Know? Patent Examiners and the Generation of Patent Citation* (working paper 2004, available at http://www.ssrn.com/abstract=548003); Deepak Hegde & Bhaven N. Sampat, *Examiner Citations, Applicant Citations, and the Private Value of Patents*, working paper (Dec. 2006). Hegde and Sampat find a statistically significant difference in applicant-cited art in the chemical and biomedical fields as opposed to other technological fields.

18. Mark Schankerman, *How Valuable Is Patent Protection? Estimates by Technology Field*, 29 RAND J. Econ. 77, 79 (1998).

19. *See* David J. Teece, *Managing Intellectual Capital*, 152 (2000) ("Much analysis appears to be based on the implicit assumption that there is a simple one-to-one correspondence between the intellectual property and the product embodying that intellectual property. Nothing could be further from the truth").

20. *See Kearns v. Gen. Motors Corp.*, 152 F.3d 945 (Fed. Cir. 1998) (unpublished decision).

21. Mark A. Lemley & Carl Shapiro, *Patent Holdup and Royalty Stacking*, 85 Tex. L. Rev. 1991 (2007).

22. *See, e.g.,* Deepak Somaya & David J. Teece, *Combining Inventions in Multi-Invention Products: Organizational Choices, Patents, and Public Policy* (2000) (discussing the component nature of innovation as a factor affecting patent value).

23. Gideon Parchomovsky & R. Polk Wagner, *Patent Portfolios*, 154 U. Pa. L. Rev. 1 (2005).

24. Jean O. Lanjouw & Mark Schankerman, *Protecting Intellectual Property Rights: Are Small Firms Handicapped?* 47 J. L. & Econ. 45, 47 (2004).

25. James Bessen & Robert M. Hunt, *An Empirical Look at Software Patents, supra,* at 39. For criticism of their empirical study, *see* Robert W. Hahn & Scott Wallsten, *A Review of Bessen and Hunt's Analysis of Software Patents* (Nov. 2003, available at http://www.ssrn.com/abstract=467484).

26. Rosemarie Ham Ziedonis, *Don't Fence Me In: Fragmented Markets for Technology and the Patent Acquisition Strategies of Firms*, 21 (Oct. 2003), available at http://www.ssrn.com/abstract=475601.

27. Allison & Lemley, *Who's Patenting What? supra*, at 2128.

28. Kimberly A. Moore, *Xenophobia in American Courts: An Empirical Study of Patent Litigation*, 97 Nw. U. L. Rev. 1497 (2003).

29. Mark A. Lemley, *Rational Ignorance at the Patent Office*, 95 Nw. U. L. Rev. 1495, 1501 (2001).

30. *See id.* at 1503–6 (discussing trophy value and defensive uses); Mark A. Lemley, *Reconceiving Patents in the Age of Venture Capital*, 4 J. Small & Emerging Bus. L. 137 (2000) (discussing value of patents in obtaining venture capital); Clarisa Long, *Patent Signals*, 69 U. Chi. L. Rev. 625 (2002) (examining patents as signaling mechanisms).

31. Parchomovsky & Wagner, *supra*; Allison et al., *supra*.

32. *See* John R. Allison et al., *Valuable Patents*, 92 Geo. L.J. 453 (2002); Jean Olson Lanjouw & Mark A. Schankerman, *Characteristics of Patent Litigation: A Window on Competition*, 32 RAND J. Econ. 1 (2000).

33. Deepak Somaya, *Firm Strategies and Trends in Patent Litigation in the United States*, in *Intellectual Property and Entrepreneurship*, 103, 111 Fig. 3 (Gary D. Libecap ed., 2004).

34. *Id.* at 126, 139.

35. *See, e.g.,* Allison et al. (finding that large companies obtain 71 percent of all patents but file only 37 percent of patent infringement lawsuits).

36. *See* John R. Allison & Mark A. Lemley, *Empirical Evidence on the Validity of Litigated Patents*, 26 AIPLA Q.J. 185, 224–25 (1998) [hereinafter Allison & Lemley, *Empirical Evidence*]; Moore, *supra* note 27.

37. Michael J. Meurer, *Controlling Opportunistic and Anti-competitive Intellectual Property Litigation*, 44 B.C. L. Rev. 509, 542 (2003).

38. For example, in *Peeler v. Miller,* 535 F.2d 647 (C.C.P.A. 1976), an application sat on an in-house patent attorney's desk for more than four years because of the backlog of applications he had to file.

39. Allison & Lemley, *Who's Patenting What? supra.*

40. Allison et al., *supra.*

41. Allison & Lemley, *supra.*

42. Julie E. Cohen & Mark A. Lemley, *Patent Scope and Innovation in the Software Industry,* 89 Calif. L. Rev. 1 (2001) (investigating software patent infringement cases and finding evidence of the latter trend).

43. Schankerman, *supra,* at 79.

44. Allison & Lemley, *Empirical Evidence, supra.*

45. Dan L. Burk & Mark A. Lemley, *Is Patent Law Technology Specific?* 17 Berkeley Tech. L.J. 1155 (2002).

46. Mark A. Lemley, *Ignoring Patents,* 2008 Mich. St. L. Rev. 19.

47. B. N. Anand & T. Khanna, *The Structure of Licensing Contracts,* 48 J. Indus. Econ. 103 (2000).

48. Ashish Arora et al., *Markets for Technology* (2001).

49. Richard C. Levin, *A New Look at the Patent System,* 76 Am. Econ. Rev., May 1986, at 199, 201 (arguing that patents may be used to measure the performance of research and redevelopment employees).

50. Parchomovsky & Wagner, *supra.*

51. *See, e.g.,* Mark A. Lemley, *Reconceiving Patents in the Age of Venture Capital,* 4 J. Sm. & Emerging Bus. L. 137 (2000).

52. We demonstrate this in exhaustive detail in Burk & Lemley, *Technology-Specific, supra.*

53. *See id.* at 1160–73.

54. *See, e.g.,* Mueller, *supra* note 76; Amir A. Naini, *Convergent Technologies and Divergent Patent Validity Doctrines: Obviousness and Disclosure Analyses in Software and Biotechnology,* J. Pat. & Trademark Ofc. Soc'y 541 (2004); Sampson, *supra;* Natalie A. Lissy, *Patentability of Chemical and Biotechnology Inventions: A Discrepancy in Standards,* 81 Wash. U. L.Q. 1069 (2003); Limin Zheng, *Note, Purdue Pharma L.P. v. Faulding Inc.,* 17 Berkeley Tech. L.J. 95, 95 (2002). Although there are a number of recent written description cases outside the biotechnology context, all of them involve patentees who changed their claims during prosecution to cover a competitor's product. *See, e.g., Chiron v. Genentech,* 363 F.3d 1247 (Fed. Cir. 2004); *Turbocore Div. of Demag Delaval Turbomachinery Corp. v. Gen. Elec. Co.,* 264 F.3d 1111 (Fed. Cir. 2001); *Hyatt v. Boone,* 146 F.3d 1348 (Fed. Cir. 1998); *Gentry Gallery, Inc. v. Berkline Corp.,* 134 F.3d 1473 (Fed. Cir. 1998). *See also* Janice M. Mueller, *Patent Misuse through the Capture of Industry Standards,* 17 Berkeley Tech. L.J. 623, 639–40 (2002) (distinguishing the biotechnology cases from written description decisions in other areas, especially *Union Oil Co. of Cal. v. Atl. Richfield Co.,* 208 F.3d 989 [Fed. Cir. 2000]). *Cf.* Matthew L. Goska, *Of Omitted Elements and Overreaching Inventions: The Principle of Gentry Gallery Should Not Be Discarded,* 29 AIPLA Q.J. 471, 484 (2001) (arguing that the written description requirement makes sense, but that it should not be applied to original claims as it has been in the biotechnology cases).

Other commentators have pointed out that the nonobviousness standard in biotechnology is lower than in other industries. *See, e.g.,* Sara Dastgheib-Vinarov, *A Higher Nonobviousness Standard for Gene Patents: Protecting Biomedical Research from the Big Chill,* 4 Marq.

Intell. Prop. L. Rev. 143, 154 (2000); John Murray, *Note, Owning Genes: Disputes Involving DNA Sequence Patents*, 75 Chi.-Kent L. Rev. 231, 247 (1999).

55. *See, e.g., Gummow v. Snap-On Tools*, 58 U.S.P.Q.2d 1414 (N.D. Ill. 2001) (holding that mechanical patents require less disclosure than biotechnology patents due to the uncertainty in biotechnology).

56. *Fonar Corp. v. Gen. Elec. Co.*, 107 F.3d 1543, 1549 (Fed. Cir. 1997).

57. *Regents of the Univ. of Calif. v. Eli Lilly & Co.*, 119 F.3d 1559, 1568 (Fed. Cir. 1997).

58. *See* U.S. Patent & Trademark Office, *Utility Examination Guidelines*, 60 Fed. Reg. 36263 (July 14, 1995) (describing the law as setting different standards for the life sciences); Timothy J. Balts, *Substantial Utility, Technology Transfer, and Research Utility: It's Time for a Change*, 52 Syracuse L. Rev. 105 (2002) (describing and criticizing the higher utility standard applied to life sciences); Philippe Ducor, *New Drug Discovery Technologies and Patents*, 22 Rutgers Computer & Tech. L.J. 369, 431–33 (1996); *cf.* Rebecca S. Eisenberg & Robert P. Merges, *Opinion Letter as to the Patentability of Certain Inventions Associated with the Identification of Partial cDNA Sequences*, 23 AIPLA Q.J. 1 (1995) (arguing that the utility doctrine may bar the patenting of "expressed sequence tags" that can be used to identify human gene sequences).

59. *In re Fisher*, 427 F.2d 833 (C.C.P.A. 1970). *Accord Spectra-Physics, Inc. v. Coherent, Inc.*, 827 F.2d 1524, 1533 (Fed. Cir. 1987); *In re Cook*, 439 F.2d 730, 734 (C.C.P.A. 1971).

60. *See Juicy Whip, Inc. v. Orange Bang, Inc.*, 185 F.3d 1364 (Fed. Cir. 1999) (saying that a patented device is useful if there is a demand for it).

61. 383 U.S. 519 (1966).

62. *See In re Brana*, 51 F.3d 1560, 1567 (Fed. Cir. 1995).

63. *In re Fisher*, 421 F.3d 1365 (Fed. Cir. 2005).

64. *Juicy Whip, Inc. v. Orange Bang, Inc.*, 185 F.3d 1364 (Fed. Cir. 1999).

65. *See* Donald S. Chisum, *Anticipation, Enablement and Obviousness: An Eternal Golden Braid*, 15 AIPLA Q.J. 57, 58 (1987).

66. Burk & Lemley, *Technology-Specific, supra*, at 1170–71.

67. *See id.* at 1170–71. There are other consequences of this rule that are less favorable to patentees. For example, because the Federal Circuit considers broad functional disclosure sufficient in software, it has held that even an oral description of the goal of the program may be sufficient to make it "ready for patenting" and therefore to trigger the on-sale bar. *Robotic Vision v. View Systems*, 249 F.3d 1307 (Fed. Cir. 2001).

68. *Philip A. Hunt Co. v. Mallinckrodt Chem. Works*, 177 F.2d 583, 585–86 (2d Cir. 1949) (noting that it is impossible to write claims of appropriate scope without using functional language to describe variants).

69. Burk & Lemley, *Technology-Specific, supra*, at 1176–77. Since the publication of that article, the Federal Circuit's decisions in *Griffin v. Bertina*, 285 F.3d 1029 (Fed. Cir. 2002), *Univ. of Rochester v. G.D. Searle & Co.*, 358 F.3d 916 (Fed. Cir. 2004), and *In re Wallach*, 378 F.3d 1330 (Fed. Cir. 2004), make clear that the biotechnology-specific nature of the written description doctrine is not an accident or an anomaly in a few cases.

70. R. Polk Wagner, *(Mostly) against Exceptionalism*, in *Perspectives on Properties of the Human Genome Project* 367 (F. Scott Kieff ed., 2003); R. Polk Wagner, *Exactly Backwards: Exceptionalism and the Federal Circuit*, 54 Case W. Res. L. Rev. 749 (2004).

71. *In re Wallach*, 378 F.3d 1330 (Fed. Cir. 2004).

72. Burk & Lemley, *Technology-Specific, supra*.

73. William Kingston, *How Realistic Are EU Hopes for Innovation?* 2004 Eur. Intell. Prop. Rev. 197, 198.

74. *See* John R. Thomas, *Formalism at the Federal Circuit*, 52 Am. U. L. Rev. 771, 773 (2003).

75. *See Wilson Sporting Goods Co. v. David Geoffrey & Assoc.*, 904 F.2d 677, 684 (Fed. Cir. 1990).

76. *See* John H. Barton, *Non-Obviousness,* 43 Idea 475, 492 (2003); Robert Hunt, *supra;* Wagner, *Against Exceptionalism, supra.*

77. *See, e.g.,* Ronald J. Mann, *Intellectual Property and Innovation in Small Software Firms* 58 (2003) ("It surely is true that patents are not as effective in appropriating the value of software inventions as they are in appropriating the value of some other kinds of inventions").

78. Wesley M. Cohen & Steven A. Merrill, *Patents in the Knowledge-Based Economy* 3 (2003) ("Empirical work by a number of economists over nearly fifty years suggests that patents play a prominent role in stimulating invention in only a few manufacturing industries").

79. James Bessen & Michael J. Meurer, *Lessons for Patent Policy from Empirical Research on Patent Litigation,* 9 Lewis & Clark L. Rev. 1, 5 (2005).

80. James Bessen & Eric Maskin, *Sequential Innovation, Patents, and Imitation* 7 (Mass. Inst. of Tech. 2006), http:// sss.ias.edu/publications/papers/econpaper25.pdf.

Chapter Six

1. John Shepard Wiley Jr., *Copyright at the School of Patent,* 58 U. Chi. L. Rev. 119, 119 (1991).

2. James Boyle, *Shamans, Software, and Spleens* 19 (1996).

3. *See, e.g.,* Ward S. Bowman Jr., *Patent and Antitrust Law* 2–3 (1973); F. M. Scherer, *Industrial Market Structure and Economic Performance* 440 (2d ed., Edward Jaffe et al. eds., 1980); John S. McGee, *Patent Exploitation: Some Economic and Legal Problems,* 9 J.L. & Econ. 135, 135–36 (1966); Rebecca S. Eisenberg, *Patents and the Progress of Science: Exclusive Rights and Experimental Use,* 56 U. Chi. L. Rev. 1017, 1024–28 (1989).

4. *See* Eisenberg, *supra,* at 1028–30 (discussing disclosure theory); *see also* Scherer, *supra,* at 440.

5. *See, e.g.,* Lawrence Lessig, *Intellectual Property and Code,* 11 St. John's J. Legal Comment. 635, 638 (1996).

6. *See Eldred v. Ashcroft,* 123 S.Ct. 769, 784–85 (2003). To be sure, the court's rejection of the public interest in *Eldred* runs counter to a large number of prior copyright cases that had emphasized the importance of the public domain in copyright. *See, e.g., Mazer v. Stein,* 347 U.S. 201, 219 (1954). *See also Fogerty v. Fantasy, Inc.,* 510 U.S. 517, 524 (1994); *Feist Publ'ns v. Rural Tel. Serv. Co.,* 499 U.S. 340, 349 (1991); *Stewart v. Abend,* 495 U.S. 207, 228 (1990); *Bonito Boats v. Thunder Craft Boats,* 489 U.S. 141, 167 (1989); *Sony Corp. v. Universal City Studios,* 464 U.S. 417, 429 (1984); *Twentieth Century Music Corp. v. Aiken,* 422 U.S. 151, 156 (1975); *Goldstein v. California,* 412 U.S. 546, 559 (1973); *Fox Film Corp. v. Doyal,* 286 U.S. 123, 127 (1932).

7. For a discussion of reward-based theories of scientific invention stemming from natural law, *see* A. Samuel Oddi, *Un-unified Economic Theories of Patents—The Not-Quite-Holy Grail,* 71 Notre Dame L. Rev. 267, 275–77 (1996); Kevin Rhodes, *Comment, The Federal Circuit's Patent Nonobviousness Standards: Theoretical Perspectives on Recent Doctrinal Changes,* 85 Nw. U. L. Rev. 1051, 1077–84 (1991).

8. *See* Mark A. Lemley, *The Economics of Improvement in Intellectual Property Law,* 75 Tex. L. Rev. 989, 1003–5 (1997).

9. *See* Julie S. Turner, *Comment, The Nonmanufacturing Patent Owner: Toward a Theory of Efficient Infringement,* 86 Cal L. Rev. 179 (1998).

10. Patent terms extend for no more than twenty years in most cases, 35 U.S.C. § 154(a)(2) (2000), while copyright lasts for the life of the author plus seventy years, 17 U.S.C. § 302(a) (2000), and trademarks can last forever as long as the mark is used in commerce.

11. Patent law confers the broad right to prevent others from making, using, selling, offering for sale, or importing the invention. 35 U.S.C. § 271(a) (2000). Unlike copyright or trade secret law, patent law does not treat independent invention as a defense. *See* Michelle Armond, *Comment, Introducing the Defense of Independent Invention to Motions for Preliminary Injunctions in Patent Infringement Lawsuits,* 91 Cal. L. Rev. 117 (2003). For proposals that it should do so, *see,* for example, Stephen M. Maurer & Suzanne Scotchmer, *The Independent Invention Defense in Intellectual Property,* 69 Economica 535 (2002); Samson Vermont, *Independent Invention as a Defense to Patent Infringement,* 105 Mich. L. Rev. 475 (2006); Armond, *supra,* at 117; John S. Liebovitz, *Note, Inventing a Nonexclusive Patent System,* 111 Yale L.J. 2251 (2002).

12. Lawrence C. Becker, *Deserving to Own Intellectual Property,* 68 Chi.-Kent L. Rev. 609 (1993).

13. Yusing Ko offered a similar taxonomy in 1992, but without the benefit of some of the more recent theoretical work on the patent system, such as the foundational theoretical work on anticommons theory and patent thickets. Yusing Ko, *Note, An Economic Analysis of Biotechnology Patent Protection,* 102 Yale L.J. 777 (1992). Like ours, Ko's work attempts to derive economic principles specific to the biotechnology industry by analyzing different theories of patent protection. *Id.* at 791–804. She is, in our view, ultimately unsuccessful because she attempts to apply a variety of different theories of patent protection to a single industry when some of them simply do not fit the profile of that industry.

14. There are other approaches that do not rise to the level of complete theories of the patent system. *See, e.g.,* Ian Ayres & Paul Klemperer, *Limiting Patentees' Market Power without Reducing Innovation Incentives: The Perverse Benefits of Uncertainty and Non-injunctive Remedies,* 97 Mich. L. Rev. 985 (1999).

15. Edmund W. Kitch, *The Nature and Function of the Patent System,* 20 J.L. & Econ. 265, 265 (1977).

16. *See id.* at 276–78; Wendy J. Gordon, *Of Harms and Benefits: Torts, Restitution, and Intellectual Property,* 21 J. Legal Stud. 449, 473–74 (1992); Robert P. Merges, *Of Property Rules, Coase, and Intellectual Property,* 94 Colum. L. Rev. 2655, 2660–61 (1994).

17. Garrett Hardin, *The Tragedy of the Commons,* 162 Sci. 1243 (1968).

18. For more on these problems, *see* Mancur Olson Jr., *The Logic of Collective Action: Public Goods and the Theory of Groups* (1965). One commentator views this internalization of (positive) externalities as a key function of property. Harold Demsetz, *Toward a Theory of Property Rights,* 57 Am. Econ. Rev. (Papers and Proc.) 347, 348 (1967).

19. *See* Ronald H. Coase, *The Problem of Social Cost,* 3 J.L. & Econ. 1, 15 (1960).

20. *See* Guido Calabresi & A. Douglas Melamed, *Property Rules, Liability Rules, and Inalienability: One View of the Cathedral,* 85 Harv. L. Rev. 1089, 1094–95 (1972) (discussing this implication of the Coase theorem).

21. For other property-based views of IP, *see* Kenneth W. Dam, *Some Economic Considerations in the Intellectual Property Protection of Software,* 24 J. Legal Stud. 321 (1995); Trotter Hardy, *Property (and Copyright) in Cyberspace,* 1996 U. Chi. Legal F. 217; Edmund W. Kitch, *Patents: Monopolies or Property Rights?* 8 Res. L. & Econ. 31 (1986).

22. *See* Lewis Edmunds, *The Law and Practice of Letters Patent for Inventions* 3 (1890).

23. *Id.* at 276.

24. *Id.*

25. *See* Anastasia P. Winslow, *Rapping on a Revolving Door: An Economic Analysis of Parody and Campbell v. Acuff-Rose Music, Inc.,* 69 S. Cal. L. Rev. 767, 780 (1996). For a discussion of what happens when we relax these unrealistic assumptions, *see* Lemley, *Economics of Improvement, supra* note 8, at 1048–72. On the importance of efficient licensing to the case for IP protection, *see* Wendy J. Gordon, *Asymmetric Market Failure and Prisoner's Dilemma in Intellectual Property,* 17 U. Dayton L. Rev. 853, 857–58 (1992). On the problems with identifying the patents one would have to transact over, *see* James Bessen & Michael J. Meurer, *Patent Failure: How Judges, Bureaucrats, and Lawyers Put Innovators at Risk* (2008).

26. *See* Herbert Hovenkamp et al., *IP and Antitrust: An Analysis of Antitrust Principles Applied to Intellectual Property Law* § 4.2 (Supp. 2003).

27. Lemley, *Economics of Improvement, supra,* at 1048–72.

28. The classic argument cited in favor of monopolists coordinating innovation is Joseph A. Schumpeter, *Capitalism, Socialism, and Democracy* 106 (6th ed. 1987). For an application to patent law, *see* F. Scott Kieff, *Property Rights and Property Rules for Commercializing Inventions,* 85 Minn. L. Rev. 697 (2001); *cf.* Suzanne Scotchmer, *Protecting Early Innovators: Should Second-Generation Products Be Patentable?* 27 RAND J. Econ. 322 (1996). David Teece has modified the strong form of Schumpeter's argument, noting that in modern capital markets small firms have access to the financial resources needed to invest, and so long as there is some departure from perfect competition there may be sufficient incentive to invest even without monopoly. David J. Teece, *Managing Intellectual Capital* 40 (2000).

29. *See* Kenneth J. Arrow, *Economic Welfare and the Allocation of Resources for Invention,* in *The Rate and Direction of Inventive Activity* 609, 619–20 (Nat'l Bureau of Econ. Research ed., 1962), *reprinted in* 5 Kenneth J. Arrow, *Collected Papers of Kenneth J. Arrow: Production and Capital* 104, 115–16 (1985). *See also* Morton I. Kamien & Nancy L. Schwartz, *Market Structure and Innovation* (1982); F. M. Scherer & David Ross, *Industrial Market Structure and Economic Performance* 660 (3d ed. 1990); Mark A. Lemley & Lawrence Lessig, *The End of End-to-End: Preserving the Architecture of the Internet in the Broadband Era,* 48 UCLA L. Rev. 925, 960–62 (2001); Howard A. Shelanski, *Competition and Deployment of New Technology in U.S. Telecommunications,* 2000 U. Chi. Legal F. 85, 87; Michele Boldrin & David K. Levine, *Perfectly Competitive Innovation,* http://www.dklevine.com/papers/pcibasic14.pdf (2005).

30. *See, e.g.,* Yochai Benkler, *Overcoming Agoraphobia: Building the Commons of the Digitally Networked Environment,* 11 Harv. J.L. & Tech. 287, 359–60 (1998); Mark A. Lemley, *Ex Ante versus Ex Post Justifications for Intellectual Property,* 71 U. Chi. L. Rev. 129 (2004).

31. *See, e.g.,* Herbert Hovenkamp, *Economics and Federal Antitrust Law* § 8.3, at 219 (1985); Herbert Hovenkamp et al., *IP and Antitrust, supra* note 26, at § 4; Nat'l Inst. on Indus. & Intellectual Prop., *The Value of Patents and Other Legally Protected Commercial Rights,* 53 Antitrust L.J. 535, 547 (1985); William Montgomery, *Note, The Presumption of Economic Power for Patented and Copyrighted Products in Tying Arrangements,* 85 Colum. L. Rev. 1140, 1156 (1985).

32. Lawrence Lessig, *The Future of Ideas: The Fate of the Commons in the Digital World* (2001). Similar arguments have been made against business method patents. *See, e.g.,* Rochelle Cooper Dreyfuss, *Are Business Method Patents Bad for Business?* 16 Santa Clara Comp. & High Tech. L.J. 263 (2000); Alan L. Durham, *"Useful Arts" in the Information Age,* 1999 B.Y.U. L. Rev. 1419 (1999); John R. Thomas, *The Patenting of the Liberal Professions,* 40 B.C. L. Rev. 1139 (1999).

The existence of open source software is often cited as an example of how the absence of IP rights can promote innovation. Paradoxically, however, the open source movement depends on the existence of IP—here, copyright—to ensure openness. *See* Robert W. Gomulkiewicz, *How Copyleft Uses License Rights to Succeed in the Open Source Software Revolution and the Implications for Article 2B*, 36 Hous. L. Rev. 179 (1999); David McGowan, *Legal Implications of Open Source Software*, 2001 U. Ill. L. Rev. 241. Open source licenses do not address patents directly. But Oren Bar-Gill and Gideon Parchomovsky have suggested that firms might precommit not to seek broad patent protection in an analog to open source software. *See* Oren Bar-Gill & Gideon Parchomovsky, *The Value of Giving Away Secrets*, 89 Va. L. Rev. 1857 (2003).

33. *See* Shelanski, *supra*; F. M. Scherer, FTC Testimony, at http://www.ftc.gov/opp/global/scherer.htm (Nov. 29, 1995). While Christopher Yoo has challenged the strength of this evidence, he has done so largely through a rather strained reading of the data, rather than through offering empirical data of his own. *See* Christopher S. Yoo, *Vertical Integration and Media Regulation in the New Economy*, 19 Yale J. on Reg. 171, 272–78 (2002).

34. William J. Baumol, *The Free Market Innovation Machine: Analyzing the Growth Miracle of Capitalism* (2002); *accord* Seungwoo Son, *Selective Refusals to Sell Patented Goods: The Relationship between Patent Rights and Antitrust Law*, 2002 U. Ill. J.L. Tech. & Pol'y 109, 142.

35. *See* Michele Boldrin & David Levine, *The Case against Intellectual Property*, 92 Am. Econ. Rev. (Papers & Proc.) 209, 209 (2002).

36. *See* Jerry R. Green & Suzanne Scotchmer, *On the Division of Profit in Sequential Innovation*, 26 RAND J. Econ. 20 (1995). *See also* John H. Barton, *Patents and Antitrust: A Rethinking in Light of Patent Breadth and Sequential Innovation*, 65 Antitrust L.J. 449, 453 (1997); Howard F. Chang, *Patent Scope, Antitrust Policy, and Cumulative Innovation*, 26 RAND J. Econ. 34 (1995); Ted O'Donoghue, *A Patentability Requirement for Sequential Innovation*, 29 RAND J. Econ. 654 (1998).

37. *See* Lemley, *Economics of Improvement*, *supra*, at 1048–72.

38. Robert P. Merges & Richard R. Nelson, *On the Complex Economics of Patent Scope*, 90 Colum. L. Rev. 839, 876–79 (1990).

39. *Id.* at 878.

40. *Id.* at 877.

41. *Id.* at 884–908. Merges has argued elsewhere that the history of innovation in almost any field shows the importance of improvement inventions. Robert P. Merges, *Rent Control in the Patent District: Observations on the Grady-Alexander Thesis*, 78 Va. L. Rev. 359, 373 n.54 (1992).

42. Robert Merges, *Intellectual Property Rights and Bargaining Breakdown: The Case of Blocking Patents*, 62 Tenn. L. Rev. 75 (1994).

43. *See* Ward Bowman Jr., *Patent and Antitrust Law: A Legal and Economic Appraisal*, 32–34 (1973); F. M. Scherer, *Industrial Market Structure and Economic Performance* 443–50 (2d ed. 1980); Martin J. Adelman, *The Supreme Court, Market Structure, and Innovation*, 27 Antitrust Bull. 457, 479 (1982); Lemley, *Economics of Improvement*, *supra*, at 993–1000; Oddi, *supra*, at 273–81; Kevin Rhodes, *The Federal Circuit's Patent Nonobviousness Standards: Theoretical Perspectives on Recent Doctrinal Changes*, 85 Nw. U. L. Rev. 1051, 1053 (1991).

44. William M. Landes & Richard A. Posner, *An Economic Analysis of Copyright Law*, 18 J. Legal. Stud. 325, 326 (1989).

45. *See, e.g.*, Kenneth W. Dam, *Intellectual Property in an Age of Software and Biotechnology*, in *Chicago Lectures in Law and Economics* 113, 114–116 (Eric A. Posner ed., 2000).

46. *See* Calabresi & Melamed, *supra.*

47. *See* Robert P. Merges, *Of Property Rules, Coase, and Intellectual Property,* 94 Colum. L. Rev. 2655 (1994). The rules for injunctive relief changed substantially with *eBay, Inc. v. MercExchange LLC,* 547 U.S. 388 (2006); we discuss the impact of this change in much more detail in chapter 10.

48. *Cf.* Louis Kaplow & Steven Shavell, *Property Rules versus Liability Rules: An Economic Analysis,* 109 Harv. L. Rev. 713, 715 (1996). For a general discussion of valuation, *see* A. Mitchell Polinsky, *An Introduction to Law and Economics* 135-38 (2d ed., Aspen Law & Business, 1989).

49. *See* Rebecca S. Eisenberg, *Patents and the Progress of Science: Exclusive Rights and Experimental Use,* 56 U. Chi. L. Rev. 1017, 1072-73 (1989); Lemley, *Economics of Improvement, supra,* at 1048-72 (1997); Merges, *Bargaining Breakdown, supra,* at 82-89; Merges & Nelson, *supra.*

50. *See* Wesley M. Cohen & Daniel A. Levinthal, *Innovation and Learning: The Two Faces of R&D,* 99 Econ. J. 569 (1989); Zvi Griliches, *The Search for R&D Spillovers,* 94 Scand. J. Econ. S29 (Supp. 1992); Richard C. Levin, *Appropriability, R&D Spending, and Technological Performance,* 78 Am. Econ. Rev. 424, 427 (1988); *cf.* Suzanne Scotchmer, *Standing on the Shoulders of Giants: Cumulative Research and the Patent Law,* 5 J. Econ. Persp. 29, 30 (1991). For a general discussion of spillovers in the IP environment, *see* Brett M. Frischmann & Mark A. Lemley, *Spillovers,* 107 Colum. L. Rev. 257 (2007).

51. *See* Jennifer F. Reinganum, *The Timing of Innovation: Research, Development, and Diffusion, in* 1 *Handbook of Indus. Org.* 850 (Richard Schmalensee & Robert Willig eds., 1989); *Rent Control, supra* note 41 , at 370-71; *cf.* Mark F. Grady & Jay I. Alexander, *Patent Law and Rent Dissipation,* 78 Va. L. Rev. 305 (1992).

52. *See* Merges, *Bargaining Breakdown, supra,* at 91-99; Merges & Nelson, *supra,* at 911; Lemley, *Economics of Improvement, supra,* at 1010-13.

53. *See* Lemley, *Economics of Improvement, supra,* at 1007-13 (distinguishing between minor, significant, and radical improvements).

54. Carol Rose, *The Comedy of the Commons: Custom, Commerce, and Inherently Public Property,* 53 U. Chi. L. Rev. 711 (1986).

55. *Cf.* Dan Hunter, *Cyberspace as Place and the Tragedy of the Digital Anticommons,* 91 Cal. L. Rev. 439, 441-42 (2003); Mark A. Lemley, *Place and Cyberspace,* 91 Cal. L. Rev. 521, 523 (2003).

56. *See* Michael A. Heller, *The Tragedy of the Anticommons: Property in the Transition from Marx to Markets,* 111 Harv. L. Rev. 621 (1998).

57. *See* Michael A. Heller & Rebecca S. Eisenberg, *Can Patents Deter Innovation? The Anticommons in Biomedical Research,* 280 Sci. 698, 698-99 (1998). *See also* Arti K. Rai, *The Information Revolution Reaches Pharmaceuticals: Balancing Innovation Incentives, Cost, and Access in the Post-Genomics Era,* 2001 U. Ill. L. Rev. 173, 192-94 (2001).

58. *See* Heller, *supra,* at 670-72.

59. For more on the holdout problem, *see* generally Mancur Olson, *The Logic of Collective Action* (1961). On its specific application in patent law, *see* Rochelle Cooper Dreyfuss, *Varying the Course in Patenting Genetic Material: A Counter-Proposal to Richard Epstein's Steady Course, in Perspectives on Properties of the Human Genome Project* 196 (2005).

60. *See* Lloyd Cohen, *Holdouts and Free Riders,* 20 J. Legal Stud. 351, 356 (1991).

61. For discussion of this problem, *see* Mark A. Lemley & Philip J. Weiser, *Should Property or Liability Rules Govern Information?* 85 Tex. L. Rev. 783 (2007); Mark A. Lemley & Carl Shapiro, *Patent Holdup and Royalty Stacking,* 85 Tex. L. Rev. 1991 (2007).

62. For a technical proof of this, *see* Carl Shapiro, *Setting Compatibility Standards: Cooperation or Collusion?* in *Expanding the Boundaries of Intellectual Property* 81, 97–101 (Rochelle Cooper Dreyfuss et al., eds., 2001). For a description of the problem in practice, *see* Ken Krechmer, *Communications Standards and Patent Rights: Conflict or Coordination?* 3, available at http://www.csrstds.com/star.html (1997). *See also* Douglas Lichtman, *Property Rights in Emerging Platform Technologies,* 29 J. Legal Stud. 615, 615 (2000).

63. *See* Matthew Erramouspe, *Staking Patent Claims on the Human Blueprint: Rewards and Rent-Dissipating Races,* 43 UCLA L. Rev. 961, 998 (1996) ("[B]y setting stricter limits on gene patentability, the patent system can make the appropriate adjustment to reduce future rent dissipation among gene hunters").

64. *See, e.g.,* Philippe Jacobs & Geertrui Van Overwalle, *Gene Patents: A Different Approach,* [2001] Eur. Intell. Prop. Rev. 505, 505; Arti K. Rai, *Fostering Cumulative Innovation in the Biopharmaceutical Industry: The Role of Patents and Antitrust,* 16 Berkeley Tech. L.J. 813, 838 (2001).

65. Robert P. Merges, *Contracting into Liability Rules: Intellectual Property Rights and Collective Rights Organizations,* 84 Calif. L. Rev. 1293 (1996).

66. Lemley, *Rational Ignorance, supra,* at 1500; Allison & Lemley, *Empirical Evidence, supra,* at 205.

67. Carl Shapiro, *Navigating the Patent Thicket: Cross Licensing, Patent Pools, and Standard Setting, in* 1 Innovation Pol'y and the Econ. 119, 121 (Adam B. Jaffe et al. eds., 2001). *See also* James Bessen, *Patent Thickets: Strategic Patenting of Complex Technologies,* available at http://www.researchoninnovation.org/online.htm#thicket (2003).

68. *See* Gideon Parchomovsky & R. Polk Wagner, *Patent Portfolios,* 154 U. Pa. L. Rev. 1 (2005).

69. *See* Bessen, *supra,* at 1.

Chapter Seven

1. Merges & Nelson are a partial exception. They acknowledge that innovation works differently in different industries, and examine the characteristics of four different types of industries. Merges & Nelson, *supra,* at 880–908. Nonetheless, they ultimately emphasize only one characteristic of each industry—its dependence on cumulative innovation.

2. *See* Richard R. Nelson & Sidney G. Winter, *An Evolutionary Theory of Economic Change* 263 (1982).

3. *See* Gardiner Harris, "Cost of Developing Drugs Found to Rise," Wall St. J., Dec. 3, 2001, at B14.

4. Estimates of the average cost of drug development and testing range from $110 million to $500 million; the latter is the industry's figure. Compare Pharm. Res. and Mfrs. of Am., "Why Do Prescription Drugs Cost So Much and Other Questions about Your Medicines," at http://www.phrma.org/publications/publications/brochure/questions/ (2000), with Pub. Citizen, "Rebuttals to PhRMA Responses to Public Citizen Report Rx [Research and Development] Myths: The Case against the Drug Industry's 'Scare Card,'<ts>" at http://www

.citizen.org/congress/reform/drug_industry/corporate/articles.cfm?ID=6514 (last visited Aug. 13, 2003) (criticizing industry estimates and offering the lower figure).

5. Stuart Luman, "Strong Medicine," *Wired*, June 2004, at 150.

6. *See* http://www.phrma.org/publications/publications/brochure/questions/. Other estimates range from seven to fifteen years. *See* Richard J. Findlay, *Originator Drug Development*, 54 Food & Drug L.J. 227, 227 (1999).

7. *See, e.g.*, James W. Hughes et al., *"Napsterizing" Pharmaceuticals: Access, Innovation, and Consumer Welfare* (Nat'l Bureau of Econ. Res. Working Paper No. 9229, 2002).

8. Cohen & Merrill, *supra*, at 12 ("Economic research has made a convincing case that in at least one area—pharmaceuticals— patents have played a critical role in stimulating technical advance").

9. James Bessen & Michael Meurer, *Patent Failure: How Judges, Bureaucrats, and Lawyers Put Innovators at Risk* (2008).

10. Although pharmaceutical companies have tried to find ways to obtain multiple patents on the same basic invention in an effort to extend the life of their patents, these efforts are aberrations that represent a failure of the system, not its normal function. *See* Lara J. Glasgow, *Stretching the Limits of Intellectual Property Rights: Has the Pharmaceutical Industry Gone Too Far?* 41 Idea 227, 233-35 (2001). The patent doctrine of "double patenting" is designed to prevent this sort of abuse. *See, e.g., Eli Lilly & Co. v. Barr Labs.*, 251 F.3d 955, 967-68 (Fed. Cir. 2001).

11. B. N. Anand & T. Khanna, *The Structure of Licensing Contracts*, 48 J. Indus. Econ. 103 (2000).

12. *See, e.g., Hotel Security Checking Co. v. Lorraine Co.*, 160 F. 467 (2d Cir. 1908). *See also* Durham, *supra;* Thomas, *supra.*

13. *See State St. Bank & Trust v. Signature Fin. Group*, 149 F.3d 1368 (Fed. Cir. 1998). The United States is the only country to patent business methods. *See, e.g.*, William van Caenegem, *The Technicality Requirement, Patent Scope and Patentable Subject Matter in Australia*, 13 Austr. Intell. Prop. J. 41, 41 (2002).

14. *See, e.g.*, Dreyfuss, *supra;* Robert P. Merges, *Patent Law and Policy* 155 (2d ed. 1997). *But cf.* Mark A. Lemley et al., *Software and Internet Law* 317-21 (2000).

15. *Cf.* Mark A. Lemley & David W. O'Brien, *Encouraging Software Reuse*, 49 Stan. L. Rev. 255, 274-75 (1997).

16. *See* Julie E. Cohen & Mark A. Lemley, *Patent Scope and Innovation in the Software Industry*, 89 Calif. L. Rev. 1, 7-16 (2001).

17. *See, e.g., League for Programming Freedom, Software Patents: Is This the Future of Programming?* Dr. Dobb's J., Nov. 1990, at 56.

18. *See* Lemley & Lessig, *supra*, at 933-38.

19. *See* Scotchmer, *supra*, at 29.

20. *See* Cohen & Lemley, *supra* note 16, at 40-42; Peter S. Menell, *Tailoring Legal Protection for Computer Software*, 39 Stan. L. Rev. 1329, 1369-70 (1987); Samuelson et al., *supra*, at 2376.

21. On reuse of existing code, both within and across companies, *see* Lemley & O'Brien, *supra.*

22. *See* Lemley & O'Brien, *supra*, at 265.

23. *See, e.g., DSC Communications Corp. v. DGI Techs., Inc.*, 81 F.3d 597, 601 (5th Cir. 1996); *Bateman v. Mnemonics, Inc.*, 79 F.3d 1532, 1539 n.18 (11th Cir. 1996); *Lotus Dev. Corp. v. Borland Int'l, Inc.*, 49 F.3d 807, 817-18 (1st Cir. 1995) (Boudin, J., concurring); *Atari Games Corp.*

v. Nintendo of America, Inc., 975 F.2d 832, 843–44 (Fed. Cir. 1992) (refusing to find reverse engineering to be copyright infringement); *Sega Enters. Ltd. v. Accolade, Inc.*, 977 F.2d 1510, 1527–28 (9th Cir. 1992); *Vault Corp. v. Quaid Software Ltd.*, 847 F.2d 255, 270 (5th Cir. 1988); *Mitel, Inc. v. Iqtel, Inc.*, 896 F. Supp. 1050, 1056–57 (D. Colo. 1995), aff'd on other grounds, 124 F.3d 1366 (10th Cir. 1997). A few early decisions rejected compatibility as a justification for copying. *See, e.g., Apple Computer, Inc. v. Franklin Computer Corp.*, 714 F.2d 1240, 1253–54 (3d Cir. 1983). And the Federal Circuit has held (over a dissent by Judge Dyk) that software companies can forbid reverse engineering in a shrink-wrap license, an approach which, if widely adopted, would render the compatibility justification essentially worthless. *Bowers v. Baystate Technologies*, 320 F.3d 1317, 1324–26 (Fed. Cir. 2003); *cf. DSC Communications Corp. v. Pulse Communications, Inc.*, 170 F.3d 1354, 1363 (Fed. Cir. 1999).

As with courts, the overwhelming majority of commentators endorse a right to reverse engineer copyrighted software, at least for certain purposes. *See, e.g.*, Jonathan Band & Masanobu Katoh, *Interfaces on Trial: Intellectual Property and Interoperability in the Global Software Industry* 167–226 (1995); Cohen, *supra;* Lawrence D. Graham & Richard O. Zerbe Jr., *Economically Efficient Treatment of Computer Software: Reverse Engineering, Protection, and Disclosure*, 22 Rutgers Computer & Tech. L.J. 61 (1996); Dennis S. Karjala, *Copyright Protection of Computer Software, Reverse Engineering, and Professor Miller*, 19 U. Dayton L. Rev. 975, 1016–18 (1994); Maureen A. O'Rourke, *Drawing the Boundary between Copyright and Contract: Copyright Preemption of Software License Terms*, 45 Duke L.J. 479, 534 (1995); David A. Rice, *Sega and Beyond: A Beacon for Fair Use Analysis . . . At Least as Far as It Goes*, 19 U. Dayton L. Rev. 1131, 1168 (1994); Pamela Samuelson, *Fair Use for Computer Programs and Other Copyrightable Works in Digital Form: The Implications of Sony, Galoob, and Sega*, 1 J. Intell. Prop. L. 49, 86–98 (1993); Timothy Teter, *Merger and the Machines: An Analysis of the Pro-Compatibility Trend in Computer Software Copyright Cases*, 45 Stan. L. Rev. 1061, 1062–63 (1993). *See also* Pamela Samuelson & Suzanne Scotchmer, *The Law and Economics of Reverse Engineering*, 111 Yale L.J. 1575, 1579 (2002); Cohen & Lemley, *supra*, at 17–21.

For a contrary view, *see generally* Anthony L. Clapes, *Confessions of an Amicus Curiae: Technophobia, Law, and Creativity in the Digital Arts*, 19 U. Dayton L. Rev. 903, 906–7 (1994); Arthur R. Miller, *Copyright Protection for Computer Programs, Databases, and Computer-Generated Works: Is Anything New since CONTU?* 106 Harv. L. Rev. 977, 1013–32 (1993) (same).

24. *See, e.g.*, Micalyn S. Harris, *UCITA: Helping David Face Goliath*, 18 J. Marshall J. Computer & Info. L. 365, 375 (1999).

25. On changes in the software industry, *see* David S. Evans & Anne Lanye-Farrar, *Software Patents and Open Source: The Battle over Intellectual Property Rights*, 9 Va. J. L. & Tech. 10 (2004).

26. For a contrary view, *see* Patrick K. Bobko, *Open-Source Software and the Demise of Copyright*, 27 Rutgers Comp. & Tech. L.J. 51, 58–60 (2001). It is trivially easy to counterfeit existing software, but it is illegal under copyright law, and the relevant costs are the costs of legal imitation under a regime without patents but with other forms of IP protection intact.

27. *See* the Digital Millenium Copyright Act, 17 U.S.C. § 1201 (2003).

28. Cohen & Lemley, *supra*, at 39–50.

29. For a detailed discussion, *see* Samuelson et al., *supra*, at 2350–56; Pamela Samuelson, *CONTU Revisited: The Case against Copyright Protection for Computer Programs in Machine-Readable Form*, 1984 Duke L.J. 663, 733.

30. Samuelson worries that software patents may be too broad, given the incremental nature of software innovation. Samuelson et al., *supra*, at 2345–46. *See also* Pamela Samuel-

son, *Benson Revisited: The Case against Patent Protection for Algorithms and Other Computer Program-Related Inventions,* 39 Emory L.J. 1025 (1990). As noted below, we share this concern, but believe that the solution is to narrow the scope of those patents.

31. *See* Lemley, *Rational Ignorance, supra,* at 1507.

32. *See generally* Richard R. Nelson, *Intellectual Property Protection for Cumulative Systems Technology,* 94 Colum. L. Rev. 2674 (1994).

33. Biotechnology products appear in a wide variety of economic sectors, from pharmaceuticals to foodstuffs to industrial processes. *See* Dan L. Burk, *Introduction: A Biotechnology Primer,* 55 U. Pitt. L. Rev. 611, 621–28 (1994). Much of our discussion here focuses on the subset of biotechnology that includes gene sequences and gene therapy.

34. For a discussion of this process, *see Eli Lilly & Co. v. Medtronic, Inc.,* 496 U.S. 661, 676 (1990).

35. *See* Dan L. Burk & Mark A. Lemley, *Biotechnology's Uncertainty Principle,* in 50 *Advances in Genetics: Perspectives on Properties of the Human Genome Project* 305 (2003); Robert A Hodges, *Black Box Biotech Inventions: When a Mere "Wish or Plan" Should Be Considered an Adequate Description of the Invention,* 17 Ga. St. U. L. Rev. 831, 832 (2001).

36. *See, e.g.,* S. M. Thomas et al., *Ownership of the Human Genome,* 380 Nature 387, 387–88 (1996).

37. *See* Rebecca S. Eisenberg, *Reaching through the Genome,* in *Perspectives on Properties of the Human Genome Project* at 209 (F. Scott Kieff ed., 2003). Efforts to write patent claims that "reach through" to cover technologies developed with a research tool have been less successful, however. *See Univ. of Rochester v. G.D. Searle, Inc.,* 249 F. Supp. 2d 216 (W.D.N.Y. 2003).

38. Iain Cockburn argues that biotechnology represents the vertical disintegration of the pharmaceutical industry. Iain M. Cockburn, *O Brave New Industry, That Has Such Patents in It! Reflections on the Economic Consequences of Patenting DNA,* in *Perspectives on Properties of the Human Genome Project* 385, 388 (F. Scott Kieff ed., 2003). If so, reversing that trend may solve the anticommons problems disintegration has created. Cockburn makes this suggestion too. *Id.* at 396–97.

39. *See* Rai, *supra,* at 833–35.

40. *See id.* at 838; *cf.* Rebecca S. Eisenberg & Robert P. Merges, *Opinion Letter as to the Patentability of Certain Inventions Associated with the Identification of Partial cDNA Sequences,* 23 AIPLA Q.J. 1 (1995). The Federal Circuit held ESTs unpatentable in *In re Fisher,* 421 F.3d 1365 (Fed. Cir. 2005).

41. *See* Robert P. Merges, *A New Dynamism in the Public Domain,* 71 U. Chi. L. Rev. 183 (2004); Stephen M. Maurer, Arti Rai, & Andrej Sali, *Finding Cures for Tropical Diseases: Is Open Source an Answer?* 1 PLoS Medicine, 183, 184 (2004).

42. David Adelman makes this argument. David E. Adelman, *A Fallacy of the Commons in Biotech Patent Policy,* 20 Berkeley Tech. L.J. 985 (2005).

43. John P. Walsh et al., *The Patenting and Licensing of Research Tools and Biomedical Innovation,* in *Patents in the Knowledge-Based Economy* (Nat'l Res. Council 2003).

44. For a suggestion that ignoring patents is quite common in many industries, and explains the avoidance of the anticommons in patent law, *see* Mark A. Lemley, *Ignoring Patents,* 2008 Mich. St. L. Rev. 1.

45. Adelman discusses the scientific literature in detail. Adelman, *supra.*

46. Fiona Murray & Scott Stern, *Do Formal Intellectual Property Rights Hinder the Free Flow of Scientific Knowledge? An Empirical Test of the Anti-Commons Hypothesis,* NBER Working Paper 11465 (2005), available at http://ssrn.com/abstract=755701.

47. Arti Rai has suggested that the best way to deal with the anticommons problem is to narrow the scope of the research tool patents. Arti K. Rai, *Genome Patents: A Case Study in Patenting Research Tools,* 77 Acad. Med. 1368, 1371 (2002). But gene therapy developers will almost certainly want to use the actual human DNA sequences, not simulacra, meaning that even narrow patents will still produce the anticommons problem.

48. R. David Kryder et al., *The Intellectual and Technical Property Components of Pro-Vitamin A Rice (GoldenRice™): A Preliminary Freedom to Operate Review,* ISAAA Briefs No. 20 (2000).

49. *See* Linda J. Demaine & Aaron Xavier Fellmeth, *Reinventing the Double Helix: A Novel and Nonobvious Reconceptualization of the Biotechnology Patent,* 55 Stan. L. Rev. 303, 414 (2002).

50. *See, e.g.,* LaPedus, *supra.*

51. *See* Bronwyn H. Hall & Rosemarie Ham Ziedonis, *The Patent Paradox Revisited: An Empirical Study of Patenting in the U.S. Semiconductor Industry, 1979–1995,* 32 RAND J. Econ. 101, 102 (2001); John H. Barton, *Antitrust Treatment of Oligopolies with Mutually Blocking Patent Portfolios,* 69 Antitrust L.J. 851, 854 (2002).

52. *See* Lemley, *Rational Ignorance, supra,* at 1504–05; Mark A. Lemley, *Reconceiving Patents in the Age of Venture Capital,* 4 J. Small & Emerging Bus. L. 143 (2000); David J. Teece, *Managing Intellectual Capital* 193–224 (2000).

53. *See* John R. Allison et al., *Valuable Patents,* 92 Geo. L.J. 453 (2004).

54. B. N. Anand & T. Khanna, *The Structure of Licensing Contracts,* 48 J. Indus. Econ. 103 (2000).

55. David J. Teece, *Managing Intellectual Capital* 222 (2000).

56. James Bessen & Eric Maskin, *Sequential Innovation, Patents, and Imitation* 7 (Mass. Inst. of Tech. 2006), http:// sss.ias.edu/publications/papers/econpaper25.pdf.

57. Gideon Parchomovsky & R. Polk Wagner, *Patent Portfolios,* 154 U. Pa. L. Rev. 1 (2005).

58. James Bessen, *Patent Thickets: Strategic Patenting of Complex Technologies* (working paper 2003), available at http://www.ssrn.com/abstract=327760.

59. *Id.*

60. Weston Headley, "Rapporteur's Report, The Stanford Workshop on Intellectual Property and Industry Competitive Standards," Stanford Law School, April 17, 1998, at 17 (quoting Michael Rostoker).

61. For a discussion of the benefits of such a market, and the potential holdout problems it might create, *see* Lemley & O'Brien, *supra.*

62. *See* Rai, *supra.*

Chapter Eight

1. We are indebted to Pam Samuelson and Suzanne Scotchmer for the term "policy levers." *See* Pamela Samuelson & Suzanne Scotchmer, *The Law and Economics of Reverse Engineering,* 111 Yale L.J. 1575, 1581 (2002).

2. *Diamond v. Chakrabarty,* 447 U.S. 303, 309 (1980).

3. *See* 35 U.S.C. § 155A (2000). On the history of private patent legislation, *see* Robert Patrick Merges & Glenn Harlan Reynolds, *The Proper Scope of the Copyright and Patent Power*, 37 Harv. J. Legis. 45, 46–50 (2000).

4. *See* Business Method Patent Improvement Act of 2000, H.R. 5364, 106th Cong.; Patent Fairness Act of 1999, H.R. 1598, 106th Cong.; Kristin E. Behrendt, *The Hatch-Waxman Act: Balancing Competing Interests or Survival of the Fittest?* 57 Food & Drug. L.J. 247, 253 (2002).

5. *See, e.g.,* Samuelson, *supra.*

6. *See, e.g.,* Matthew G. Wells, *Internet Business Method Patent Policy*, 87 Va. L. Rev. 729, 770–73 (2001).

7. *See, e.g.,* Peter S. Menell, *Tailoring Legal Protection for Computer Software*, 39 Stan. L. Rev. 1329 (1987); Samuelson et al., *supra*, at 2310–12. For a somewhat different proposal, *see* Lester C. Thurow, *Needed: A New System of Intellectual Property Rights*, Harv. Bus. Rev. Sept.–Oct. 1997, at 94.

8. For discussion, *see* John C. Phillips, *Sui Generis Intellectual Property Protection for Computer Software*, 60 Geo. Wash. L. Rev. 997 (1992); Leo J. Raskind, *The Uncertain Case for Special Legislative Protecting Computer Software*, 47 U. Pitt. L. Rev. 1131 (1986); Pamela Samuelson, *Modifying Copyrighted Software: Adjusting Copyright Doctrine to Accommodate a Technology*, 28 Jurimetrics J. 179 (1988); Richard Stern, *The Bundle of Rights Suited to New Technology*, 47 U. Pitt. L. Rev. 1229, 1262–67 (1986).

9. *See, e.g.,* Dan L. Burk, *Copyrightability of Recombinant DNA Sequences*, 29 Jurimetrics J. 469 (1989); S. Benjamin Pleune, *Trouble with the Guidelines: On Urging the PTO to Properly Evolve with Novel Technologies*, 2001 J.L. Tech. & Pol'y 365.

10. For a critical analysis of such proposals, *see* Dan L. Burk, *Biotechnology and Patent Law: Fitting Innovation to the Procrustean Bed*, 17 Rutgers Computer & Tech. L.J. 1 (1991).

11. *See, e.g.,* Dan L. Burk, *Patenting Transgenic Human Embryos: A Nonuse Cost Perspective*, 30 Hous. L. Rev. 1597, 1600, 1658–65 (1993); Mark O. Hatfield, *From Microbe to Man*, 1 Animal L. 5, 6, 9 (1995); Kojo Yelpaala, *Owning the Secret of Life: Biotechnology and Property Rights Revisited*, 32 McGeorge L. Rev. 111, 200 (2000). For a very different argument against the patenting of cDNA sequences, *see* Eisenberg & Merges, *supra.*

12. *See, e.g.,* Hodges, *supra*, at 835; Janice M. Mueller, *The Evolving Application of the Written Description Requirement to Biotechnological Inventions*, 13 Berkeley Tech. L.J. 615, 633–49 (1998); Harris A. Pitlick, *The Mutation on the Description Requirement Gene*, 80 J. Pat. & Trademark Off. Soc'y 209, 222–25 (1998); Cliff D. Weston, *Chilling of the Corn: Agricultural Biotechnology in the Face of U.S. Patent Law and the Cartagena Protocol*, 4 J. Small & Emerging Bus. L. 377, 389–92 (2000).

For the related argument that the biotechnology written-description cases are really about enablement and serve to obscure the real purposes of the written description requirement, *see* Mark D. Janis, *On Courts Herding Cats: Contending with the "Written Description" Requirement (and Other Unruly Patent Disclosure Doctrines)*, 2 Wash. U. J.L. & Pol'y 55 (2000).

13. *See* Karen I. Boyd, *Nonobviousness and the Biotechnology Industry: A Proposal for a Doctrine of Economic Nonobviousness*, 12 Berkeley Tech. L.J. 311, 311–13 (1997).

14. *See, e.g.,* Rai, *supra*, at 838.

15. *See* Rai, *supra*, at 838–44.

16. *See* Craig R. Miles, *Goldilocks Patent Protection for DNA Inventions: Not Too Thick, Not Too Thin, But Just Right*, 2 Modern Trends in Intell. Prop. 3 (1998).

17. *See* Nancy Gallini & Suzanne Scotchmer, *Intellectual Property: When Is It the Best Incentive System?* in *Innovation Policy and the Economy,* 51, 53, 71 (Adam B. Jaffe et al. eds., 2001); Robert P. Merges & Richard R. Nelson, *On the Complex Economics of Patent Scope,* 90 Colum. L. Rev. 839, 843 (1990); *cf.* John R. Allison & Mark A. Lemley, *The Growing Complexity of the U.S. Patent System,* 82 B. U. L. Rev. 77, 142–44 (2002) (noting that patents are more industry-specific than they used to be, and that this is likely to lead to calls for industry-specific patent reform).

18. For a discussion of the possible international problems with industry-specific legislation, with specific reference to software, *see* Rochelle Cooper Dreyfuss, *Information Products: A Challenge to Intellectual Property Theory,* 20 N.Y.U. J. Int'l L. & Pol'y 897, 912–18 (1988).

19. *See* TRIPs, *supra* note 2, art. 27 (1), at 93–94.

20. *See* Burk & Lemley, *Technology-Specific, supra* at 1183–85.

21. *See, e.g.,* Erwin J. Basinski, *The European Union's Proposed Directive on Computer-Implemented Inventions: What Price 'Interoperability'?* 3 World eCommerce & IP Report (August 2003).

22. For an exploration of legal issues related to nanotechnology, *see* Mark A. Lemley, *Patenting Nanotechnology,* 58 Stan. L. Rev. 601 (2005); Frederick A. Fiedler & Glenn H. Reynolds, *Legal Problems of Nanotechnology: An Overview,* 3 S. Cal. Interdisc. L.J. 593 (1995).

23. *See, e.g., Symposium on Bioinformatics and Intellectual Property Law: Open Source Genomics,* 8 B.U. J. Sci. & Tech. L. 254, 254–62 (2002).

24. *See* John R. Allison & Mark A. Lemley, *Who's Patenting What? An Empirical Exploration of Patent Prosecution,* 53 Vand. L. Rev. 2099, 2114 n.45 (2000).

25. John R. Allison & Mark A. Lemley, *The Growing Complexity of the United States Patent System,* 82 B.U. L. Rev. 77 (2002) (documenting the increase from 1.37 to 1.49 technology areas per invention between the 1970s and the 1990s).

26. *See Brooktree Corp. v. Advanced Micro Devices,* 977 F.2d 1555 (Fed. Cir. 1992); *Altera Corp. v. Clear Logic Corp.,* 424 F.3d 1079 (Fed. Cir. 2005).

27. *See* Mark A. Lemley et al., *Software and Internet Law* 411 (1st ed. 2000) (making this point).

28. *See In re Ochiai,* 71 F.3d 1565 (Fed. Cir. 1995).

29. *See* Mark D. Janis & Jay P. Kesan, *U.S. Plant Variety Protection: Sound and Fury . . . ?* 39 Houston L. Rev. 727 (2002) (United States PVPA); Stephen M Maurer et al., *Europe's Database Experiment,* 294 Science 789 (2001) (EU Database Directive).

30. European Commission, *DG Internal Market and Services Working Paper: First Evaluation of Directive 96/9/EC on the Legal Protection of Databases* (Dec. 12, 2005).

31. The Supreme Court upheld the validity of such patents in *J.E.M. Ag Supply v. Pioneer Hi-Bred Int'l,* 534 U.S. 124 (2001).

32. *See* Guido Calabresi, *A Common Law for the Age of Statutes* (1982).

33. *See* Suzanna Sherry, *Haste Makes Waste: Congress and the Common Law in Cyberspace,* 55 Vand. L. Rev. 309 (2002).

34. *See* Daniel A. Farber & Philip P. Frickey, *The Jurisprudence of Public Choice,* 65 Tex. L. Rev. 873 (1987).

35. *See, e.g.,* John R. Allison & Emerson H. Tiller, *The Business Method Patent Myth,* 18 Berkeley Tech. L.J. 987 (2003).

36. On the unnecessary complexity of the copyright laws, *see* Jessica Litman, *Digital Copyright* 25 (2001); Jessica Litman, *Revising Copyright Law for the Information Age,* 75 Or.

L. Rev. 19, 22–23 (1996); Jessica Litman, *The Exclusive Right to Read,* 13 Cardozo Arts & Ent. L.J. 29, 34 (1994).

37. 35 U.S.C. § 103(b) (biotechnological processes), § 155A (private patent relief), § 156 (pharmaceutical patent term extension), and § 287 (medical process patents).

38. *See Andrx Pharm., Inc. v. Biovail Corp.,* 256 F.3d 799 (D.C. Cir. 2001), cert. denied, 535 U.S. 931 (2002); *In re Cardizem CD Antitrust Litig.,* 332 F.3d 896 (6th Cir. 2003). On the legality of such collusion, *compare* Roger D. Blair & Thomas F. Cotter, *Are Settlements of Patent Disputes Illegal Per Se?* 47 Antitrust Bull. 491, 532–38 (2002) *with* Herbert Hovenkamp et al., *Anticompetitive Settlements of Intellectual Property Disputes,* 87 Minn. L. Rev. 1719, 1728–29 (2003) (arguing that per se illegality is appropriate in some cases).

39. *eBay, Inc. v. MercExchange LLC,* 547 U.S. 388 (2006).

40. *MedImmune Inc. v. Genentech Corp.,* 127 S.Ct. 764 (2007).

41. *KSR Corp. v. Teleflex Corp.,* 127 S.Ct. 1727 (2007).

42. *In re Seagate Technology LLC,* 497 F.3d 1360 (Fed. Cir. 2007) (en banc).

43. *Tafas v. Dudas,* 541 F. Supp. 2d 805 (E.D. Va. 2008).

44. *See* Dan L. Burk & Mark A. Lemley, *Policy Levers in Patent Law,* 79 Va. L. Rev. 1575 (2003); Dan L. Burk & Mark A. Lemley, *Is Patent Law Technology Specific?* 17 Berkeley Tech. L.J. 1155 (2002).

45. Gilmore, *supra,* at 96.

46. *Id.*

47. *See, e.g.,* Richard Gilbert & Carl Shapiro, *Optimal Patent Length and Breadth,* 21 RAND J. Econ. 106, 106 (1990); Robert P. Merges & Richard R. Nelson, *On the Complex Economics of Patent Scope,* 90 Colum. L. Rev. 839, 839, 916 (1990).

48. The body of literature on this topic is extensive. *See, e.g.,* Louis Kaplow, *Rules versus Standards: An Economic Analysis,* 42 Duke L.J. 557 (1992); Duncan Kennedy, *Form and Substance in Private Law Adjudication,* 89 Harv. L. Rev. 1685 (1976); Russell B. Korobkin, *Behavioral Analysis and Legal Form: Rules vs. Standards Revisited,* 79 Or. L. Rev. 23 (2000); Eric A. Posner, *Standards, Rules, and Social Norms,* 21 Harv. J.L. & Pub. Pol'y 101 (1997); Frederick Schauer, *Playing by the Rules: A Philosophical Examination of Rule-Based Decision-Making in Law and in Life* (1991); Pierre Schlag, *Rules and Standards,* 33 UCLA L. Rev. 379 (1985); Cass R. Sunstein, *Problems with Rules,* 83 Cal. L. Rev. 953 (1995).

For a debate on the merits of rules and standards in patent law, *see* Robert P. Merges & John Fitzgerald Duffy, *Patent Law and Policy* 805–06 (3d ed. 2002); John R. Thomas, *Formalism at the Federal Circuit,* 52 Am. U. L. Rev. 771 (2003); R. Polk Wagner, *Reconsidering Estoppel: Patent Administration and the Failure of* Festo, 151 U. Pa. L. Rev. 159, 234–37 (2002).

49. *See* Frederick Schauer, *Profiles, Probabilities, and Stereotypes,* 299 (2007). Another version of this problem appears in the literature on "default rules" where some law is characterized as inflexible and mandatory and other law is characterized as a permissive default that can be waived or varied by private contract adapted to the situation of particular contracting parties. For discussion of this paradigm of default rules, *see* Ian Ayres & Robert Gertner, *Filling Gaps in Incomplete Contracts: An Economic Theory of Default Rules,* 99 Yale L.J. 87 (1989); Ian Ayres & Robert Gertner, *Strategic Contractual Inefficiency and the Optimal Choice of Legal Rules,* 101 Yale L.J. 729 (1992); Randy E. Barnett, *The Sound of Silence: Default Rules and Contractual Consent,* 78 Va. L. Rev. 821, 831–55, 860–73 (1992); Einer Elhauge, *Preference-Eliciting Statutory Default Rules,* 102 Colum. L. Rev. 2162 (2002); Einer Elhauge, *Preference-Estimating Statutory Default Rules,* 102 Colum. L. Rev. 2027 (2002).

50. *Cf.* Gordon Tullock, *Trials on Trial: The Pure Theory of Legal Procedure*, 28–30, 199 (1980).

51. Grant Gilmore, *The Ages of American Law* 95 (1977).

52. *See* Burk & Lemley, *Policy Levers, supra.*

53. *See* Einer Elhauge, *Does Interest Group Theory Justify More Intrusive Judicial Review?* 101 Yale L.J. 31, 67–68 (1991); A. C. Pritchard & Todd J. Zywicki, *Finding the Constitution: An Economic Analysis of Tradition's Role in Constitutional Interpretation,* 77 N.C. L. Rev. 409, 494 (1999).

54. *Cf.* Rochelle Cooper Dreyfuss, *The Federal Circuit: A Case Study in Specialized Courts,* 64 N.Y.U. L. Rev. 1, 14–15 (1989); Rochelle Cooper Dreyfuss, *The Federal Circuit: A Continuing Experiment in Specialization, 54 Case W. Res. 769 (2004).*

55. *See* Calabresi, *supra* at 46–47.

56. *Id.* at 48.

57. *See, e.g.,* Arti K. Rai, *Engaging Facts and Policy: A Multi-Institutional Approach to Patent System Reform,* 103 Colum. L. Rev. 1035 (2003); Arti K. Rai, *Allocating Power over Fact-Finding in the Patent System, 19 Berkeley Tech. L.J. 907 (2004).*

58. *See Dickinson v. Zurko,* 527 U.S. 150 *(1999).*

59. *See Merck & Co., Inc. v. Kessler,* 80 F.3d 1543 (Fed. Cir. 1996) (pre-*Zurko* Federal Circuit decision holding that the Patent Office is not an administrative agency with rulemaking powers that would require deference to the Office's interpretation of statutes).

60. *Cf.* Orin S. Kerr, *Rethinking Patent Law in the Administrative State,* 42 Wm & Mary L. Rev. 127 (2000) (arguing that private innovation incentives are better served by stringent judicial oversight of the Patent Office).

61. *Marbury v. Madison,* 5 U.S. (1 Cranch) 137 (1803).

Chapter Nine

1. 383 U.S. 519 (1966).

2. *See, e.g., Juicy Whip, Inc. v. Orange Bang, Inc.,* 185 F.3d 1364, 1367 (Fed. Cir. 1999); *Whistler Corp. v. Autotronics, Inc.,* 14 U.S.P.Q.2d (BNA) 1885, 1886 (N.D. Tex. 1988; *Ex parte* Murphy, 200 U.S.P.Q. (BNA) 801, 802 (Bd. Pat. App. and Inter. 1977) (rejecting proposition that immoral gambling invention lacked utility).

3. *See, e.g., Juicy Whip,* 185 F.3d at 1365–67.

4. *See* Margo A. Bagley, *Patent First, Ask Questions Later: Morality and Biotechnology in Patent Law,* 45 Wm. & Mary L. Rev. 469 (2003).

5. Robert P. Merges, *Intellectual Property in Higher Life Forms: The Patent System and Controversial Technologies,* 47 Md. L. Rev. 1051 (1988).

6. *See, e.g.,* U.S. Patent No. 4,998,724 (issued Mar. 12, 1991) ("Thumb-Wrestling Game Apparatus with Stabilizing Handle"); U.S. Patent No. 5,031,161 (issued Jul. 9, 1991) ("Life Expectancy Timepiece"); U.S. Patent No. 5,076,262 (issued Dec. 31, 1991) ("Ear-Flattening Device").

7. Robert P. Merges & John F. Duffy, *Patent Law and Policy,* 229 (4th ed. 2007).

8. *Whistler Corp. v. Autotronics, Inc.,* 14 U.S.P.Q.2d 1885 (N.D. Tex. 1988).

9. 383 U.S. 519 (1966).

10. *In re Fisher,* 421 F.3d 1365 (Fed. Cir. 2005); Request for Comments on Proposed Utility Examination Guidelines, 60 Fed. Reg. 97, 98 (Jan. 3, 1995).

11. Request for Comments on Proposed Utility Examination Guidelines, 60 Fed. Reg. 97, 98 (Jan. 3, 1995).

12. *See In re Brana*, 51 F.3d 1560, 1567 (Fed. Cir. 1995).

13. *See, e.g., In re Ziegler*, 992 F.2d 1197, 1203 (Fed. Cir. 1993).

14. The proper showing of utility necessary for ESTs has been the subject of considerable academic debate. *See* Robert P. Merges & Rebecca S. Eisenberg, *Opinion Letter as to the Patentability of Certain Inventions Associated with the Identification of Partial cDNA Sequences,* 23 AIPLA Q.J. 1, 20 (1995); Julian David Forman, *A Timing Perspective on the Utility Requirement in Biotechnology Patent Applications,* 12 Alb. L.J. Sci. & Tech. 647, 679–81 (2002).

15. Utility Examination Guidelines, 66 Fed. Reg. 1092, 1098 (Jan. 5, 2001).

16. *In re Fisher*, 421 F.3d 1365 (Fed. Cir. 2005).

17. 72 U.S.P.Q. 2d 1020 (Bd. Pat. App. and Int. 2004).

18. The European rules are more straightforward about the fact that they apply only to gene sequences. EU Biotechnology Directive article 5(3); European Patent Convention r.23e(3).

19. *See, e.g., In re Kirk*, 376 F.2d 936, 961 (C.C.P.A. 1967) (Rich, J., dissenting). Forman endorses the use of utility as a technology-specific policy lever, though he believes the doctrine as applied to biotechnology is currently too powerful. Julian David Forman, *A Timing Perspective on the Utility Requirement in Biotechnology Patent Applications,* 12 Alb. L.J. Sci. & Tech. 647, 650 (2002).

20. *Brenner*, 383 U.S. at 534.

21. *See, e.g.,* Eric Mirabel, *Practical Utility Is a Useless Concept,* 36 Am. U. L. Rev. 811 (1987); A. Samuel Oddi, *Beyond Obviousness: Invention Protection in the Twenty-First Century,* 38 Am. U. L. Rev. 1097, 1127 (1989); Charles E. Smith, *Comment, Requirements for Patenting Chemical Intermediates: Do They Accomplish the Statutory Goals?* 29 St. Louis U. L.J. 191, 202–04 (1984).

22. 97 U.S. 126 (1877).

23. *See, e.g., Pfaff v. Wells Elecs.*, 525 U.S. 55, 64 (1998).

24. *See, e.g., Lough v. Brunswick Corp.*, 86 F.3d 1113, 1120 (Fed. Cir. 1996).

25. *Atlanta Attachment Co. v. Leggett & Platt, Inc.,* 516 F.3d 1361 (Fed. Cir. 2008).

26. *Whittemore v. Cutter,* 29 F. Cas. 1120, 1121 (C.C.D. Mass. 1813) (No. 17,600).

27. *See, e.g., Roche Prods. v. Bolar Pharm. Co.,* 733 F.2d 858, 862–63 (Fed. Cir. 1984); *Madey v. Duke Univ.,* 307 F.3d 1351 (Fed. Cir. 2002). There is also a separate statutory experimental use defense that is limited to uses by generic drug makers of patented products during preparations for FDA approval of abbreviated new drug applications (ANDAs). 35 U.S.C. § 271(e)(1). That statutory doctrine was construed narrowly by the Federal Circuit in *Integra LifeSciences Inc. v. Merck KGaA,* 331 F.3d 860 (Fed. Cir. 2003). The statutory experimental use defense does of course treat pharmaceutical inventions differently than other industries, but because it is a statutory rather than a judicially created policy lever we don't discuss it further here.

28. *Madey v. Duke Univ.,* 307 F.3d 1351 (Fed. Cir. 2002).

29. *See, e.g.,* Rebecca Eisenberg, *Patents and the Progress of Science: Exclusive Rights and Experimental Use,* 56 U. Chi. L. Rev. 1017, 1021 (1989); Janice Mueller, *No Dilettante Affair: Rethinking the Experimental Use Exception to Patent Infringement for Biomedical Research Tools,* 76 Wash. L. Rev. 1 (2001); Suzanne T. Michel, *The Experimental Use Exception to Infringement Applied to Federally Funded Inventions,* 7 High Tech. L.J. 369, 372 (1992).

30. *See, e.g., Micro Chems. Ltd. v. Smith Kline & French InterAmerican Corp.,* [1972] S.C.R. 506, 520, 2 C.P.R.(2d) 193 (Sup. Ct. Canada); Rebecca S. Eisenberg, *Patent Swords and Shields,* 299 Sci. 1018, 1018 (2003).

31. Cohen & Lemley, *supra*, at 16–21.

32. Katherine J. Strandburg, *What Does the Public Get? Experimental Use and the Patent Bargain*, 2004 Wisc. L. Rev. 81. Jian Xiao argues for a similar distinction in the *statutory* experimental use exemption for FDA trials in 35 U.S.C. § 271(e)(1). Jian Xiao, *Carving Out a Biotechnology Research Tool Exception to the Safe Harbor Provision of 35 U.S.C. § 271(e)(1)*, 12 Tex. Intell. Prop. L.J. 23 (2003).

33. *See Newman v. Quigg*, 877 F.2d 1575, 1581–82 (Fed. Cir. 1989).

34. *Orthokinetics, Inc. v. Safety Travel Chairs, Inc.*, 806 F.2d 1565 (Fed. Cir. 1986). But *cf. Exxon Eng'g v. United States*, 265 F.3d 1371 (Fed. Cir. 2001) (treating indefiniteness as a question of law).

35. *See* Craig Allen Nard, *A Theory of Claim Interpretation*, 14 Harv. J. L. & Tech. 1, 6 (2000).

36. *Graver Tank & Mfg. Co. v. Linde Air Prods. Co.*, 339 U.S. 605, 609 (1950).

37. *See Hilton Davis Chem. Co. v. Warner-Jenkinson Co.*, 62 F.3d 1512, 1519 (Fed. Cir. 1995) (en banc), rev'd on other grounds, 520 U.S. 17 (1997).

38. Becky Eisenberg argues that the PHOSITA standard is underutilized in practice, because Federal Circuit cases in the obviousness line mistakenly discourage the examiner from relying on their own knowledge in the field, requiring instead a focus on documentary suggestions to combine references. Rebecca Eisenberg, *Consulting PHOSITA*, 19 Berkeley Tech. L.J. 885, 888 (2004).

39. John R. Allison & Mark A. Lemley, *Empirical Evidence on the Validity of Litigated Patents*, 26 AIPLA Q.J. 185 (1998).

40. *KSR, Inc. v. Teleflex, Inc.*, 127 S.Ct. 1727 (2007).

41. 383 U.S. 1 (1966).

42. *See, e.g., Ruiz v. A.B. Chance Co.*, 234 F.3d 654, 662–63 (Fed. Cir. 2000).

43. *See Brown & Williamson Tobacco Co. v. Philip Morris, Inc.*, 229 F.3d 1120, 1129 (Fed. Cir. 2000).

44. *See Custom Accessories v. Jeffrey-Allan Indus.*, 807 F.2d 955, 960 (Fed. Cir. 1986).

45. *KSR, Inc. v. Teleflex, Inc.*, 127 S.Ct. 1727 (2007).

46. Daralyn Durie & Mark A. Lemley, *A Realistic Approach to the Obviousness of Inventions*, William & Mary L. Rev. (forthcoming 2009).

47. *See, e.g.,* Robert P. Merges, *Economic Perspectives on Innovation: Patent Standards and Commercial Success*, 76 Calif. L. Rev. 803, 823–27 (1988); Edmund Kitch, *Graham v. John Deere Co.: New Standards for Patents*, 1966 Sup. Ct. Rev. 293, 330–335; Rochelle Cooper Dreyfuss, *The Federal Circuit: A Case Study in Specialized Courts*, 64 N.Y.U. L. Rev. 1, 9–10 (1989).

48. *Cf.* Robert M. Hunt, *Patentability, Industry Structure, and Innovation*, 52 J. Indus. Econ. 401 (2004).

49. *See Gentry Gallery v. Berkline Corp.*, 134 F.3d 1473, 1479 (Fed. Cir. 1998); *In re Gosteli*, 872 F.2d 1008, 1012 (Fed. Cir. 1989).

50. *See, e.g., Gentry Gallery*, 134 F.3d at 1479–80; *Hyatt v. Boone*, 47 U.S.P.Q.2d (BNA) 1128, 1131 (Fed. Cir. 1998); *In re DiLeone*, 436 F.2d 1404, 1405 (C.C.P.A. 1971).

51. *See, e.g., Chiron Corp. v. Genentech, Inc.*, 363 F.3d 1247 (Fed. Cir. 2004).

52. *Regents of the Univ. of Cal. v. Eli Lilly & Co.*, 119 F.3d 1559 (Fed. Cir. 1997); *Fiers v. Revel*, 984 F.2d 1164, 1171 (Fed. Cir. 1993). But *cf. Singh v. Brake*, 317 F.3d 1334, 1343–44 (Fed. Cir. 2003).

53. *Fiers v. Revel*, 984 F.2d 1164 (Fed. Cir. 1993).

54. *Id.* at 1170–71.

55. *Id.*

56. *See also* Adang v. Fischhoff, 286 F.3d 1346 (Fed. Cir. 2002) (disclosure of genetically altered tobacco plant did not enable claim to genetically altered tomato plant); *Hitzeman v. Rutter*, 243 F.3d 1345 (Fed. Cir. 2001) (conception of biotechnology invention simultaneous with reduction to practice).

57. 984 F.2d at 1357.

58. 119 F.3d 1559 (Fed. Cir. 1997).

59. cDNA, or complementary DNA, is produced by reverse transcribing the messenger RNA transcript of genomic DNA. David Freifelder & George M. Malacinski, *Essentials of Molecular Biology* 278 (2d ed. 1993). This process reverses the usual flow of genetic information from DNA to RNA, but the cDNA transcript is not necessarily identical to the genomic DNA template, as mRNA sequence may have been edited after translation. *Id.*

60. *Fiers v. Revel*, 984 F.2d at 1170–71.

61. *Id.* at 1171.

62. *Eli Lilly*, 119 F.3d at 1567.

63. *Id.* at 1568 (citations omitted).

64. *Fiers*, 984 F.2d at 1171.

65. *Moba v. Diamond Automation*, 325 F.3d 1306 (Fed. Cir. 2003) (Rader, J., concurring).

66. Many of these cases involve enablement and best mode, for the simple reason that the court doesn't normally apply the written description requirement to software at all.

67. *See Fonar Corp. v. General Electric Co.*, 107 F.3d 1543, 1549 (Fed. Cir. 1997); *see also* Lawrence D. Graham & Richard O. Zerbe Jr., *Economically Efficient Treatment of Computer Software: Reverse Engineering, Protection, and Disclosure*, 22 Rutgers Computer & Tech. L.J. 61, 96–97 (1996); Anthony J. Mahajan, *Note, Intellectual Property, Contracts, and Reverse Engineering after ProCD: A Proposed Compromise for Computer Software*, 67 Fordham L. Rev. 3297, 3317 (1999).

68. 908 F.2d 931 (Fed. Cir. 1990).

69. *Northern Telecom, Inc. v. Datapoint Corp.*, No. CA3–82–1039–D (N.D. Tex. Aug. 31, 1988).

70. 908 F.2d 931 at 943 (Fed. Cir. 1990).

71. *Id.* at 941.

72. *Id.*

73. *Id.* at 941–42.

74. *Id.* at 942 (quoting *Ex rel Sherwood*, 613 F.2d 809, 817, n.6 (Ct. Cust. Pat. App. 1980).

75. 107 F.3d 1543 (Fed. Cir. 1997).

76. *Id.* at 1549 (citations omitted).

77. *See Robotic Vision Sys., Inc. v. View Eng'g, Inc.*, 112 F.3d 1163 (Fed. Cir. 1997) (best mode); *In re Dossel*, 115 F.3d 942 (Fed. Cir. 1997) (written description).

By contrast, in *White Consol. Indus., Inc. v. Vega Servo-Control, Inc.*, 713 F.2d 788 (Fed. Cir. 1983), the Federal Circuit had invalidated a patent for a machine tool control system that was run by a computer program. Part of the invention was a programming language translator designed to convert an input program into machine language, which the system could then execute. The patent specification identified an example of a translator program, the so-called SPLIT program, which was a trade secret of the plaintiff. The court held that the program translator was an integral part of the invention, and that mere identification of it was not sufficient to discharge the applicant's duty under Section 112. The court seemed concerned that maintaining the translator program as a trade secret would allow White Consolidated Industries to extend the patent beyond the seventeen-year term then specified in the patent code.

Although *White* suggests that it is not sufficient merely to identify the program or its functions, more recent Federal Circuit authority is overwhelmingly to the contrary. *See, e.g., In re Dossel,* 115 F.3d at 946 (Fed. Cir. 1997) ("While the written description does not disclose exactly what mathematical algorithm will be used to compute the end result, it does state that 'known algorithms' can be used to solve standard equations which are known in the art." This was deemed sufficient to describe the invention).

78. *See Union Pacific Resources v. Chesapeake Energy Corp.,* 236 F.3d 684, 690–92 (Fed. Cir. 2001).

79. *Id.* at 691.

80. One decision even found that a specification that provided inconsistent and inaccurate guidance as to how the invention worked was not rendered indefinite by a lack of enablement. *See S3 Inc. v. Nvidia Corp.,* 259 F.3d 1364 (Fed. Cir. 2001). *But see id.* at 1371 (Gajarsa, J., dissenting).

81. *Enzo Biochem v. Gen-Probe, Inc.,* 296 F.3d 1316, 1324–25 (Fed. Cir. 2002).

82. *Diamond v. Chakrabarty,* 447 U.S. 303, 309 (1980) (quoting S. Rep. No. 82–1979, at 5 (1952) and H.R. Rep. No. 82–1923, at 6 [1952]).

83. Most notably, the *Diamond v. Chakrabarty,* 447 U.S. 303 (1980) decision restricted the scope of the products of nature exception, and the *State Street Bank v. Signature Financial Services,* 149 F.3d 1368 (Fed. Cir. 1998), court eliminated the business methods exception. By contrast, in *In re Ngai,* 367 F.3d 1336 (Fed. Cir. 2004), the court, perhaps surprisingly, retained the patentability exception for printed matter.

84. 56 U.S. (15 How.) 62 (1853).

85. 56 U.S. at 113.

86. *Diamond,* 447 U.S. 303.

87. *Brenner v. Manson,* 383 U.S. 519, 534 (1966).

88. *See* Nelson & Winter, *supra,* at 263; William Kingston, *Direct Protection of Innovation* 13 (William Kingston ed., 1987).

89. *But see* Mark D. Janis & Jay P. Kesan, *Weed-Free I.P.: The Supreme Court, Intellectual Property Interfaces, and the Problem of Plants* 33 (Illinois Public Law and Legal Theory Research Papers Series, Working Paper No. 00–07, 2001).

90. *Hilton Davis,* 62 F.3d at 1518.

91. *Graver Tank,* 339 U.S. at 608.

92. *See, e.g., Warner-Jenkinson Co. v. Hilton Davis Chem. Co.,* 520 U.S. 17, 39–40 (1997).

93. *See Hilton Davis,* 62 F.3d at 1519.

94. 925 F.3d 1444, 1449 (Fed. Cir. 1991).

95. *See, e.g., Amgen, Inc. v. Chugai Pharm. Co.,* 927 F.2d 1200, 1208–09 (Fed. Cir. 1991); Burk & Lemley, *Uncertainty Principle, supra.*

96. Antony L. Ryan & Roger G. Brooks, *Innovation vs. Evasion: Clarifying Patent Rights in Second-Generation Genes and Proteins,* 17 Berkeley Tech. L.J. 1265, 1265 (2002).

97. *Warner-Jenkinson Co. v. Hilton Davis & Co.,* 530 U.S. 17 (1997); *Pennwalt Corp. v. Durand-Wayland Corp.,* 833 F.2d 931 (Fed. Cir. 1987) (en banc).

98. Dan L. Burk & Mark A. Lemley, *Quantum Patent Mechanics,* 9 Lewis & Clark L. Rev. 29 (2005).

99. Michael J. Meurer & Craig Allen Nard, *Invention, Refinement, and Patent Claim Scope: A New Perspective on the Doctrine of Equivalents* 93 Geo. L.J. 1947, n.233 (2005) ("certain technologies require fewer limitations").

100. Whether software patents are construed to have many different elements or not may depend on whether the patent claim is drafted to cover only the software or whether it simply includes software in a larger machine. Cohen & Lemley argue that "the element-by-element approach . . . may not help in many software cases, where the software-related part of the invention is often described in a single element." Cohen & Lemley, *supra*, at 44.

101. *See* Antony L. Ryan & Roger G. Brooks, *Innovation vs. Evasion: Clarifying Patent Rights in Second-Generation Genes and Proteins*, 17 Berkeley Tech. L.J. 1265, 1284–85 (2002) ("some commentators suggest that each nucleotide in a gene patent and each amino acid in a protein patent may constitute a separate claim element. But most amino acids in any particular protein do not perform a known function of their own. . . . Thus, it makes no sense to consider each amino acid to be a separate claim element").

102. *See, e.g., Morley Sewing Mach. Co. v. Lancaster,* 129 U.S. 263 (1889); *Miller v. Eagle Mfg. Co.,* 151 U.S. 186, 207 (1894); *Perkin-Elmer Corp. v. Westinghouse Elec. Corp.,* 822 F.2d 1528, 1532 (Fed. Cir. 1987); John R. Thomas, *The Question concerning Patent Law and Pioneer Inventions,* 10 High Tech. L.J. 35, 37 (1995).

103. *Wright v. Herring-Curtiss Co.,* 211 F. at 655.

104. *Autogiro Co. v. United States,* 384 F.2d 391 (Ct. Cl. 1967).

105. *Warner-Jenkinson Co. v. Hilton Davis & Co.,* 530 U.S. 17, n.4 (1997).

106. *Compare Augustine Med., Inc. v. Gayman Indus.,* 181 F.3d 1291, 1301 (Fed. Cir. 1999) *with Sun Studs Inc. v. ATA Equip. Leasing,* 872 F.2d 978, 987 (Fed. Cir. 1989). The Federal Circuit did endorse the pioneering patent doctrine in an unpublished opinion in 2003, *see Molten Metal Equip. Innovations v. Metaullics Sys.,* 56 Fed. App. 475, 4 (Fed. Cir. Jan. 2003), but unpublished decisions cannot of course be relied upon in subsequent litigation.

107. *See, e.g.,* Michael J. Meurer & Craig Allen Nard, *supra;* Thomas, *supra* note 108, at 58–59.

108. *See* Oddi, *supra,* at 1127.

109. *See Westinghouse v. Boyden Power Brake Co.,* 170 U.S. 537, 562 (1898). For a detailed discussion, *see* George M. Sirilla et al., *The Doctrine of Equivalents: Both a Sword and a Shield,* 13 Fed. Cir. Bar J. 75 (2004).

110. 279 F.3d 1357, 1368 (Fed. Cir. 2002).

111. *Contra Scripps Clinic and Research Found. v. Genentech,* 927 F.2d 1565, 1581 (Fed. Cir. 1991).

112. *See Amgen, Inc. v. Hoechst Marion Roussel,* 314 F.3d 1313, 1351 (Fed. Cir. 2003).

113. *See* Robert P. Merges, *A Brief Note on Blocking Patents and the Reverse Doctrine of Equivalents in Biotechnology Cases,* 73 J. Pat. & Trademark Off. Soc'y 878, 883 (1991); Mark A. Lemley, *The Economics of Improvement in Intellectual Property Law,* 75 Tex. L. Rev. 989, 1023–24 (1997).

114. *See, e.g., Scripps Clinic,* 927 F.2d at 1581.

115. *Id.*

116. Karl Bozicevic, *The "Reverse Doctrine of Equivalents" in the World of Reverse Transcriptase,* 71 J. Pat. & Trademark Ofc. Soc'y 353, 360–69 (1989).

117. *Panduit Corp. v. Stahlin Bros. Fibre Works, Inc.,* 575 F.2d 1152 (6th Cir. 1978).

118. The classic, fifteen-factor test is set out in *Georgia-Pacific Corp. v. U.S. Plywood,* 318 F. Supp. 1116, 1123 (S.D.N.Y. 1970), *aff'd,* 446 F.2d 295 (2d Cir. 1971).

119. *See* Mark A. Lemley & Carl Shapiro, *Patent Holdup and Royalty Stacking,* 85 Tex. L. Rev. 1991 (2007).

120. *Monsanto Corp. v. McFarling,* 488 F.3d 973 (Fed. Cir. 2007) (affirming a "reasonable" royalty six times the actual license fee charged in the market); *Golight Inc. v. Wal-Mart Stores,* 355 F.3d 1327, 1338 (Fed. Cir. 2004) (upholding a reasonable royalty that exceeded the infringer's profits from the product); Amy L. Landers, *Let the Games Begin: Incentives to Innovation in the New Economy of Intellectual Property Law,* 46 Santa Clara L. Rev. 307, 311–22 (2006).

Chapter Ten

1. For a detailed elucidation of the ideas in this paragraph, *see* Robert P. Merges, *Uncertainty and the Standard of Patentability,* 7 High Tech. L.J. 1 (1992).

2. In using this typology, we follow Joseph Schumpeter. *See* Richard R. Nelson & Sydney G. Winter, *An Evolutionary Theory of Economic Change* 263 (1982) (attributing the distinction between invention and innovation to Schumpeter).

3. 35 U.S.C. § 282 (2000).

4. *Al-Site Corp. v. VSI Int'l,* 174 F.3d 1308, 1323 (Fed. Cir. 1999).

5. *See* Doug Lichtman & Mark A. Lemley, *Rethinking Patent Law's Presumption of Validity,* 60 Stan. L. Rev. 45 (2007); Mark A. Lemley et al., *What to Do about Bad Patents,* Regulation, Winter 2005–2006, at 10; Jay P. Kesan, *Carrots and Sticks to Create a Better Patent System,* 17 Berkeley Tech. L.J. 763, 765–66 (2002); Mark A. Lemley, *Rational Ignorance at the Patent Office,* 95 Nw. U. L. Rev. 1495, 1527–29 (2001).

6. *See In re Lee,* 277 F.3d 1338, 1342 (Fed. Cir. 2002); *In re Oetiker,* 977 F.2d 1443, 1449 (Fed. Cir. 1992) (Plager, J., concurring); John R. Thomas, *Collusion and Collective Action in the Patent System: A Proposal for Patent Bounties,* 2001 U. Ill. L. Rev. 305, 325. This results from the court's reading of 35 U.S.C. § 102, which provides that an applicant shall be entitled to a patent "unless" specified conditions are satisfied.

7. *See, e.g., Kahn v. Gen. Motors,* 135 F.3d 1472, 1480 (Fed. Cir. 1998) ("The presentation of evidence that was not before the examiner does not change the presumption of validity"); *Applied Materials, Inc. v. Advanced Semiconductor Materials Am.,* 98 F.3d 1563, 1569 (Fed. Cir. 1996) ("The presentation at trial of additional evidence that was not before the PTO does not change the presumption of validity or the standard of proof, although the burden may be more or less easily carried because of the additional evidence").

8. *See, e.g., Mfg. Research Corp. v. Graybar Elec. Co.,* 679 F.2d 1355, 1360–61 (11th Cir. 1982) (adopting the "considered art only" rule); *NDM Corp. v. Hayes Prods.,* 641 F.2d 1274, 1277 (9th Cir. 1981) (same); *Lee Blacksmith Inc. v. Lindsey Bros.,* 605 F.2d 341, 342–43 (7th Cir. 1979) (same).

9. *KSR Corp. v. Teleflex Corp.,* 127 S.Ct. 1727 (2007).

10. *See FMC Corp. v. Hennessy Indus.,* 836 F.2d 521, 526 n.6 (Fed. Cir. 1987) ("As a general rule, there is no duty to conduct a prior art search").

11. Iain M. Cockburn & Rebecca Henderson, *The 2003 Intellectual Property Owners Association Survey on Strategic Management of Intellectual Property* F6 (working paper 2004) (a survey of IP managers found that 67 percent disagreed with the statement "we always do a patent search before initiating any RandD or product development effort"). For an explanation of why companies don't want to read other patents, *see* Mark A. Lemley & Ragesh K. Tangri, *Ending Patent Law's Willfulness Game,* 18 Berkeley Tech. L.J. 1275 (2003). For discussion of how to encourage prior art searches, *see* Kesan, *supra* note 5, at 770; Jay P. Kesan &

Mark Banik, *Patents as Incomplete Contracts: Aligning Incentives for RandD Investment with Incentives to Disclose Prior Art*, 2 Wash. U. J.L. & Pol'y 23, 26 (2000).

12. *See, e.g.,* Julie E. Cohen, *Reverse Engineering and the Rise of Electronic Vigilantism: Intellectual Property Implications of "Lock-Out" Programs*, 68 S. Cal. L. Rev. 1091, 1178–79 (1995).

13. John R. Allison & Emerson Tiller, *The Business Method Patent Myth*, 18 Berkeley Tech. L.J. 987 (2003) (arguing that Internet business method patents appear to be no worse than the average patent).

14. Mark A. Lemley & Bhaven Sampat, *Is the Patent Office a Rubber Stamp?* 58 Emory L.J. (forthcoming 2008).

15. John R. Allison, *On the Feasibility of Improving Patent Quality One Technology at a Time: The Case of Business Methods*, 21 Berkeley Tech. L.J. 729 (2006).

16. Lemley & Sampat, *supra*.

17. *See, e.g.,* John R. Allison & Mark A. Lemley, *Who's Patenting What? An Empirical Exploration of Patent Prosecution*, 53 Vand. L. Rev. 2099, 2130–31 and tbl.13 (2000).

18. *See, e.g.,* Doug Lichtman & Mark A. Lemley, *Rethinking Patent Law's Presumption of Validity*, 60 Stan. L. Rev. 45 (2007); Mark A. Lemley et al., *What to Do about Bad Patents*, Regulation, Winter 2005–2006, at 10.

19. For a general discussion of patent misuse, *see* 1 Herbert Hovenkamp et al., *IP and Antitrust*, § 3.

20. 1 Herbert Hovenkamp et al., *IP and Antitrust*, § 3.2b–c.

21. *See* 35 U.S.C. § 261 (2000) (permitting territorially restricted patent licenses).

22. *See B. Braun Med. Co. v. Abbott Labs.*, 124 F.3d 1419, 1426 (Fed. Cir. 1997).

23. *See Brulotte v. Thys*, 379 U.S. 29, 32 (1964); 1 Herbert Hovenkamp et al., *IP and Antitrust*, ch. 3. *But cf. Scheiber v. Dolby Labs.*, 293 F.3d 1014, 1017–19 (7th Cir. 2002) (following *Brulotte*, but criticizing its reasoning).

24. 1 Herbert Hovenkamp et al., *IP and Antitrust*, § 3.4a.

25. *See In re Napster Inc. Copyright Litig.*, 191 F. Supp. 2d 1087 (N.D. Cal. 2002).

26. *Alcatel*, 166 F.3d at 792–94; *DGI*, 81 F.3d at 601.

27. *See* Mark A. Lemley et al., *Software and Internet Law*, 198 (2d ed. 2003).

28. *See Alcatel USA v. DGI Techs.*, 166 F.3d 772, 792–94 (5th Cir. 1999); *DSC Communications Corp. v. DGI Techs.*, 81 F.3d 597, 601 (5th Cir. 1996).

29. *See* 2 Herbert Hovenkamp et al., *IP and Antitrust*, § 33.9; Herbert Hovenkamp et al., *Anticompetitive Settlements of Intellectual Property Disputes*, 87 Minn. L. Rev. 1719, 1739 (2003).

30. *See C.R. Bard, Inc. v. M3 Sys.*, 157 F.3d 1340, 1373 (Fed. Cir. 1998) (no general concept of "wrongful use" outside of specified categories); *B. Braun Med. Co. v. Abbott Labs.*, 124 F.3d 1419, 1426 (Fed. Cir. 1997) (categorizing patent misuse claims). For similar formalist readings of antitrust cases involving patents, *see CSU v. Xerox*, 203 F.3d 1322, 1325 (Fed. Cir. 2000); *Intergraph Corp. v. Intel Corp.*, 195 F.3d 1346, 1362 (Fed. Cir. 1999).

31. *See* Mark A. Lemley, *The Economic Irrationality of the Patent Misuse Doctrine*, 78 Calif. L. Rev. 1599, 1614–20 (1990).

32. For the classic formulation of such a rule, *see* Guido Calabresi & A. Douglas Melamed, *Property Rules, Liability Rules, and Inalienability: One View of the Cathedral*, 85 Harv. L. Rev. 1089, 1092 (1972).

33. *See* Robert P. Merges et al., *Intellectual Property in the New Technological Age* 355 (rev. 4th ed. 2007).

34. *See* Edward J. Kessler et al., *Preliminary Injunctions in Patent and Trademark Cases,* 80 Trademark Rep. 451 (1990) (discussing historical treatment and current criteria).

35. *See, e.g., H.H. Robertson Co. v. United Steel Deck, Inc.,* 820 F.2d 384, 390 (Fed. Cir. 1987) (holding that there is a rebuttable presumption of irreparable harm for the purposes of granting preliminary injunctions in patent cases).

36. *See, e.g., Amazon.com v. Barnesandnoble.com,* 239 F.3d 1343, 1350–51 (Fed. Cir. 2001) (rejecting a preliminary injunction where there are any serious questions about the merits of the case).

37. *See N.Y. Times v. Tasini,* 533 U.S. 483, 505 (2001); *Campbell v. Acuff Rose Music, Inc.,* 510 U.S. 569, 578 n.10 (1994); *see also Abend v. MCA,* 863 F.2d 1465 (9th Cir. 1988) (refusing to grant injunctive relief), aff'd on other grounds sub nom. *Stewart v. Abend,* 495 U.S. 207 (1990).

38. 492 F.2d 1317 (2d Cir. 1974).

39. *Id.* at 1324; *see also E.I. du Pont de Nemours & Co. v. Phillips Petroleum Co.,* 835 F.2d 277, 278 (Fed. Cir. 1987) (refusing to grant an injunction to a patentee that was exiting the industry because it would not suffer irreparable harm); *Hybritech, Inc. v. Abbott Labs,* 4 U.S.P.Q.2d 1001 (C.D. Cal. 1987), *aff'd,* 849 F.2d 1446 (Fed. Cir. 1988).

40. 146 F.2d 941, 945 (9th Cir. 1944); *see also City of Milwaukee v. Activated Sludge, Inc.,* 69 F.2d 577, 593 (7th Cir. 1934) (refusing to enjoin an infringement where the result would create public health problems); *Bliss v. Brookllyn,* 3 F. Cas. 706 (C.C.E.D.N.Y. 1871) (refusing to enjoin use of a patented fire hose because doing so would create a safety hazard).

41. *Vitamin Technologists,* 146 F.2d at 945.

42. *Milwaukee v. Activated Sludge,* 69 F.2d 577 (7th Cir. 1934).

43. *Nerney v. New York,* 83 F.2d 409, 411 (2d Cir. 1936).

44. 247 F. Supp. 2d 1011 (N.D. Ill. 2003), *aff'd on other grounds,* 403 F.3d 1331 (Fed. Cir. 2005) (en banc).

45. *See* 1 Herbert Hovenkamp et al., *IP and Antitrust,* § 6.5c; F. M. Scherer, *The Economic Effects of Compulsory Patent Licensing* (1977).

46. *eBay Inc. v. MercExchange LLC,* 126 S.Ct. 1837 (2006).

47. *Paice v. Toyota,* 2006 WL 2385139 (E.D. Tex. Aug. 16, 2006).

48. *CSIRO v. Buffalo Technology, Inc.,* 492 F. Supp. 2d 600 (E.D. Tex. 2007).

49. Richard Epstein, *Steady the Course: Property Rights in Genetic Material* 37 (John M. Olin Law and Econ., Working Paper No. 152, Mar. 2003); Robert P. Merges et al., *Intellectual Property in the New Technological Age* 299–302 (3d ed. 2003). For a nontraditional argument against injunctive relief, *see* Ian Ayres & Paul Klemperer, *Limiting Patentees' Market Power without Reducing Innovation Incentives: The Perverse Benefits of Uncertainty and Non-injunctive Remedies,* 97 Mich. L. Rev. 985, 1020–23 (1999); *cf.* Dan L. Burk, *Muddy Rules for Cyberspace,* 21 Cardozo L. Rev. 121 (1999) (favoring unclear or muddy rules for online entitlements).

50. Colleen Chien studied examples of compulsory licenses in the pharmaceutical industry and found that they did not affect innovation incentives, for example. Colleen Chien, *Cheap Drugs at What Price to Innovation: Does the Compulsory Licensing of Pharmaceuticals Hurt Innovation?* 18 Berkeley Tech. L.J. 853 (2003). By contrast, Jean Lanjouw finds that price controls imposed by developing world countries delay the introduction of new drugs in those countries. Jean O. Lanjouw, *A Patent Policy for Global Diseases: Legal and International Issues,* 16 Harv. J. L. & Tech. 86 (2002).

51. *See* Julie S. Turner, *The Nonmanufacturing Patent Owner: Toward a Theory of Efficient Infringement,* 86 Calif. L. Rev. 179 (1998) (making this argument); Michelle Armond, *Intro-*

ducing the Defense of Independent Invention to Motions for Preliminary Injunctions in Patent Infringement Lawsuits, 91 Calif. L. Rev. 117, 122 (2003) (making a similar argument limited to denial of preliminary injunctive relief); *see also Foster v. Am. Mach. & Foundry Co.,* 492 F.2d 1317, 1324 (2d Cir. 1974) (taking into consideration whether party practiced welding system patent).

52. *See, e.g., Water Techs. Corp. v. Calco, Ltd.,* 850 F.2d 660, 671 (Fed. Cir. 1988) ("[A] lost profits award is appropriate only if [the patentee] proved that it would have made sales of its . . . product," but for infringement). Nonmanufacturing patentees, of course, cannot meet this burden.

53. Michael A. Heller, *The Tragedy of the Anticommons: Property in the Transition from Marx to Markets,* 111 Harv. L. Rev. 621, 623 (1998).

54. For an argument in favor of compulsory licensing of DNA to solve the anticommons problem, *see* Donna M. Gitter, *International Conflicts over Patenting Human DNA Sequences in the United States and the European Union: An Argument for Compulsory Licensing and a Fair-Use Exception,* 76 N.Y.U. L. Rev. 1623, 1628 (2001).

55. *See, e.g.,* Andrew Beckerman-Rodau, *Patent Law—Balancing Profit Maximization and Public Access to Technology,* 4 Colum. Sci. & Tech. L. Rev. 1 (2002) (arguing for a compulsory licensing scheme to correct the failure of the free market to deliver drugs to developing nations); Susan K. Sell, *TRIPS and the Access to Medicines Campaign,* 20 Wis. Int'l L.J. 481, 504–5 (2002) (endorsing compulsory licensing and stressing the importance of greater access to medicine by the developing world); Ellen t' Hoen, *TRIPS, Pharmaceutical Patents, and Access to Essential Medicines: A Long Way from Seattle to Doha,* 3 U. Chi. J. Int'l L. 27, 45–46 (2002) (discussing the need to reconcile TRIPS with the need to address health concerns in developing countries); *cf.* Alan O. Sykes, *TRIPS, Pharmaceuticals, Developing Countries, and the Doha "Solution,"* 3 U. Chi. J. Int'l L. 47, 49 (2002) (questioning the Doha Declaration in light of what it may do to the TRIPS agreement).

Judge Posner's decision in *SmithKline Beecham v. Apotex,* 247 F. Supp. 2d 1011 (N.D. Ill. 2003) is specific to pharmaceuticals, but for a different reason: He concluded that the patentee was trying to extend its proprietary rights beyond their lawful term by asserting a new patent. In any event, he found that permanent injunctive relief was inappropriate even if the patent was infringed.

56. Christopher A. Cotropia, *"After-Arising" Technologies and Tailoring Patent Scope,* 61 N.Y.U. Ann. Surv. Am. L. 151 (2005).

Chapter Eleven

1. The Pharmaceutical Research and Manufacturers of America estimate that the total time spent from the beginning of a research project to the marketing of a successful drug is twelve to fifteen years, 1.8 years of which is due to the FDA approval process. *See* Pharm. Research and Mfrs. of Am., "Why Do Prescription Drugs Cost So Much?" (June 2000), http://www.phrma.org/publications/publications/brochure/questions/. Estimates of the average cost of drug development and testing range from $150 million to over $800 million; the latter is the industry's figure. Compare *id.* with Public Citizen, "Rebuttals to PhRMA Responses to the Public Citizen Report, "Rx R&D Myths: The Case against the Drug Industry's R&D 'Scare Card,'" at http://www.citizen.org /congress/reform/drug_industry/corporate/articles.cfm?ID=6514 (Nov. 28, 2001); Gardiner Harris, "Cost of Developing Drugs Found to Rise," Wall St. J., Dec. 3, 2001, at B14.

2. For example, the Centocor sepsis antibody, a highly promising biotechnology treatment, succeeded in passing many years of costly trials, but failed in the last phase of FDA approval. Burk & Lemley, *Uncertainty Principle, supra,* foot.

3. For a discussion of how the patent and FDA rules interact to provide protection for developers of new drugs, *see* William Ridgway, *Realizing Two-Tiered Innovation Policy through Drug Regulation,* 58 Stan. L. Rev. 1221 (2006).

4. 21 U.S.C. § 355(j)(2)(A)(i) (2000).

5. 858 F.2d 731 (Fed. Cir. 1988).

6. 802 F.2d 1367 (Fed. Cir. 1986).

7. *See* Burk & Lemley, *Technology-Specific, supra,* at 1178–79.

8. *See, e.g.,* Kenneth J. Burchfiel, *Biotechnology and the Federal Circuit* § 6.2, at 84–85 (1995) (objecting on numerous grounds to the Federal Circuit's treatment of the obviousness requirement); Philippe Ducor, *New Drug Discovery Technologies and Patents,* 22 Rutgers Computer & Tech. L.J. 369, 371 (1996); Arti K. Rai, *Intellectual Property Rights in Biotechnology: Addressing New Technology,* 34 Wake Forest L. Rev. 827 (1999); *cf.* Jonathan M. Barnett, *Cultivating the Genetic Commons: Imperfect Patent Protection and the Network Model of Innovation,* 37 San Diego L. Rev. 987, 1028 (2000). *See generally* John M. Golden, *Biotechnology, Technology Policy, and Patentability: Natural Products and Invention in the American System,* 50 Emory L.J. 101 (2001).

9. *See* Boyd, *supra;* Robert P. Merges, *One Hundred Years of Solicitude: Intellectual Property Law, 1900–2000,* 88 Cal. L. Rev. 2187, 2225–27 (2000) [hereinafter Merges, *Solicitude*]; Merges, *Uncertainty, supra,* at 4.

10. *See* Robert P. Merges & John Fitzgerald Duffy, *Patent Law and Policy,* 727–28 (3d ed. 2002); *see also* Giorgio Sirilli, *Patents and Inventors: An Empirical Study,* 16 Res. Pol'y 157, 164–66 (1987) (finding that patents give most inventors more incentive to commercialize than incentive to invent). One way to think of this is to conceive of patents as a financing mechanism: By providing definable rights, patents enable companies to obtain the funding they need to turn an invention into a product. *See* Fritz Machlup, *Patents,* in 11 *Int'l Encyclopedia of the Social Sciences* 461, 467 (David L. Sills ed., 1968); Golden, *supra* note 8, at 167–72; Mark A. Lemley, *Reconceiving Patents in the Age of Venture Capital,* 4 J. Small & Emerging Bus. L. 137 (2000).

11. *See, e.g., Plant Genetic Sys. v. DeKalb Genetics Corp.,* 315 F.3d 1335 (Fed. Cir. 2003); *Regents of the Univ. of Cal. v. Eli Lilly & Co.,* 119 F.3d 1559, 1567–68 (Fed. Cir. 1997). *But see Amgen, Inc. v. Hoechst Marion Roussel,* 314 F.3d 1313, 1332 (Fed. Cir. 2003). Although *Amgen* reads the written description requirement more loosely than *Lilly,* it appears to have limited its holding to cases in which those of skill in the art already know of a correspondence between function and structure before the invention, *Amgen,* 314 F.3d at 1332, something that will not be true in the DNA patent cases. Similarly, *Capon v. Eshhar,* 418 F.3d 1349 (Fed. Cir. 2005), held that the written description requirement does not automatically require disclosure of the nucleotide sequence of claimed DNA, but only when the sequence is already known in the prior art.

12. *See* Kenneth G. Chahine, *Enabling DNA and Protein Composition Claims: Why Claiming Biological Equivalents Encourages Innovation,* 25 AIPLA Q.J. 333 (1997).

Curiously, Merges doesn't *see* this as a major problem, suggesting that in general "the Federal Circuit has overall been quite successful at integrating biotechnology cases into the fabric of patent law." Merges, *Solicitude, supra,* at 2228. We think the written description cases and the correspondingly narrow scope afforded biotechnology patents are a more serious problem than Merges acknowledges.

One might question why, if the written description requirement is producing such narrow DNA patents, the biomedical industries consistently cite patent protection as extremely important to them. *See, e.g.,* Cohen et al., *supra* (reporting the results of a survey in which biomedical companies rated patents more important than did companies in any other industry); Levin et al., *supra* (same). We note that the industries that count patents as extremely valuable tend to be chemistry and pharmaceuticals, not biotechnology per se, and certainly not those in the business of discovering and using DNA sequences. Second, the biotechnology written description cases are relatively new, and the industry-specific studies are somewhat older, so their understanding of the value of patents may not reflect modern realities.

13. *See, e.g.,* Mark J. Stewart, *The Written Description Requirement of 35 U.S.C. § 112(1): The Standard after* Regents of the University of California v. Eli Lilly & Co., 32 Ind. L. Rev. 537, 557–58 (1999).

14. Burk & Lemley, *Technology-Specific, supra,* at 1202–05.

15. Merges, *Uncertainty, supra.*

16. *See* Heller & Eisenberg, *supra;* Arti K. Rai & Rebecca S. Eisenberg, *Bayh-Dole Reform and the Progress of Biomedicine,* 66 Law & Contemp. Probs. 289 (2002).

17. For example, suppose a patentee isolates the DNA sequence for human beta-interferon, but because of the lowered disclosure requirement is entitled to claim all mammalian beta-interferon. The lowered obviousness requirement may mean that future inventors can patent rat, bat, and cat beta-interferon respectively if they discover those particular sequences; it is well established that a patent on a genus does not necessarily render obvious claims to a previously undisclosed species within that genus. *See Corning Glass Works v. Sumitomo Elec. U.S.A.,* 868 F.2d 1251, 1262 (Fed. Cir. 1989). Those later patents will be subservient to, but block, the original broad patent to mammalian beta-interferon.

18. For detailed discussions, *see* Lemley, *Economics of Improvement, supra;* Merges, *supra,* at 75. There is some evidence that the reverse doctrine of equivalents may play a greater role in the biotechnology arena than elsewhere. *See, e.g., Scripps Clinic & Research Found. v. Genentech,* 927 F.2d 1565, 1581 (Fed. Cir. 1991).

19. *See* Eisenberg & Merges, *supra;* Heller & Eisenberg, *supra* (discussing the anticommons).

20. *See also* Eisenberg, *supra,* at 26. Merges himself notes that increasing the scope of patents is an alternative to lowering the obviousness threshold. *See* Merges, *Uncertainty, supra,* at 47. He does not pursue that alternative in his paper, however.

21. Indeed, Hunt suggests that lowering the nonobviousness threshold actually creates a trade-off, increasing the probability of acquiring a patent but reducing the value of any given patent, thus possibly weakening the incentive to innovate. Robert M. Hunt, *Nonobviousness and the Incentive to Innovate: An Economic Analysis of Intellectual Property Reform* (Federal Reserve Bank Working Paper No. 99-3, Mar. 1999).

22. *See Ex Parte Kubin,* 83 U.S.P.Q.2d (BNA) 1410 (BPAI 2007).

23. *See* Janice Mueller, *Chemicals, Combinations, and 'Common Sense': How the Supreme Court's KSR Decision Is Changing Federal Circuit Obviousness Determinations in Pharmaceutical and Biotechnology Cases,* 35 N. Ky. L. Rev. (forthcoming 2008).

24. *Ortho-McNeil Pharmaceutical v. Mylan Labs, 520 F.3d 1358 (Fed. Cir. 2008).*

25. *See* Heller & Eisenberg, *supra;* Rai & Eisenberg, *supra,* at 289.

26. F. M. Scherer, *The Innovation Lottery,* in *Expanding the Boundaries of Intellectual Property* 3 (2001).

27. *See* Mark A. Lemley, *Ignoring Patents,* 2008 Mich. St. L. Rev. 19.

28. Rai and Eisenberg take this approach. *See* Rai & Eisenberg, *supra,* at 291.

29. *See, e.g., In re Vaeck,* 947 F.2d 488, 496 (Fed. Cir. 1991).

30. *See* Arti K. Rai & James Boyle, *Synthetic Biology: Caught between Property Rights, the Public Domain, and the Commons,* 5 PLoS BIOLOGY, http://biology.plosjournals. org/perlserv/?request=get-document&doi=10.1371%2Fjournal.pbio.0050058&ct=1 (Mar. 13, 2007).

31. *See, e.g., Amgen Inc. v. Chugai Pharm. Co., Ltd.,* 13 U.S.P.Q.2d (BNA) 1737 (D. Mass. 1990).

Chapter Twelve

1. John R. Allison & Ronald S. Mann, *The Disputed Quality of Software Patents,* 85 Wash. U. L.Q. 297, 304–13 (2007); Julie E. Cohen & Mark A. Lemley, *Patent Scope and Innovation in the Software Industry,* 89 Calif. L. Rev. 1, 1–12 (2001) (documenting the unsuccessful efforts to exclude software from patentability in the 1980s and 1990s).

2. Cohen & Lemley, *supra,* at 5–6.

3. *See* Merges, *Uncertainty, supra,* at 29–32.

4. *See* Burk & Lemley, *Technology-Specific, supra,* at 1170–73.

5. *See Pfaff v. Wells Elecs.,* 525 U.S. 55, 67–69 (1998).

6. *See Robotic Vision Sys. v. View Eng'g,* 249 F.3d 1307, 1311–13 (Fed. Cir. 2001) (finding a software invention on sale under § 102(b) more than one year before it was actually made).

7. The success of the open source movement suggests that significant innovation can occur in the software industry in the absence of intellectual property protection, though it does not follow that we would get as much or the same kinds of innovation were we to abolish intellectual property protection for software outright. For discussions of the open source movement, *see* Yochai Benkler, *Coase's Penguin, or, Linux and the Nature of the Firm,* 112 Yale L.J. 369 (2002); David McGowan, *Legal Implications of Open-Source Software,* 2001 U. Ill. L. Rev. 241 (2001).

8. Jim Bessen and Robert Hunt find that software patents tend to be issued to manufacturing companies, not software developers, and that they are consistent with strategic "patent thicket" behavior. James Bessen & Robert M. Hunt, *An Empirical Look at Software Patents* (May 2003) (working paper). If they are correct, it is further evidence that the scope of software patents should be reduced to eliminate the overlap problem.

9. For this suggestion, *see* Burk & Lemley, *Technology-Specific, supra,* at 1202–05.

10. *See, e.g.,* Burk & Lemley, *Uncertainty Principle, supra* (suggesting cost and uncertainty of postinvention development as a new secondary consideration supporting nonobviousness).

11. *See generally* Richard R. Nelson, *Intellectual Property Protection for Cumulative Systems Technology,* 94 Colum. L. Rev. 2674 (1994) (discussing the need to reduce the scope of patents in the software industry).

12. John R. Allison & Mark A. Lemley, *The (Unnoticed) Demise of the Doctrine of Equivalents,* 59 Stan. L. Rev. 955 (2007).

13. Mark A. Lemley & Carl Shapiro, *Patent Holdup and Royalty Stacking,* 85 Tex. L. Rev. 1991 (2007).

14. *See, e.g.,* Cohen & Lemley, *supra* (discussing the policy issues in detail and citing numerous authorities).

15. Maureen A. O'Rourke, *Toward a Doctrine of Fair Use in Patent Law,* 100 Colum. L. Rev. 1177 (2000).

16. *See, e.g.,* U.S. Patent No. 5,179,765 (issued Jan. 19, 1993) (for a "Plastic Paper Clip").

17. Pamela Samuelson and her colleagues argue that certain features of computer programs are readily apparent to competitors and are therefore vulnerable to copying. Samuelson et al., *supra,* at 2333. Their argument, however, depends not only on the vulnerability of programming innovations to casual inspection, but also on the ability of competitors to reverse engineer and analyze the design know-how lying "near the surface" of a program. *Id.* at 2335–37. If patent law precludes reverse engineering, it also precludes this sort of knowledge. It is true that certain types of computer program innovations, particularly user interfaces, are necessarily available to even the casual user, at least in part. It is unlikely, however, that these innovations are the most significant parts of a new computer program or the parts most likely to be patented. Further, those innovations for which precise understanding is most important (such as application program interfaces) are also those that will not be available to casual inspection.

18. For further discussion of the implied license and exhaustion doctrines that confer such a right, *see* Cohen & Lemley, *supra,* at 30–35.

19. It seems clear that generating even temporary instantiations of a patented product "makes" that product for purposes of patent infringement. This principle is firmly established in the pharmaceutical context, where courts have held that a patent is infringed when the patented product is generated by metabolization of a different drug within the human body and that chemical intermediates temporarily generated in the course of making a final product may infringe a patent covering those intermediates. *See Hoechst-Roussel Pharm. v. Lehman,* 109 F.3d 756, 759 (Fed. Cir. 1997); *Zenith Labs. v. Bristol-Myers Squibb,* 19 F.3d 1418, 1422 (Fed. Cir. 1994); *see also* Keith E. Witek, *Software Patent Infringement on the Internet and on Modern Computer Systems—Who Is Liable for Damages?* 14 Santa Clara Computer & High Tech. L.J. 303, 323–24 (1998) (arguing that since patent law lacks a fixation requirement, even near-instantaneous duplication of patented software is a prohibited "making" of the patented product).

20. Thus, an article-of-manufacture claim to a particular program "encoded on a computer hard drive" might be infringed by a reverse engineered copy temporarily stored on a computer hard drive. One limit to this principle was established in *In re Nuijten,* 500 F.3d 1346 (Fed. Cir. 2007), which held that a computer program could be patented when incorporated in some media (disks, electronic circuits), even temporarily, but not when incorporated in wires during transmission of the program from one site to another.

21. One possible argument that the copies are noninfringing is that most copies made during the reverse engineering process are nonfunctional, either because they are only partial or because they are converted to assembly language or source code form. Theoretically, a source code readout of a computer program could be considered a description of the invention, rather than a copy of the invention itself. Nonetheless, decompilation also involves the generation of object code "copies" of the patented program, at least in RAM.

22. Cohen and Lemley have explained how the doctrines of exhaustion and experimental use might be modified to create a right to reverse engineer patented software. Cohen & Lemley, *supra,* at 29–35.

23. *Quanta Comp. v. LG Elecs.,* 128 S.Ct. 2109 (2008).

24. *See* Cohen & Lemley, *supra,* at 23–25.

25. This macro lever may nonetheless be tailored, for example, by adopting a rule privileging only reverse engineering done for certain laudable purposes. This case-specific tailoring does not change the character of the policy lever, however, which is still industry-specific.

26. *See* Mark A. Lemley et al., *Software and Internet Law,* 274 (2d ed. 2003).

27. *See* John H. Barton, *Antitrust Treatment of Oligopolies with Mutually Blocking Patent Portfolios,* 69 Antitrust L.J. 851, 852 (2002) (arguing that patents may support innovation in the semiconductor industry by restricting entry to an oligopoly, permitting a supracompetitive price that supports R&D expenditures).

28. *See* Mark F. Grady & Jay I. Alexander, *Patent Law and Rent Dissipation,* 78 Va. L. Rev. 305, 306–08 (1992); Robert P. Merges, *Rent Control in the Patent District: Observations on the Grady-Alexander Thesis,* 78 Va. L. Rev. 359, 360 (1992).

29. *See* Hall & Ziedonis, *supra,* at 109–10.

30. Merges, *Uncertainty, supra,* at 47–49.

31. Lemley & Sampat, *supra.*

32. For more on the importance of standard-setting organizations (SSOs) to clearing rights in the semiconductor industry, *see* Mark A. Lemley, *Ten Things to Do about Patent Holdup of Standards (and One Not To),* 48 B.C. L. Rev. 149 (2007); Mark A. Lemley, *Intellectual Property Rights and Standard-Setting Organizations,* 90 Cal. L. Rev. 1889 (2002). For more on patent pools as a form of collective rights organization serving similar goals, *see* Merges, *Collective Rights, supra,* at 1293; *cf.* Lemley, *supra,* at 1951–54 (suggesting ways SSOs are better suited than patent pools to serve this function). *But see Rambus, Inc. v. Infineon Tech.,* 318 F.3d 1081, 1096–1105 (Fed. Cir. 2003) (reading narrowly and refusing to apply an SSO policy requiring disclosure of patents).

33. *See, e.g.,* Mark A. Lemley, *Patenting Nanotechnology,* 58 Stan. L. Rev. 601 (2005); Ted Sabety, *Nanotechnology Innovation and the Patent Thicket: Which IP Policies Promote Growth?* 1 Nanotech. L. & Bus. 262 (2004).

Conclusion

1. Christopher A. Cotropia, *"After-Arising" Technologies and Tailoring Patent Scope,* 61 N.Y.U. Ann. Rev. Am. L. 151 (2005).

2. Richard J. Gruner, *Everything Old Is New Again: Obviousness Limitations on Patenting Computer Updates of Old Designs,* 9 B.U. J. Sci. & Tech. L. 209 (2003).

3. Michael John Gulliford, *Much Ado about Gene Patents: The Role of Foreseeability,* 34 Seton Hall L. Rev. 711 (2004).

4. David E. Adelman, *A Fallacy of the Commons in Biotech Patent Policy,* 20 Berkeley Tech. L.J. 985 (2005).

5. Steven W. Usselman, *Regulating Railroad Innovation: Business, Technology, and Politics in America, 1840–1920* (2002).

Index

DATE DUE

GAYLORD			PRINTED IN U.S.A.